CORPORATE

SCANDALS

THE MANY FACES OF GREED

3/06

CORPORATE

SCANDALS

THE MANY FACES OF GREED

THE GREAT HEIST, FINANCIAL BUBBLES, AND THE ABSENCE OF VIRTUE

Kenneth R. Gray
Larry A. Frieder
George W. Clark, Jr.

PARAGON HOUSE
St. Paul, Minnesota

HV
6769
.G73
2005

First Edition 2005

Published in the United States by
Paragon House
2285 University Avenue West
St. Paul, MN 55114

Library of Congress Cataloging-in-Publication Data

Gray, Kenneth R., 1952-
  Corporate scandals : the many faces of greed / Kenneth R. Gray, Larry A. Frieder,
George W. Clark, Jr.-- 1st ed.
    p. cm.
  Includes bibliographical references and index.
  ISBN 1-55778-838-3 (pbk. : alk. paper) 1. Commercial crimes--United States. 2.
Corporations--Corrupt practices--United States. I. Frieder, Larry A., 1948- II. Clark,
George W. (George William), 1944- III. Title.

  HV6769.G73 2005
  364.16'8'0973--dc22

                          2004014788

The paper used in this publication meets the minimum requirements of American
National Standard for Information Sciences—Permanence of Paper for Printed
Library Materials, ANSIZ39.48-1984.

Manufactured in the United States of America
10 9 8 7 6 5 4 3 2 1

For current information about all releases from Paragon House,
visit the web site at http://www.paragonhouse.com

DEDICATION

To my wife, Doris Herr Gray, who has always been there for me in the highs and especially in the lows.

—*Ken*

To my nieces, Laura, Lindsay, Kimberly, and Nicole. These girls have always provided great joy in all endeavors.

—*Larry*

To my mother, Justina Elizabeth Clark, because the virtues of a parent are like the wind that blows beneath the wings of the child in flight.

—*George*

Acknowledgements

As with any undertaking this large, the authors are indebted to the many people who supported our work in this book project of more than two years' life. As our efforts are now completed, it is most appropriate that we offer our thanks and acknowledge the support of the following people.

This project required significant data collection and research assistance. In this regard, we were fortunate to have a cadre of superb graduate research assistants who greatly contributed and provided extensive support during our endeavors to being this project to completion; given the continuous ongoing events that is happening on Wall Street. Specifically, we acknowledge the following MBA candidates at the Florida A & M University (FAMU) School of Business and Industry (SBI): Renita Canady, Rodney Clayton, Wayne Goodall, Allison Groomes, Yvette Holmes, and Zena King. We would also like to thank Kenneth B. Clark, a graphic arts major at FAMU, whose timely assistance in the use of the Photoshop Graphics program was sincerely appreciated.

We benefited immensely from the critical reviews by Dr. Harvey Rosenblum of the Federal Reserve Bank of Dallas, Dr. Stan Smith of the University of Central Florida, and John Baker of the Banc Funds, Chicago, Illinois.

Our presentations relied on various financial data sets. Henry "Chip" Dickson, Senior Investment Strategist of Lehman Brothers and his staff were most helpful in these endeavors.

The production work on the project was endless. To meet the challenge, we received enormous support from the School of Business and Industry (SBI), Florida A and M University. We thank SBI Dean Amos Bradford and our Academic Programs Director, Dr. Charles Evans, who both have been terrific supporters of this project. Also, Dr. LaQuita Booth, SBI's Director of Administration who provided great administrative assistance. Special thanks goes to Ms. Nell Wright, Manager of SBI's Services Center, who constantly "turned the work out."

We would also like to express our appreciation for the editorial assistance provided by Jayme Harpring and Beverly Dayton. They were incredibly patient, generous, and meticulous in working with us.

Special thanks to all the great folks at Paragon House Publishing who labored on our behalf. Specifically, Gordon Anderson and Rosemary Yokoi, who worked diligently on the numerous drafts of the manuscript.

As we express appreciation to all those who helped make this book a reality, we regret that we cannot mention individually the great number of people who have influenced our thinking over the years. Each of the authors has spent virtually all of their adult lives in business education and Corporate America, and in doing so we have had the opportunity to work with many outstanding people of like mind who have a similar passion for our free enterprise system. Undoubtedly, many of the ideas that were put forth in this book emanated from various discussions, projects, and panels that we have enjoyed over the years with our professional colleagues. To each of them we give a sincere and warmhearted "thanks" and we look forward to our continued associations in the future.

If, for any reason, we have inadvertently omitted anyone, we apologize in advance.

Kenneth R. Gray, Ph.D.
Tallahassee, Florida

Larry A. Frieder, Ph.D.
Tallahassee, Florida

George W. Clark, Jr., Ph.D.
Tallahassee, Florida

CONTENTS

Acknowledgements vii
List of Tables and Figures xiv
List of Abbreviations and Acronyms xv
Foreword by Sybil C. Mobley xix

CHAPTER 1: CORPORATE SCANDALS 1

The Need to Restore Trust and Integrity 3
Root Causes of the Current Crisis 5
Remedies to the Current Crisis 7
Corruption and Greed on Wall Street 8
Overview of the Text 9

CHAPTER 2: A SHORT HISTORY OF BUSINESS SCANDALS. . 13

The Mississippi Company Bubble of France .15
The South Sea Company Bubble of England .17
The Age of the Railways 20
Railroad Scandals 21
Railway Stocks, Jay Cooke, and the U.S. Stock Market
    Crash of 1873 23
The Ponzi Pyramid Scheme of Finance 26
Swindles of the Boom Era of the 1920s 27
    Kreuger and Toll 28
    The Middle West Utilities Holding Company 29
    Albert Wiggins Sells Short 30
    Charles Mitchell's Financial Supermarket 31
Government Regulation: The United States' Response to the
    Stock Market Crash and Corporate Misdeeds 33
    The Bank Act of 1933 33
    Securities and Exchange Act of 1934 36
More Scandals—McKesson & Robbins Company 37
Savings & Loan Scandals 38
Final Thoughts 40

CHAPTER 3: CORPORATE MALFEASANCE: FRAUD,
THEFT, AND REGULATORY LAXITY. 47

Major American Corporations Lose Their Way 49
    Enron 49

Tyco 57
WorldCom 61
Global Crossing 64
Qwest 66
Adelphia 67
ImClone 68
Scandals Appear in Europe 71
Missing Oil Reserves At Shell 71
Royal Ahold 72
Parmalat 73
Other European Scandals 75
International Reactions 76
Conclusion 78

CHAPTER 4:   ADDRESSING CORPORATE SCANDALS: THE
              SARBANES-OXLEY ACT AS A PANACEA? 83
The Public Company Accounting Oversight Board (PCAOB) 84
Corporate Self-Regulation 84
CEO/CFO Reporting Certification 84
Disgorgement of CEO and CFO Compensation and Profits 85
Ban on Personal Loans to Executive Officers and Directors 86
Accelerated Reporting of Trades by Insiders 86
Prohibition on Insider Trades During Pension Fund Blackout Periods 86
New Audit Committee Standards 87
HealthSouth: An Early Test of the Sarbanes-Oxley Act 88
Sarbanes-Oxley Paying Dividends 91
Demise of Arthur Andersen 92
The Plight of Other Accounting Firms 95
Freddie Mac Suppresses Profits 96
Broad Effects of Corporate Malfeasance 98
Assessment and Final Thoughts 99

CHAPTER 5:   SCANDAL SPREADS TO WALL STREET 103
Pressures Mount in Washington: SEC Chairman, Harvey Pitt,
    at Center of Controversy 104
Bush's Reaction: Status Quo? 105
The Martin Act Addresses Wall Street Wrongdoing 106
Eliot Spitzer—The Public's Hero 108
Reforms Start: The Global Settlement for Investment Banks 109
Penalties, Disgorgement, Funds for Independent Research, and
    Investor Education 111
Summary of the Enforcement Actions 112
Summary of Global Settlement 114

CONTENTS

Celebrity Investment Analysts Investigated 114
    Henry Blodget's Resignation. 114
    Mary Meeker Never Indicted 115
    Jack Grubman: Permanently Barred from the Securities Industry 117
    Frank Quattrone: The Master of Technology IPOs. 118
The New York Stock Exchange (NYSE): Another
  Self-Regulation Failure 120
    Richard Grasso: From Hero to Goat. 120
    Carl McCall Avocates Separating Trading and Regulation 126
    John Reed Begins Work 127
Violations of "Trade-Through Rules". 129
Final Thoughts and Conclusion. 131

CHAPTER 6: MUTUAL FUNDS SCANDALS: MORE THAN A
             FEW BAD APPLES 133

Mutual Fund "Late Trading" and "Market Timing" Scandals 134
    Canary Capital Partners 136
    Bank of America—Nations Funds Family 137
    Putnam Investments. 139
    The Strong Funds 140
    Janus Capital Group. 143
    Massachusetts Financial Services Company 145
    Alliance Capital Management 146
    Other Prominent Firms 146
Mutual Fund Fees Questioned. 150
Illegal Sales Practices—Directed Brokerage Businesses 152
Fund Trustees As Chihuahuas 155
Fidelity's Johnson Argues Against Proposed Board Reform. 155
Commission Bundling and Soft Dollar Payments 156
Malfeasance at Insurance Companies. 157
Cash Withdrawal and the Effect on Funds Size 157
SEC Reform 158
Final Thoughts 161

CHAPTER 7: EXECUTIVE PERVERSION OF FINANCIAL
             MANAGEMENT. 163

Agency Theory. 164
The Agency Problem in Full Bloom. 166
Leveraged Buyouts and Junk Bonds. 167
Options: The Major By-Product of the LBO Movement 167
The Economic Boom of the 1990s 168
Dividend Conventions Violated. 169
The Fundamentals of Share Repurchase Strategies 170

Buybacks Substituted For Dividends 171
The Inappropriate Use of Share Buybacks 172
Anything But Chump Change. 173
What Happened at the End of the Day? 175
A Trillion Dollar Heist. 176
What About Agency Theory?. 178
Concluding Thoughts and Analysis 179

CHAPTER 8:   MARKET SYSTEM AND SOCIAL INSTITUTIONS
             CALLED INTO QUESTION. 181
Institutions Establish the Rules of the Game 182
The Role of Organizations. 184
The Market Economy as an Institution 185
Public Education is Necessary to Avoid "Atrophied Personalities" 186
Transaction Costs and Property Rights Create Institutions. 188
Non-Market Institutions that Counter the Negative Effects
    of the Market 190
    The Family as an Institution. 190
    The State as an Indispensable Institution 191
    The Nation and Cultural Institutions. 192
    Professional Associations Let Us Down 193
Choices Devoid of Meaning. 194
Spill-Over Effects of the Market. 195
Organization Theory: Incentives Versus Leadership 197
Executive Compensation 198
    Paying for Performance as a Joke 198
    CEO Compensation Excesses: How Much is Enough?. 200
Transparency as a Panacea 201
Final Thoughts and Analysis 203

CHAPTER 9:   VIRTUE: MEDICINE FOR BUSINESS ETHICS. . . 207
Reflections on the Virtuous Life: Early Philosophies 209
The Study of Virtue in History 210
    Adam Smith Relates Morality to the Invisible Hand. 214
    Confucius 219
Developing Character Through Virtuous Behavior 224
Blindsided By Greed 226
Education and Business Ethics. 229
Final Thoughts and Analysis 231

CONTENTS

CHAPTER 10: REFLECTIONS ON CORPORATE SCANDALS . . . 235

Six Key Questions 236
A Central Villain? 245

Appendix 1: Caux Round Table 249
Appendix 2: Listing of Virtues 257
Notes 263
Bibliography 279
Index 289

LIST OF TABLES AND FIGURES

CHAPTER 3

Figure 3-1: Dow Jones Industrial Average 1998-2004 48
Table 3-1: Enron's Political Contacts 51
Table 3-2: Enron Timeline 54
Table 3-3: Tyco Timeline 60
Table 3-4: Main Players in WorldCom Fraud 64
Table 3-5: Corporate Legal and Ethical Violations 70
Table 3-6: Parmalat Timeline 74
Table 3-7: Prominent European Company Ethical Violations 76

CHAPTER 5

Table 5-1: Specific Settlement Payments 111
Table 5-2: Investment Bank Analysts 120
Figure 5-1: Richard Grasso's Compensation 122

CHAPTER 6

Table 6-1: SEC Reform Initiatives 159

CHAPTER 7

Figure 7-1: S&P 500 Dividend Yield Since 1871 169
Figure 7-2: Share Repurchases Compared to Dividends 172
Figure 7-3: S&P 500 Share Repurchases and Equity Issuance 174
Figure 7-4: Market Value of U.S. Corporate Equities and Foreign
             Depository Receipts Owned by U.S. Residents 177

CHAPTER 9

Table 9-1: Universal Symmetry: The Golden Rule Across Cultures . . . 212
Table 9-2: Virtues that Support Business Transactions 218
Table 9-3: Six Core Virtues 227
Table 9-4: The Seven Capital Sins and The Seven Capital Virtues 228

LIST OF ABBREVIATIONS AND ACRONYMS

.com	commercial
.edu	education
.gov	government
.org	organization
AA	Arthur Andersen
AA, LLP	Arthur Andersen, Limited Liability Partnership
AACSB	Association to Advance Collegiate Schools of Business (formerly) American Assembly of Collegiate Schools of Business
ABN	Algemene Bank Nederland
AFL-CIO	American Federation of Labor–Congress of Industrial Organizations
AMG	Affiliated Managers Group
AMRO	Amsterdam–Rotterdam Bank (Now AMRO)
AT&T	American Telephone and Telegraph
B.C.	before Christ
BBC	British Broadcasting Company
BofA	Bank of America Corporation
CalPERS	California Public Employees' Retirement System
CEO	Chief Executive Officer
CESR	Committee of European Securities Regulators
CFO	Chief Financial Officer
CIT	Commercial Investment Trust
CNBC	Cable National Broadcasting Company
CNN	Cable News Network
COO	Chief Operating Officer
CPA	Certified Public Accountant
CSFB	Credit Suisse First Boston LLC
DOJ	Department of Justice
EPS	Earnings Per Share
EU	European Union

FASB	Financial Accounting Standards Board
FBI	Federal Bureau of Investigations
FDA	Federal Drug Administration
FDIC	Federal Deposit Insurance Corporation
GAAP	Generally Accepted Accounting Principles
GDP	Gross Domestic Product
GLBA	Gramm-Leach-Bliley Act
GSE	Government Sponsored Enterprise
HBS	Harvard Business School
ICI	Investment Company Institute
ING	International Netherlands Group Bank
IOU	I Owe You
IPO	Initial Public Offerings
IRS	Internal Revenue Service
JEDI	Joint Energy Development Investments
KKR	Kravis, Kohlberg, and Roberts
KPMG	Klynveld Peat Marwick Goerdeler
LBO	Leverage Buyout
LDDS	Long-Distance Discount Service
LLC	Limited Liability Company
MBA	Masters of Business Administration
MCI	Microwave Communications Incorporated
MD	Doctor of Medicine (from L. Midicinae Doctor)
MFS	Massachusetts Financial Services
NASD	National Association of Securities Dealers
NBC	National Broadcasting Company
NCB	National City Bank
NCC	National City Company
NPR	Northern Pacific Railroad
NPV	Net Present Value
NYAG	New York Attorney General
NYSE	New York Stock Exchange
OFHEO	Office of Federal Housing Enterprises Oversight
P/BV	Price Divided by Book Value
P/E	Price Divided by Earnings per share

PBHG Funds   Pilgram, Baxter, Hoyt and Greg Funds
PCAOB   Public Company Accounting Oversight Board
PhD   Doctor of Philosophy (from L. Philosophiae Doctor)
PIMCO   Pacific Investment Management Company
PwC   Price-Waterhouse-Coopers
RCN   Residential Communications Network
S&Ls   Savings and Loans
S&P   Standard and Poor's
SEC   Securities and Exchange Commission
SLF   Sun Life Financial Inc.
SOA   Sarbanes-Oxley Act
SOP   Standard Operating Procedure
SPE   Special Purpose Entity
SRO   Self-Regulated Organization
SRS   Share Repurchase Strategy
SSB   Salomon Smith Barney Inc.
UBS AG   Union Bank of Switzerland (Zurich)
UBS   UBS Warburg LLC
UK   United Kingdom
US   United States
USA   United States of America
VIA   Values In Action

FOREWORD

In *Corporate Scandals: The Many Faces of Greed*, Professors Kenneth R. Gray, Larry A. Frieder, and George W. Clark, Jr. dissect one of our country's most devastating economic periods. The three authors are uniquely qualified for this task. Their writing brings important insights, as well as a sense of candor about our free enterprise system that is often missing from public and academic discourse.

Dramatic corporate malfeasance marked the end of the 1990's and the beginning of the new millennium. Industrial and financial sector scandals filled newspaper headlines. Nowhere could anyone find proponents of the status quo in business and finance, yet few emerged to constructively address what can only be characterized as a crisis or breakdown of major proportions. The authors put forth a masterful effort in analyzing the pervasive institutional failures that contributed to the systemic shock we all experienced during this time.

Earlier, I mentioned the authors' unique qualifications to execute their work. As their longtime Academic Dean of the School of Business & Industry (SBI) at Florida A & M University, I have had the opportunity to observe their constant and inquisitive participation in SBI's Professional Development Program. These professors interacted almost daily with major corporate CEO's and other high level executives of numerous large corporations, many of which actually were involved in various issues examined in this book. These exchanges occurred in the course of faculty luncheons, Executive Forum Series, and SBI's television series, "Today's Leaders Face Tomorrows." This book evidences all the productive insights that derived from these valuable high-level interactions.

We are very fortunate to have the team of Kenneth Gray, Larry Frieder, and George Clark exploring and explaining the numerous scandals and ramifications covered in this book. Ken, as SBI's Eminent Scholar Chair of Global Business, specializes in business strategy, policy, and international management. In his role as a professor, he has thoughtfully researched and published on numerous topics related to global corporate management and the effects of complex institutions on modern corporations. Larry, Florida A & M's Eminent Scholar Chair Professor of Financial Services is deeply rooted in the study of commercial banking consolidation and "best practices." Several U.S. and global banks, with approximately $1 trillion in asset size, bear the mark of Larry's insights. George holds Florida A & M's distinguished 3M Professorship. He has been a leader in the field of business ethics and is quite knowledgeable in the area of organizational behavior. As this book's title underscores, greed and the absence of virtue are central to an examination of corporate malfeasance, and these are topics that George has been focusing on for decades. Now we all can benefit from his learning experiences and from the remarkable perspectives all three authors share with their readers.

Much has been reported in the popular press about the financial scandals of the previous decade and their specific resolutions. This book does more than recount events however. Rather, it provides all the background needed to allow the reader to better appreciate how such problems came into being and how one can constructively address resultant challenges. I believe this work has much to teach those engaged in business, education, and government regulation.

Given my forty years as an academician in the field of accounting, over thirty years as SBI's Dean, and twenty years of service on the corporate boards of several corporations, this book really hits home. That is, it speaks to the deep failure of public auditors and the accounting profession, the need to address breakdowns in corporate governance, and the potential opportunities that exist in business education. Having spent my entire professional life in these areas, I can confidently say that readers of this book will be well served.

Sybil C. Mobley, C.P.A., Ph.D.
Dean Emeritus
School of Business & Industry
Florida A & M University

1

CORPORATE
SCANDALS

The *Oxford English Dictionary* defines "scandal" as "an action or event regarded as morally or legally wrong and causing general public outrage." Often associated with matters of sex and money, scandals are violations of societal norms; they imply loss of loyalty, fidelity, and trust in relationships, and sometimes violations of the law. Typically they are associated with famous or widely popular figures and often involve large sums of money.

Within the context of business, the relationships that have fallen victim to scandals most recently concern managers and their shareholders. Through profoundly unscrupulous dealings, scurrilous managers used both legal and illegal means to enrich themselves at the expense of their shareholders to the tune of millions and sometimes billions of dollars.

In its short history, the twenty-first century has witnessed unprecedented corporate scandal, malfeasance, and financial crisis. The energy company Enron, the seventh largest company in the United States, collapsed into a painful and ignomious bankruptcy. Telecommunications giants Global Crossing and WorldCom also declared bankruptcies. Corporate profit claims received sharp public scrutiny. Over a four-year period Xerox Corporation overstated its profits by $1.4 billion.

The federal homeowner lending organization nicknamed Freddie-Mac understated its profits by more than $4 billion. In fact, in 2002 some 250 American public companies had to restate their accounts compared with only 92 in 1997 and 3 in 1983.[1]

Further many U.S. chief executive officers, chief financial officers, and other high-ranking managers have been arrested, tried, and convicted for fraud, conspiracy and other misdeeds. Prestigious accounting firms, such as Arthur Andersen, traditionally the guardians of integrity, have been found guilty of negligence and obstruction of justice. Additionally, allegedly independent Wall Street stock analysts violated their fiduciary obligation to investors by becoming servants not of their cleints but of their investment banking departments. In satisfying blatant corporate and individual greed, these analysts completely destroyed their credibility.

Corporate boards of directors, public accountants, auditors, and other self-regulated professionals, such as lawyers and investment bankers, have also been consumed by greed. In addition, the Securities and Exchange Commission (SEC) and the U.S. stock market exchanges (e.g., the NASD and NYSE), which are responsible for policing our nation's financial system have been ineffective regulators. Even our legal system is implicated in these scandals: White-collar criminals are treated far more leniently than "street" criminals, even though the economic and social magnitude of their acts are much greater.

The grand result of these diverse crimes is an unprecedented assault on the integrity of U.S. corporations. The effects of these waves of scandalous corporate practices have been worldwide and severe. Employees who were innocent of any wrongdoings have lost their jobs. Many loyal workers who had invested in company 401(k)s, pensions, and mutual funds had seen their life savings wiped out. Not surprisingly, the U.S. is suffering the effects of a considerable loss in investor confidence and an even greater loss of trust in corporations and their executives.

What has happened to the public trust in corporate America and the moral fidelity of corporate leaders? Is there no place for ethical concern within our market system? How can public corporations be made accountable?

THE NEED TO RESTORE TRUST AND INTEGRITY

The integrity of America's economic system relies on the confidence of investors in the guardians of our financial capital. This point extends far beyond just accountancy and audit issues. In economic terms, the absence of trust, truth, and loyalty create costs. Trustworthiness increases the efficiency of the wider economic system. To work well, markets need both a robust legal framework and a behavioral infrastructure of accepted rules and codes of conduct, that is, ethical principles involving truth, trust, and honesty. When laws, rules, and codes are flaunted, transaction costs go up. Corporate misconduct delegitimizes the creation of wealth. Corporate scandals give protectionist politicians and anti-globalization protesters propaganda gifts to use on those in the developed world who seriously question the underlying tenets of free enterprise. Hence, governments committed to wealth creation must sanitize the operation of the corporate engines that deliver rising standards of living.

In what way, and to what degree, does the concept of ethics influence economic activity? The 1998 Nobel laureate in Economic Science, Amartya Sen, observes, "A basic code of good business behavior is a bit like oxygen: we take an interest in its presence only when it is absent."[2] Clearly, the recent financial scandals call for ethical conduct that can recreate the valuable sense of trust among investors. *Webster's Collegiate Dictionary* defines "trust" as, "the assured reliance on the character, ability, strength, or truth of someone or something."[3] If such assured reliance can be reestablished, then the monitoring and transaction costs in many companies and in the wider economy can be reduced as well. Ethics scholar Norman Bowie notes:

> The essential point is that trusting relationships change the nature of monitoring. In non-trusting relationships, the supervisor functions as a policeman; in trusting relationships, as a mentor....[trust] reduces the amount of bias in forecasts and budgetary requests....[and] one would expect to see more joint ventures between corporations that have higher levels of trust.[4]

At a fundamental level, shared ethical principles are a low-cost substitute for internal control and external regulation. If corporations conceal facts and truth and thereby erode trust, then the conduct of business becomes more risky and costly. Indeed, the transactions themselves may become unreliable. The broader system is then forced to absorb the additional costs to create vitality and reliability.

Auditors are the guardians of the integrity of our capitalist system. Former U.S. Chief Justice Warren Burger explained it this way: "The public watchdog function demands that the accountant maintain total independence from the client at all times and requires complete fidelity to the public trust."[5] Ethical behavior is thus a necessary prerequisite if investors are to benefit from auditor's conclusions about financial statements. Auditors must have the skill and competence to detect misrepresentations or omissions in financial statements, as well as the ethical standards necessary for rendering trustworthy opinions.

The hiring and pay of public auditors are decided by the management of the firms they audit. Auditor independence is compromised at the outset, because practicing impartial, competent auditing could lead to their loss of future income. Controls exist to counteract unethical practices: stigma and disrepute if audits are inaccurate, the threat of costly litigation, loss of client trust and contracts, or the potentially catastrophic consequences of a criminal investigation by the U.S. Justice Department. These problems ruined Arthur Andersen, the oldest and most respected accounting firm in the nation, with major clients and name recognition around the globe. Yet it is clear that the threat of such sanctions did not stop Andersen from squandering its reputation as the most rigorous of the Big Five audit firms and becoming excessively pliant and conspiratorial with its top-paying clients. No solution to this problem exists until the innate conflict of interest in the auditor-client relationship is rectified.

In the Andersen case, another problem was the unresolved conflict of interest between the firms auditing and consulting functions. The relationship between the two was so close that human bias got in the way of a principled, professional disinterest.[6] The suggestion of a hypothetical relationship with a client distorts an auditor's judgment and a long-standing relationship involving tens of millions of dollars would surely magnify this distortion. Harvard business professor Max Bazerman and his research associates concluded that auditors should ideally be regarded "as more like tax collectors than partners or advisers."[7]

Corporate executives, as overachievers, sometimes test the borders of ethics. Each new and more inflated level of a stock market bubble tests executives' integrity. Society suffers when industry captains succumb to greed. Our economic system needs penalties and incentives that control this egocentric, self-interest motive that pervades our system. One reason the U.S. capital market model has "slipped off the rails" is precisely that existing rewards and punishments have been inadequate.

ROOT CAUSES OF THE CURRENT CRISIS

In a market economy a key for shareholder success is to attain the highest possible price for their stock. A company's share price determines the wealth of its stockholders. Thomas Kochan, of the MIT Workplace Center, comments that a root cause of the current crisis is the "overemphasis American corporations have been forced to give in recent years to maximizing shareholder value without regard for the effects of their actions on other stakeholders."[8]

Since the 1980s, Wall Street has encouraged the relentless drive to maximize share prices. Increasingly, large private and institutional investors demanded *immediate* returns on investments. Executives often sought to meet short-term expectations of investment analysts by restructuring operations to boost earnings.[9] Corporate Boards of Directors and compensation consultants restructured executive contracts to better align management incentives with investor interests. Boards turned to Chief Executive Officers (CEOs) who could best manage relations with the financial community and project an image of confidence. The era of the charismatic CEO was born.[10]

Wall Street, the business media and press, and business school case writers reinforced these trends by committing a classic attribution error. They credited the successes of organizations to the leadership and vision of the CEO and the top executive team. This error increased the perceived value of CEOs and dramatically escalated CEO's salaries. By 2000, the salaries of top corporate CEOs were, on average, six hundred times greater than the pay of an average worker. By comparison, the ratio was 42:1 in 1980. As a result, power and financial rewards became densely concentrated at the top levels of corporate management.

The increasingly frequent awards of stock options to U.S. CEOs and the dramatically high and rising salaries of corporate executives are classic examples of unintended consequences. In 1993, the U.S. government attempted to cap CEOs' pay by imposing a $1 million limit on tax deductibility and the Financial Accounting Standards Board (FASB) insisted that the cost of options be expensed on the profit-and-loss statement, but both suggestions were defeated by the big business lobby. Business leaders have thought that they are justified in awarding large stock options because it is believed to align top executives' interest with those of the shareholders. In reality these large option awards create a powerful incentive for the company to buy-back more of its stock because by doing so, the company avoids an explosion of its outstanding shares and the consequent dilution of profits-per-share that would undoubtedly create investor outrage. Since many companies tend to buy back stock at bubble-inflated prices their economic value is reduced. So higher stock earnings-per-share and higher stock prices as a result of share buybacks never materialize.

The Commission on Public Trust and Private Enterprise set up by the Conference Board, a business-led research organization reported:

> The commission shares the public's anger over excessive executive compensation, especially to executives of failed or failing companies, and finds that compensation abuses have contributed to a dramatic loss of confidence in the governance of American publicly held corporations—with visible and damaging financial market effects.[11]

A pressing need exists to address the conditions that have created incentives for misconduct. If they are not corrected, the same thing will happen again.

REMEDIES TO THE CURRENT CRISIS

Suggestions abound for addressing the ongoing crisis of corporate behavior. One suggestion encourages publicly traded companies to take out insurance on their financial statements.[12] This would cover investors against losses arising from misrepresentation and the insurers would have incentive to appoint and pay auditors. An alternative would shift control over the auditors' appointments and pay to a public agency that serves as a public sector watchdog. This shift would create a system similar to the U.S. Internal Revenue Service: a cadre of auditors would evaluate publicly traded companies. Both approaches create more independent auditors.

In the case of stock options, similarly ineffective checks and balances exist. For example, institutional investors such as mutual funds and pension funds, which control vast amounts of money in the United States, do not adequately monitor corporate management. Few fund managers have protested egregiously large stock options. Additionally, ineffective mutual fund trusteeship needs to be addressed. Also, many cases exist where non-executive directors' independence has been compromised by consultancy contracts and the granting of stock options.

Despite some strong rhetoric from the Bush administration in the wake of the Enron scandals, reform was left mostly to the Securities and Exchange Commission (SEC), the chief financial regulator in the United States. However, then-SEC chairman Harvey Pitt seemed reluctant to shake up the system. Yet the revelation of egregious fraud at WorldCom—now called MCI—changed the atmosphere.

Public outrage stirred politicians of all persuasions to unite around the sweeping reform plans of Paul Sarbanes, a Democrat in charge of the Senate Banking Committee. At the same time, Michael Oxley, Republican Chairman of the House Committee on Financial Services, proposed a similar, though less stringent, bill. The tougher provisions proposed by Senator Sarbanes mostly prevailed, and the Sarbanes-Oxley Act (SOA), the United States' most far-reaching financial legislation in 70 years, became law in August of 2002.

The business community quickly criticized the SOA. Executives cautioned that the cost of compliance to businesses could involve millions of dollars. Other critics suggested that executives' need to focus on compliance would inhibit their ability to take entrepreneurial risks. There was also considerable confusion about the effect of the legislation on non-U.S. companies—some of the world's largest—that list their shares on U.S. exchanges. Despite these alleged flaws, observers universally agree that the Act has forced those in the executive suite and boardroom to concentrate on accurate and more transparent financial disclosure, effective corporate governance, and new working relationships with public audit firms.

To clean up the auditing process, the Act created the Public Company Accounting Oversight Board (PCAOB) to oversee auditors and strengthen the independence of auditors by rotating audit partners every five years. The Act also requires executives to certify financial statements, expands rules governing conflicts of interest, and heightens criminal penalties. It imposes tougher penalties on directors and places restrictions on auditors providing non-audit services. However, it does not address the more fundamental conflict inherent in management's appointment and remuneration of auditors.

CORRUPTION AND GREED ON WALL STREET

Not only was the SEC slow to address corporate malfeasance and the associated public accounting failures in the non-financial sector, but also it was equally lax and ineffective in patrolling the financial marketplace generally and Wall Street particularly. However, the New York State Attorney General, Eliot Spitzer, using an obscure New York law—the Martin Act—stepped in to fill the gap. Investigations by his office concluded that investment bankers and security analysts regularly violated their fiduciary responsibility to investors by colluding to promote deals. Spitzer also pursued and prosecuted the mutual fund companies which engaged in market timing, late trading, illegal sales practices, and other violations of their own prospectuses.

Such efforts will not in themselves provide a long-term solution. Neither does the business environment sufficiently constrain companies. There was a time when leading investment banks, accounting firms, institutional investors, and law firms would not connive to set up dubious special purpose entities or engage in questionable accounting practices, and they would have paid attention to conflicts of interest between managers and company shareholders.

Restoring positive values and a sense of trust within the business community is, of course, more difficult than passing laws and introducing regulations. Ethical organizational cultures that foster trust must be established to reinforce legal restraints and bolster ethical behavior. The social-political-economic leadership of the United States must stress our economic system's ethical dimensions.

OVERVIEW OF THE TEXT

Our journey begins in chapter two with a brief survey of corporate scandals throughout history. Great waves of exploration and innovation have propelled often worthless speculative ventures that grew until they burst, hence the name "bubble." Financial scandals followed. A look at some of history's more infamous financial bubbles provide numerous insights relevant today. Many bubbles grew from the enthusiasm generated by world exploration, and from the subsequent colonial land grabs. The discovery of new territories initiated speculative bursts of capital expansion that produced both the South Seas and the Mississippi Company bubbles. Two centuries later, the steam engine and the railroad boom created an investment bubble that was similar to the technology bubble of the 1990s. Interestingly, the public and lawmakers usually overreact to bubble-related scandals and produce legislation that curtails innovation and economic activity. This was the case during the stock market crash of 1929.

Chapters three to six discuss the systematic evolution of corporate malfeasance and corruption both on and off Wall Street, noting the laxity of the SEC and of various self-regulated professions and stock exchanges. Chapter three explores recent high profile corporate breakdowns. How did these problems come to be? How did they come to light? Enron was the first prominent firm to exhibit the direct results of stock market pressures, corporate malfeasance, questionable oversight by the board of directors, as well as dubious conduct by its public auditors, law firms, and investment bankers.

Evidence of a general breakdown of the corporate culture arose when the public discovered similar problems at several other prominent companies: Tyco, WorldCom, Global Crossing, Qwest, ImClone, HealthSouth, and Adelphia for example. Scandal also rocked the European firms Royal Ahold and Parmalat.

Chapter four presents the Sarbanes-Oxley Act and the Public Company Accounting Oversight Board (PCAOB). The SOA sought to restore investor confidence during the general economic decline that followed the waves of scandal. The PCAOB plays a central role in the effort to restore confidence. The chapter discusses the case of HealthSouth as an example of how effective SOA may be as a tool for corporate policing.

Chapter five focuses on Wall Street. Beginning with a discussion of the SEC and its embattled Chairman, Harvey Pitt, we detail SOA's development and Pitt's resignation. The chapter examines New York State Attorney General Eliot Spitzer's efforts to address the unfolding Wall Street scandal and it discusses the $1.6 billion settlement that he reached with ten major investment banks. The chapter also reviews the plight of high profile investment analysts Henry Blodgett, Jack Grubman, and Mary Meeker and analyzes the breakdown of the venerable New York Stock Exchange (NYSE), with attention to the roles of its celebrated CEO, Richard Grasso, the NYSE Board of Directors, its new chief administrator, John Reed, and the SEC.

Chapter six explores the scandals and corruption afflicting the $7 trillion mutual fund industry, including Canary Capital, Bank of America, Janus, Strong, Putnam, Massachusetts Financial Services and Alliance Capital. Again, Eliot Spitzer, and not the SEC, brought these issues to light and pursued an effective remedy.

Chapter seven focuses on a subplot we call "the great heist": the perversion of corporate financial management practices that facilitated excessive and ruinous executive compensation. Dramatically rising executive salaries, benefits, and awards triggered a major shift in the historical role of corporate dividend policy. Rates of return were increasingly driven by share repurchase strategies as opposed to dividend yields. Share repurchase strategies applied in the 1990s not only destroyed stock value at the various firms, but also left the door open to a $1.679 trillion "heist" by corporate management that we uncover. Massive share buybacks masked an explosive issuance of executive stock options by which management acquired vast wealth without actual conspiracy or illegality.

Chapters eight and nine identify how our society can address fundamental economic and corporate problems.

Chapter eight examines social institutions and the incentives that guide social welfare. The market system is a social institution. Non-market institutions—such as family, educational and cultural organizations, and professional associations—seek to constrain socially undesireable traits, promote attractive values, and balance individual behavior.

The spill-over of marketplace values to other non-market institutions is one of the great challenges of our time. Social instituions and cultural norms set parameters for executive compensation. Do growing CEO compensation packages signal a change in social norms or a violation of those norms? What unintended consequences may arise from efforts to constrain such compensation?

Chapter nine looks at business ethics from the point of view of virtue across history in Western and Eastern philosophy. The chapter considers Plato, Aristotle, Adam Smith, G.W.F. Hegel, Confucius, and the Caux Roundtable. Since business schools usually fail to instill ethical ideals in their graduates, the chapter offers an alternative pedagogy.

The final chapter of this book is reflective. In considering the broad, systemic breakdowns in accounting, regulation, and Wall Street practices, several problems and issues emerge. We frame six key questions to assess these breakdowns and related issues:

1. Why did our financial caretakers fail to use history's lessons to guard against the developing bubble and its subsequent burst?

2. To what extent is the free enterprise system broken? How well has it been fixed?

3. New York State Attorney Eliot Spitzer led the reform of Wall Street investment banking as well as mutual fund practices. How enduring will these reforms be?

4. How do the media and other cultural influences feed greed?

5. Are the current high levels of CEO pay appropriate? How can we improve our management compensation systems?

6. Does the shift of wealth to a management elite signify a larger social problem?

The book ends with an attempt to establish the central villains of the saga *Corporate Scandals: The Many Faces of Greed.*

CHAPTER ONE QUESTIONS:

CORPORATE SCANDALS

1. What makes a particular wrongdoing in business qualify as a scandal?

2. Why has the public lost trust in corporate America? What are some of the root causes of this loss of trust?

3. What is the purpose of the Securities and Exchange Commission (SEC)?

4. How does ethical behavior affect economic activity?

5. Why is it important for auditors to have a sense of integrity?

6. What are some of the root causes of American business scandals?

8. What are some remedies for the problem of corporate behavior?

2

A SHORT HISTORY OF BUSINESS SCANDALS

B usiness history is replete with misjudgments, mistakes in financial management, and financial skullduggery. In addition to fraud, misrepresentation, and blatant lying, unscrupulous entrepreneurs have diverted funds from one stated use to another, paid dividends out of capital or borrowed money, issued company stock based on inside knowledge, sold securities without full disclosure of new knowledge, made noncompetitive purchases from or extended loans to insiders, and altered company books. These illegal activities and unethical transactions violate basic trust and misrepresent corporate motives.

In the early stages of capitalist economic development during the fifteenth and sixteenth centuries, codes of conduct provided for honor and trust only within the family. In these settings nepotism was efficient and even sensible, since a stranger virtually had a license to steal. At the beginning of the eighteenth century, a firm bought a man's services but not his loyalty. In a time when embezzlement and fraud were not regarded as crimes, to be a clerk was an invitation to start a new competitive business.[1] Until 1799 it was not illegal in the United States for bank officers to borrow bank funds.[2]

Some of the earliest documented financial scandals involved the governments of France and Britain. In the early 1700s these governments each used a chartered company, the Mississippi Company and the South Sea Company, respectively, to restructure national debts accumulated during the wars of 1689 to 1714. The two companies, whose shares became objects of speculation in 1719-1720, were nominally monopolistic trading companies, but their real function was to convert large government debt into private debt held as stock shares. In time, the Mississippi Company and the South Sea Company became involved in two of the largest cases of corporate scandal and financial bubbles in history.

Charles Kindleberger, a noted economic historian, defines a "financial bubble" as a dramatic rise in stock prices over an extended period of time, yet eventually and unexpectedly the price of the stock bursts and collapses.[3] Financial bubbles reflect dramatically rising prices and stock values that are unjustifiable and unsustainable due to irrational concentrations of capital. While not all bubbles are swindles, they are often the product of a greedy appetite for wealth. The South Sea Company bubble arose from a scam; the Mississippi Company bubble grew from two mistaken ideas. The first mistaken belief regarded stocks and bonds as money. That is, people believed money was a medium of exchange rather than a store of intrinsic value (it is really both). Further, the prevailing notion of "money" was quite broad, including paper currency, bonds, credit notes, and "company shares."[4] The second mistaken notion held that issuing more money as demand increased would not be inflationary. People did not yet understand that the rate of inflation is directly proportionate to an increase in the money supply.

Unfortunately for the Mississippi Company, during the eighteenth century, equity shares were difficult to evaluate accurately. Returns were not guaranteed and were contingent on a host of often poorly understood circumstances affecting the economics of the companies. Such conditions contributed to mis-pricing. Further compounding the difficulties of the Mississippi Company was the tendency of its top managers to mislead investors with unrealistic expectations of profits.

THE MISSISSIPPI COMPANY BUBBLE OF FRANCE

John Law (1671-1729), a Scottish financier and speculator, founded the Mississippi Company.[5] The company's rise fueled financial specula-tion that led to a financial collapse greater than the Wall Street stock market crash of 1929.[6] Law, an entrepreneur who came to France to make his fortune, set up the Banque Générale, the first bank charged with issuing bank notes in France. Law's plan was to introduce paper money to rescue France from its rampant inflation, shortage of coins, and unstable currency. The public gradually accepted Law's bank notes, due in large part to the notes' convertibility into fixed quantities of gold, which stabilized the debased French coins.

Law's bank invested heavily in the Compagnie d'Occident (Com-pany of the West), which controlled of large grants of land around the Mississippi River and held exclusive trading rights in the territory for 25 years. The company, a trading concession from the French govern-ment, had been relinquished by its previous owner in lieu of tax arrears.[7] Law offered to turn it into a joint-stock company, exchanging shares for short-term government notes and reducing the interest on the national debt. In effect, Law was converting part of the French national debt into shares in his company. The territory, later to become part of the Louisiana Purchase, was the company's greatest asset, and Law needed to develop the French colony rapidly to maintain public confidence in the bank. Law sought to foster emigration to the Americas to occupy the territory and acquire control and monopoly of all tobacco conces-sions. In pursuit of his goals, he undertook a promotional campaign that brought several thousand settlers to New Orleans.

In 1719, the Compagnie d'Occident absorbed the rival East India and China Company, and the Banque Générale became the state bank of France.[8] These mergers produced a monopoly that controlled the entire colonial trade of one of the most powerful nations of its time. The crown appointed Law as Counselor of State and Comptroller General of Finances. When the public was invited to invest in shares of the Mississippi venture (which Law re-christened the Mississippi Com-pany), a great wave of speculation drove the price of the shares up over fourteen thousand percent. At the same time, Law's bank was flooding the country with paper money.

Law issued a large number of shares in his businesses, but kept speculative fever high by announcing generous dividends and allowing existing shareholders to buy additional shares at a preferential rate. His boldest move came later in 1719 when he offered to convert the entire national debt of France from annuities into company shares. He also offered a huge sum for the right to take over the royal tax collection. Law financed all of this by issuing even larger numbers of shares.

Under this new scheme the government of France agreed to pay 3 percent interest annually on that portion of its 1,500 million units of the new French currency in outstanding debt that the Compagnie d'Occident was able to trade for its equity. Any government security acquired, besides providing a steady source of interest income, could be collateralized to support loans to finance the Compagnie's overseas expansion. Simultaneously, Law sought to build up the enterprise's capital surplus account by manipulating the market value of its shares so that it sold at a premium over the par value of the debt acquired.

The inevitable collapse of France's first national bank came in 1720 after a royal decree by Louis XV halved the value of the bank notes. People hoarded and debased silver and gold coins to retain their value, thus dramatically shrinking the amount circulating. Prices of goods and services rose enormously. Shares of Law's company, which had been amalgamated with his bank, sank in price as rapidly as they had risen and the Banque Générale had to suspend dividend payments. It soon became clear that speculators, who found their shares worthless, had had no intention of actually taking part in the emigration to the Mississippi region sponsored by the Compagnie des Indes. Emigration to this area in the new world had remained largely limited to forced deportations of convicts and undesirables. Law was forced to leave France secretly. He settled in Venice, where he died in 1729, poor and forgotten.

Law's control of both the central bank and the stock market allowed him to avoid questions concerning what his company actually did. Law mistakenly considered money the source of public wealth, rather than the result of it. Accordingly, he believed that the state would prosper by increasing the issuance of paper currency. He used investors' shares and limitlessly issued french currency without reserves to support the value of the shares and currency.

THE SOUTH SEA COMPANY BUBBLE OF ENGLAND

The South Sea Company of England was founded in 1711 and had a monopoly on trade with Spanish America. The monopoly came about with the Treaty of Utrecht, which terminated the War of Spanish Succession. Following the war, Britain extracted from Spain the right to trade with the Spanish colonies. The term "South Seas" in the company name referred to an area just off the western coasts of South America; it had nothing at all to do with the part of the world located in Polynesia. Nevertheless, the term captured the imagination of the British:

> In the South Seas of the Englishman's misconception there were fabulous lands where gold was lying upon the ground waiting to be picked up, and where natives would exchange marvelous artifacts for a pittance.[9]

Yet the enormous wealth of South America could be had only if an efficient organization was created to exploit the riches. This was the purpose of the South Sea Company.

The South Sea bubble was not quite as large a scandal as that of the Mississippi Company. The parliamentary political system in Britain greatly limited the possibility that the company would succeed in gaining control of all the key financial institutions, as Law had done in France. Also, the South Sea officials were never able to use exchange-control regulations when the price of their shares began to fall since such regulations did not exist. As in France, the principal objective of the British government was to transform the national debt into the share capital of a company. In other words, the South Sea Company sought to convert annuities into equities and thus, it was hoped, reduce the cost of the national debt.[10]

By 1719, Britain's war with Spain was strangling South Sea business. So the company directors decided to focus instead on the market for public debt. The architect of the scheme was John Blunt, the son of a prosperous English shoemaker. In the early part of 1720, a parliamentary announcement proclaimed that the Company would take over the entire British national debt, absorbing annuities with a capital value of more than $150 million. Companies of all kinds were floated to take advantage of the public interest in obtaining South Sea Company stock. Soon speculation carried the stock to ten times its nominal value.

Having discovered the enormous power of advertising, the South Sea directors worked hard at exciting the market and the financial press by using the same sorts of devices that John Law used for the Mississippi Company. The directors were in the business of orchestrating a dream. Quotations for South Sea stock appeared in local papers and an enthusiastic public bought huge quantities. As Baskin and Miranti described it:

> A fever of speculation gripped England. The entire population was infected. Everyone invested, rich and poor alike.... Half of continental Europe too, was gambling in South Sea stock.[11]

A flood of fresh proposals for new companies engulfed the government as the South Sea Company's success spawned a large number of imitators. This prompted South Sea directors to persuade their political allies to pass the Bubble Act of June 1720, making it extremely difficult to set up a new joint-stock company. To do so required a charter granted from parliament. The Bubble Act reduced the number of enterprises that could compete with the South Sea Company for capital. Further, the people of England were now advised to distrust the many unsound enterprises that had already been established.

A debate ensued in the House of Commons over a proposal to limit the conversion of South Sea stock, but was opposed for reasons that were not public knowledge. The directors of the Company secretly provided several members of the government and the court of King George I with an allocation of shares in the South Sea Company. These shares were issued at a premium to the market price yet no deposit was required. Because the shares did not in fact exist, the bribes offered to government officials functioned much in the same way as a modern executive stock-option scheme: If the share price rose, then the recipients could redeem the shares and take their profits. Once holding fictitious shares or options, then these influential persons had an interest in seeing the South Sea Company share price rise without regard to the cost to the nation.

John Blunt and his insiders deliberately sought to make profits on stock issues to themselves against loans secured by the stock itself. As the capital gains were drawn off, they were converted into estates that were purchased from the proceeds of previous sales of company stock. In fact, at the time of the South Sea Company's collapse, Blunt held six contracts to buy land. In September 1720 the collapse of the South Sea Company was set in motion when people began to unload their stock. By the end of the month, South Sea stock had dropped 92 percent. When chairman John Blunt and some directors sold their shares and cashed out, the bubble burst, and the stock completely collapsed. Thousands of stockholders were ruined. Parliamentary investigation later revealed complicity by some company officials.

Apart from the bribes paid to Ministers (positions comparable to U.S. cabinet members) and members of Parliament (comparable to members of U.S. Congress), four factors tended to propel the price of the stock upwards. First, the company never committed itself to a fixed conversion price for the old debt it was acquiring.[12] Second, stock was not made available for transfer until the end of the year, eight months after the first issue. Third, as in France, although one could pay for shares in installments over long periods, buyers could instantly use the shares as collateral for loans from the company. Buyers usually used the loans to purchase more shares of the company. Finally, as with the Mississippi Bubble in France, exchange rate and the other interest rate data indicate the existence of large-scale foreign speculation in the South Sea Company, first from France and later from Holland. As was the case with the Mississippi Company, the foreign investors sold their shares when share prices were at their peak.[13] This left local investors holding worthless shares of stock in the company. In addition, London bankers refrained from participation in the last issuance of stock of the South Sea Company. The departure of the more experienced market operators at or near the peak of a bubble is a common feature of speculative booms. The proximity of the Mississippi Company and South Sea Company bubbles shows how the contagion of speculation can pass from one country and financial center to another, in this case not just from France to England, but throughout Europe to Amsterdam, Hamburg, and even Lisbon.[14]

In the latter part of 1720, the British government effectively nationalized the South Sea Company, leaving the investors with large losses, but saving most of the financial system. Nevertheless, credit had dried up, paper money was almost worthless, banks closed, prices collapsed, unemployment rose, and food riots ensued. The collapse also destroyed business confidence. As the country set about with an official enquiry, South Sea company officials frantically set about altering the books and burning their accounts. Found guilty for their part in allowing the financial scandal to unfold, the Chancellor of the Exchequer (similar to the U.S. Chairman of the Federal Reserve Board) and several directors of the Company, including Blunt, had their estates confiscated by an act of Parliament and were imprisoned in the Tower of London.

The Age of the Railways

The nineteenth century saw the start of a great economic expansion that changed finance in fundamental ways. The age of global exploration had arrived. The new lands in the Western Hemisphere, brimming with untapped resources, were to provide economic growth. However, in the aftermath of this exploration, the subsequent boundaries imposed by the closure of geographic horizons underlined the need for the conservation of dwindling natural stocks. A more efficient use of existing resources was sought to continue economic expansion.

The new arenas that arose as a result of technological innovation led to dramatic increases in industrial output. The substitution of coal for wind and water as the energy source for industry, for example, was a major advance. Significant improvements in steam engine design led steam energy to revolutionize transportation. All of this led to the extension of railroad and telegraph services which, in turn, contributed to the rise of great urban-industrial economies. The advent of regular, all-season rail service made possible the establishment of high-volume manufacturing units capable of efficiently distributing their output to increasing numbers of consumers concentrated in growing cities. An early milestone in this transformation was the completion of a rail line connecting Liverpool and Manchester in 1830. Such progress in transportation, as well as in manufacturing, accelerated the pace of investment in productive assets creating a "railway mania" for investors. During the boom period of the 1840s, railway expansion was financed by the public, which bought bonds (called scripts, i.e. subscriptions) that paid up to four times the prevailing rate of interest. The public trust in the railway revolution was growing. Besides being a more efficient means of transportation, the railroads gave local investors an opportunity to invest their funds in tangible ventures whose operations could be observed daily. These investors often had direct knowledge of key determinants of railroad profitability. They could observe the intensity of traffic flows, the quantities and types of cargoes hauled, and how well roadbeds and equipment were serviced.

The closest parallel to the nineteenth century Railway Mania is the more recent expansion of the Internet in the mid-1990s. The present-day changes wrought by the latest "Information Revolution" are expressed in language strikingly similar to descriptions of the "Railway Revolution" of the 1840s. Whereas in the 1840s, the crowds around the provincial stock exchanges sustained the speculative fever, a century and a half later the Internet nourished the fever. Just as the railway boom spawned new stock exchanges, the Internet itself became a stock market of sorts enabling companies to trade their shares in cyberspace.

RAILROAD SCANDALS

In 1846, George Hudson simultaneously positioned himself as the chairman of four railways in England. Once called the "Railway King," Hudson became its longest suffering victim. He largely acted in secrecy, keeping his fellow directors in the dark about his use of dubious accounting methods. This manner of conducting business allowed him to appropriate shares, taking funds belonging to the York and North Midland railways.[15] As a private individual he also made contracts containing special price preferences with various companies of which he was also an officer. Hudson's behavior was in direct violation of the Clauses Consolidation Act, a measure enacted by the Federal authority to stop economic discrimination by prohibiting a common carrier from charging one person more than another for carrying the same amount of freight. Dividends of both the York and North Midland railways were paid out of capital.

On a different front, Hudson raised the dividend of the Eastern Counties Railway from 2 to 6 percent, then altered the accounts to justify the payments. He defended his course of action against similar accusations related to the Yorkshire, Newcastle and Berwick Railway by noting that he had personally advanced funds to the railway to extend its network. The risk was his, Hudson argued, and he was entitled to the advantages that ultimately accrued to himself and the other guaranteeing parties.

In 1840, a fatal accident on the York and North Midland line occurred after Hudson had employed an elderly train driver with defective eyesight in order to save on wages. Similar accidents became frequent on his railways and Hudson's critics accused him of sacrificing public safety for profitability.[16] From Hudson's own point of view, however, his actions were entirely justifiable, since lower costs enabled him to pay higher prices when buying rival railway companies and to distribute greater dividends to his shareholders.

The railway expansion crashed in 1847. Precipitated by poor economic conditions in the nation, the Bank of England raised its interest rates after a decline in its reserves. It announced that it would no longer make advances on public securities. After an unstable period, the House of Commons finally brought an end to the crisis by repealing the Bank Act of 1845, which had put a limit on the amount of notes the bank could issue.

Railway directors were accused of manipulating their accounts and paying dividends out of capital invested in the company, a practice clearly at odds with the more typical method of paying dividends out of profits made on the capital invested. Two of Hudson's companies were specifically mentioned. Early in 1849, Hudson's rule over the railway world came to an abrupt end. At a shareholders' meeting in February, Hudson was accused of profiting from the sale at above market prices of shares in one of his companies to another of his companies (of which he was chairman). Shortly after, he failed to attend a meeting of his shareholders. In 1849, several investigations of Hudson's management of his companies concluded that he had exaggerated revenues and paid exorbitant dividends out of capital in several companies. Later that year, Hudson's brother-in-law and a fellow railway director committed suicide.

In his own defense, Hudson admitted that his private affairs and those of his companies had unfortunately become intertwined. The practice of charging certain expenses to capital accounts was common at the time and had been accepted when the railways were successful. Although Hudson was never charged with criminal wrongdoing, he had taken advantage of the absence of regulation by acting in secrecy, bullying fellow directors to bow to his will, and opposing any outside supervision of the accounts or any general regulation of the railways. His false accounting and generous dividends misled speculators into believing that the railways were more profitable than they actually were.

Having paid back the money taken from his companies, he spent much of his time in France and Germany in order to escape his creditors. He lost his parliamentary seat in 1859 and was arrested for unpaid debt six years later. When he died in the winter of 1871, his estate, which at one time had been estimated to be in the millions, consisted of only a pitiful three hundred dollars.

RAILWAY STOCKS, JAY COOKE, AND THE U.S. STOCK MARKET CRASH OF 1873

In the nineteenth century, a prerequisite for forming financial markets capable of attracting capital from wide geographic areas was the need to develop procedures to enable investors to evaluate the underlying worth of traded securities. A lack of reliable information was a major difficulty for outside investors in the East India Company, the Mississippi Company, the South Sea Company, and other early joint-stock companies. Poor information heightened the risk that one could lose money by selecting weak stocks. At that time and today, the problem of selecting a high performing stock highlights the difficulty of distinguishing between the price paid for a financial asset and some truly informed discounted net value of the asset. This problem is less significant for risk-less bonds held to maturity but virtually impossible to avoid for other classes of financial assets. By the mid-1800s, the U.S. government issued bonds to finance the railway expansion opening up the western frontier.

Jay Cooke (1821–1905), a successful financier during the U.S. Civil War, was perhaps America's first investment banker. Cooke leaves his legacy of being one of the first investment bankers to begin marketing corporate securities. The large banking houses at that time, including Cooke, originally had concentrated on government finance. Between 1865 and 1887, Cooke was instrumental in doubling the size of the rail system in America, adding some 30,000 miles of track at a cost of nearly $1.5 billion. However, the rail lines offered an excuse for a gigantic land grab. Cooke assumed, as did many others, that the railroads would produce rapid settlement of the uninhabited west, which in turn would lead to a spectacular rise in the value of the railroad's landholdings.

In 1869, Cooke purchased the Northern Pacific Railroad (NPR) and was given a land grant larger than the entire territory of New England—nearly fifty million acres in the Northwest. Cooke financed the acquisition by using a network of agents, just as he had done during the Civil War, to sell $100 million in bonds. His publicist described the property as a "vast wilderness waiting like a rich heiress to be appropriated and enjoyed."[17]

Almost right from the beginning, however, Cooke began to have problems. The building of the railroad was eating through his capital as quickly as Cooke could raise it from investors. Bridges collapsed, roadbeds washed out, and by early 1873, NPR was paying its workers in scrip (which amounted to IOUs). As the year progressed, fears of a financial crisis mounted as NPR became deeply overdrawn at its banks. At the same time, trading volume in the New York Stock Exchange soared and margin activity picked up. One publication of the time decried that the Stock Exchange was fostering a "growing mania for gambling." Another publication called the Northern Pacific Railroad "a South Sea Bubble ready to burst."

Also in 1873, U.S. president Ulysses S. Grant's administration was fending off reports of political corruption. Reckless speculation in railroads and wholesale stock manipulation, coupled with increasingly hard times in Europe, fed the public's fear of an impending financial crisis. By mid-year several railroads were having trouble refinancing outstanding loans, and newspapers were carrying stories about forged bonds, as well as forged shares, finding their way into circulation. Cooke thought he had come up with a solution to the impending financial crisis by marketing a $300 million U.S. Government bond issue to European investors. While the underwriting fee was minimal, the proceeds of the sale did not have to be turned over to the government until the end of 1873. The bonds sold slowly in Europe, however, leaving the most prominent banker in the U.S. bankrupt. A crisis was imminent. The American people reacted with disbelief to the collapse of America's leading banker. Soon the contagion spread to Europe, where markets crashed as well. In September, the New York Stock Exchange announced that it would close for the first time in its history.

After the initial panic, industrial plants and commercial establishments shut down, railway construction halted, and over half of the railroads defaulted on their bonds. The crisis touched off by Cooke's miscalculation exposed the weaknesses in the economy as a whole and its institutions. With no central bank (the Federal Reserve System would not be established until 1913), the country had no way to increase its currency supply or make cash available to faltering firms. The boom had been fueled by too much unsecured debt, and speculation had driven stock prices far beyond rational valuations. As debts led to business failures and closures, the economy collapsed like an avalanche.

As for Cooke, by 1880 he had met all of his financial obligations. Through an investment in a silver mine in Utah he again became wealthy.

THE PONZI PYRAMID SCHEME OF FINANCE

Charles (Carlo) Ponzi (1882-1949) developed the archetypal "pyramid scam." Ponzi was the embodiment of "the swindler"—cunning, independent, and flamboyant, mocking the rule-keepers as well as the rules. Ponzi's success was grounded in his belief that people are swindled because they are after a quick-and-easy profit in the first place. Although con artists had for centuries worked the sort of swindle concocted by Ponzi, his name became synonymous with a particular type of financial activity in which the interest charges of a business exceed cash flows from operations. The "Ponzi game of financing" is to finance and repay the debt by issuing new debt.

At the age of 17, Ponzi came to America from Italy with $2.50 in cash and "a million dollars in hope."[18] One might say he achieved wealth by borrowing from Peter to pay Paul: He used the money he received from one group of investors to pay his debts to a previous group of investors. What sets Ponzi schemes apart from more intricate swindles is the simplicity of its design: the money investors put up is not invested in anything and profits are paid out of new money from subsequent investors. Eventually there are not enough newcomers to keep the snowball rolling and the entire game collapses. While it is not known if a Ponzi operator has ever found a way to close out his swindle successfully, it is clear that when a Ponzi game collapses, all of the latecomers lose. In order to profit from a Ponzi fraud, then, you must not only be the first one in, but the first one out as well.

Ponzi promised his investors a return of fifty percent for the use of deposits for ninety days. To those sufficiently patient to wait six months, the deal would double their money. Ponzi's plan was to arbitrage foreign exchange between actual depreciated exchange rates at which foreign currencies—and with them, International Postal Union coupons—could be bought abroad in 1920, and the higher fixed rates at which these coupons would be redeemed for U.S. stamps. A postal coupon bought in Europe with European money for the equivalent of .50 U.S. cents could be cashed into a full American dollar in the U.S. Ponzi took in $7.9 million and had all but $61 worth of stamps and postal coupons on the premises when he was arrested in Boston in 1920.[19]

After Ponzi's release in 1924 he was re-arrested and tried again on remaining charges. He ultimately served an additional nine years in jail before being deported to Italy, where he obtained a job with an Italian airline and was sent to Rio de Janeiro. When the airline folded Ponzi wound up in a charity ward. Half blind and partly paralyzed, he died a few years later.

We can surmise that swindles proliferate in cyclical patterns through history as investment opportunities arise with the exploration of new territory, invention, and innovation. Most importantly, the rising tide of investment spearheads rampant inflation, leaving people desperate for ways to beat soaring prices and quick to take a swindler's bait. In addition, when unemployment mounts, people without jobs seek profit by investing their savings.

In Ponzi's time, the most fraudulent stock schemes were so transparent that critics said they had no more merit than "the blue sky above." As a result, in 1911 states began passing so-called "blue sky" laws to control bogus stock sales. After the Great Depression of 1929, virtually all states passed similar types of laws. In 1921, the Martin Act, New York's Blue Sky law, prohibited fraudulent dealing in securities. New York State Attorney General Eliot Spitzer used these laws eighty years later to lead the charge against widespread corruption on Wall Street. Without a body of well-defined rules, fraud is difficult to prove. This was especially the case in the laissez-faire 1920s, when regulatory agencies were starved for resources.[20]

SWINDLES OF THE BOOM ERA OF THE 1920S

The decade of the 1920s in the United States has been called "the greatest era of crooked high finance the world has ever known."[21] In the financial world, a good deal of discussion focused on a "new economy" based on new technologies (electrical power, the internal combustion engine, and chemicals) which many historians regard as more justified than recent claims about the economic impact of the computer and the Internet. The number of overall investors grew rapidly as first-time investors entered the market, drawn by the promise of easy capital gains. However, the pre-depression era boom culminated in several climatic events: the bankruptcies of the Bank of the United States, the Kreuger and Toll Company, and the Middle West Utilities Holding Company. These companies were the Enrons, Tycos, and WorldComs of their day.

The lack of mandatory standards for financial disclosure in the 1920s also undermined the position of the public accountants who certified financial statements. They found it difficult to constrain overly aggressive clients who sought to incorporate false or misleading accounting into their financial statements. The strongest action that such public accountants could take was the economically damaging step of withdrawing from an engagement. Not surprisingly, this did not happen often.

For many current observers and investors, the crisis of confidence that characterizes Wall Street today has appeared out of nowhere. Yet many experts point to the 1920s as a similar situation. Back then, a glaring example of corporate misconduct was conducted by Ivar Kreuger, a Swedish entrepreneur whose pyramid scheme fleeced market players from widows to bankers and led to the largest bankruptcy then on record.

KREUGER AND TOLL

Kreuger was the founder of Kreuger & Toll, an international conglomerate that built a monopoly in wooden matches, which were needed in most homes around the world to ignite coal or wood. The company's stock was the most widely traded security in the world, largely because it paid a high annual dividend—up to 20 percent. Kreuger solidified his company's market dominance by lending money to foreign governments in return for nationwide match monopolies. The money for loans derived not from his marginally profitable match business, but from sales of his stock and bonds to unwary Americans. He also used money from new investors to pay the high dividends that previous investors had come to expect.

The company's business scheme fell apart with the market crash, which occurred the week *Time* magazine lauded Kreuger on its cover.[22] As investors fled Wall Street and the Great Depression set in, it became impossible for Kreuger to raise money to pay dividends, and his empire collapsed. An audit, after his 1932 suicide, revealed nearly $250 million in assets on the books that never existed, a huge sum at that time.

It was largely in reaction to Kreuger that Congress in 1934 created the Securities & Exchange Commission (SEC), which subsequently implemented accounting and financial reporting rules for publicly traded companies.

THE MIDDLE WEST UTILITIES HOLDING COMPANY

Samuel Insull (1859—1938) was CEO of the Middle West Utilities Holding Company. He was a business partner and co-founder, with Thomas Edison, of General Electric. Insull rose from poverty to become one of the most admired businessmen of the roaring 1920s.[23] Born in London, Insull in his early twenties moved to Chicago and became the personal secretary of Edison. Insull soon set about assembling an empire, ultimately making Chicago the base of a gigantic pyramid of utility and transportation companies.

Insull helped to develop the mass production of electricity that made it cheap and widely available. Electric utilities companies sought to own or acquire electric railroads, such as inter-urban underground and elevated inner-city trains and streetcar systems. Each were large electricity consumers. Without Insull's immediate capital improvements it is unlikely that these inter-urbans would have survived the Great Depression. Insull's generous civic spirit and love for the Chicago area also seemed to not only intensify his desire to increase the bottom line, but also to improve and expand the electrical transportation system in the city of Chicago.

Insull was so involved with the electrical industry that at one point he held sixty-five chairmanships, eighty-five directorships, and eleven presidencies.[24] Insull also went on a buying binge, acquiring badly run companies for multiples of their net worth. In this way, he burdened his holding company with a mountain of debt and associated interest payments, wiping out the common stock equity when the utilities' revenues decreased in the depression. The stock market crash of 1929 brought his pyramid tumbling down.

Eventually, Insull was tried but acquitted in each of three separate securities fraud trials in the mid-1930s. Historians speculate that Insull was set up as a scapegoat to take partial blame for the financial woes of the country. Broken financially by his exhausting court trials and the Great Depression, Insull retired in France. He died there in 1938, penniless, in a Paris subway station.

ALBERT WIGGINS SELLS SHORT

Albert Henry Wiggins (1868–1951), son of a Unitarian minister, became a bank clerk at the age of seventeen, and by 1904 he had become the youngest vice-president ever at Chase National Bank in New York. He became chairman in 1917. Wiggins then went on an acquisition spree that led Chase to swallow up six New York institutions by 1929, making the bank the second largest in the world after National City Bank (now Citigroup). Wiggins further expanded Chase's traditional business, opening up additional branches throughout New York City, and even expanding into overseas markets. He also served on fifty-nine corporate boards, taking advantage of his business and social connections to help him gain support beyond his own ventures.

By the autumn of 1929, when the stock market crashed, Wiggins had established six private corporations, three in America and three in Canada. Using this setup (discovered by a 1933 Senate investigation examining the causes of the 1929 financial crash), Wiggins organized investment pools to speculate on shares of Chase Securities and Chase National Bank. He profited handsomely during the "bull run" through the first half of 1929. An investigation later revealed that Wiggins and his family also took out loans of $8 million from Chase even though their own large net worth suggested that loans were not needed.

Wiggins had enjoyed a reputation as "the most popular man on Wall Street"[25] until the Senate investigation that exposed him as self-dealing at the expense of his bank, its subsidiaries, and its clients. As the market fell—during the 1929 crash—he was found "selling short" his own company's shares. That is, he was speculating that the value of his company's stock would fall. In short, Wiggins received a high salary from the company to enhance its prospects and protect its shareholders, yet he planned his affairs on the expectation that the company would decline. His unscrupulous strategy proved to be a smart bet, since he earned profits in excess of $4 million from this activity.

Wiggins used his offshore shell companies to hide his profits and avoid paying taxes, a fact uncovered in his testimony before the Senate in 1933. At the congressional hearing Wiggins did not admit any wrongdoing. In his testimony he stated, "I think it is highly desirable that the officers of the bank should be interested in the stock of the bank."[26]

Wiggins retired from Chase in 1932, at which point he was awarded a $100,000 pension by the bank's board, only to be forced to renounce it when the new chairman questioned the validity of the award. As a final humiliation, he was sued by a group of Chase shareholders and settled the suit for $2 million. Once the most popular man on Wall Street, Wiggins died in relative obscurity in 1951.

CHARLES MITCHELL'S FINANCIAL SUPERMARKET

Charles E. Mitchell (1873—1955) was an Irish-American immigrant raised in the Boston suburb of Chelsea. At the age of thirty-eight, he became president of National City Company (NCC), the securities arm of National City Bank (NCB). In 1916, after five years of running the subsidiary, Mitchell was elevated to the top position of CEO.

During the 1920s, American commercial banks were forbidden to deal in securities, but all of them had arms like NCC that were involved in both the stock and bond markets. In 1922, there were 600 thousand

Americans with annual incomes in excess of $5,000. By 1929, over 1 million Americans made over this amount.[27] Mitchell sought to take advantage of this untapped market for potential investors and began to market to the growing middle class.

Focusing at first on selling bonds as conservative investments to largely naïve investors, Mitchell was responsible for building NCB and NCC into the first financial supermarket, with sixty-nine branch offices in over fifty cities by 1929. In addition, Mitchell was the first of the modern securities managers to institute sales quotas and offer incentives to his sales force.

Mitchell's downfall began when he undertook to market securities intensely, all the while knowing, on the basis of inside information, that the profits of the companies concerned were declining rapidly or that the foreign governments had stopped paying interest on their bonds. For example, NCC sold from its books about $100 million invested in the paper industry of Brazil, Peru, and Chile, even as the bank received word by cable that the governments would have a difficult time meeting the interest payments. Mitchell saw no problem in withholding this information from investors while NCC rid itself of its exposure.

On the equity side, NCC sold shares at inflated prices of issues like Anaconda Copper to an unsuspecting public, which then watched the shares drop from $125 to $4 in a span of a few months. Sale of these shares resulted in $20 million of profits for the shareholders of the NCB holding company.

When the U.S. Federal Reserve (the Fed) proposed measures to rein in the markets, Charles Mitchell, newly elected director of the Federal Reserve Bank of New York, said that if Federal Reserve Bank Chairman Roy Young went through with his measures, then Mitchell's NCB would lend up to $25 million to traders to thwart the Fed's proposed actions. In 1928 Mitchell was quoted as saying: "Business is entering the New Year upon a high level of activity and with confidence in the continuation of prosperity....No complaint regarding the level of stock prices (is) justified except from the standpoint of credit strain."[28]

When the stock market crashed on October 29 that year, Mitchell personally borrowed millions of dollars from National City Bank in an attempt to support his own institution's share price. Unfortunately, his tactic did not work, as NCB's stock price sank from $455 to $300 that very day. Eventually, Mitchell was forced to resign from National City in 1933 and was tried for income tax evasion in 1934. Somehow he was acquitted even though he admitted he had not paid taxes for years. Mitchell later became chairman of Blythe & Co., rebuilt his fortune, and paid off his debt. He died in 1955 with his reputation on Wall Street largely restored.

GOVERNMENT REGULATION: THE UNITED STATES' RESPONSE TO THE STOCK MARKET CRASH AND CORPORATE MISDEEDS

THE BANK ACT OF 1933

New Deal legislation created the basic structure of financial regulation and governance in existence today. Until recently, the Bank Act of 1933, commonly known as the Glass-Steagall Act, has remained one of the pillars of banking law. By erecting a wall between commercial banking and investment banking, the law prevented commercial banks from underwriting financial securities. The Glass-Steagall Act also laid the groundwork for legislation that would allow the Federal Reserve to let banks into the securities business in a limited way if eventually deemed appropriate.

In order to fully understand the rationale behind the passage of the Glass-Steagall Act, it is important to remember that, by 1933, the U.S. was in one of the worst economic depressions of its history. A quarter of the formerly working population was unemployed. The nation's banking system was in chaos. Over eleven thousand banks had failed or been forced to merge, reducing the number of banks from twenty-five thousand to fourteen thousand. The governors of several states had closed their state banks and in March of that year President Franklin D. Roosevelt closed all the banks in the United States.

The Bank Act of 1933 was probably the most important response of the newly elected Roosevelt administration to the nation's distressed financial and economic system. Unfortunately, the Act did not change the most important weaknesses of the American banking system: unit banking within states and the prohibition of nationwide banking. This early structure of the banking system is the principal reason for the failure of U.S. banks during the depression period, as 90 percent of pre-Depression banks were unit banks with under $2 million in assets. (Canada, in contrast, with its nationwide banking, suffered no bank failures.) Further, only a few of the over 11,000 banks in the U.S. that failed or merged were branch banks. Instead of allowing for nationwide banking, the Banking Act of 1933 established new approaches to financial regulation. The Act created deposit insurance and the legally separated most aspects of commercial and investment banking.

The primary force behind the Glass-Steagall Act was Carter Glass, a seventy-five-year-old senator who at one point in his career had served as Treasury Secretary. Glass also had made large contributions to the formation of the Federal Reserve System and was a critic of banks that engaged in what he considered the risky business of investing in stocks. Henry Steagall, the Democratic chairman of the House Banking and Currency Committee, was the co-sponsor of the law. Steagall's passion for helping farmers and rural banks emerged from his childhood in the Ozarks of Arkansas. He had little interest in separating banking from Wall Street, but signed on to the bill after Glass agreed to attach Steagall's amendment, which authorized bank deposit insurance for the first time.

The Glass-Steagall Act of 1933 was not signed and passed into law, however, until revelations concerning National City Bank were brought forth in the Senate Committee on Banking and Currency hearings on stock exchange practices. The ambiguity between speculators and securities merchants carried over from investment bankers to commercial bankers; in fact, the two were often the same. The intertwining of investment and banking functions that was brought to light during these hearings proved convincing enough to persuade legislators to pass the Bank Act of 1933.

The original arguments for legally separating commercial and investment banking included:

- reduce risk of losses
- eliminate conflicts of interest and other abuses
- avoid improper banking activity
- produce needed constraints on competition
- limit the scope of the Federal "safety net"
- prohibit unfair competition; and
- impede concentrations of power and less-than-competitive performance

The original provisions of the Glass-Steagall Act were directed at some of these key issues. First, banks were investing their own assets in securities with consequent risk to commercial and savings deposits. Immediately prior to the enactment of the Glass-Steagall Act, the concern of Congress with blocking such risky practices was made evident in the report of the Senate Banking and Currency Committee. Second, banks were making unsound loans in order to shore up the price of securities or the financial position of companies in which a bank had invested its own assets. Third, a commercial bank's financial interest in the ownership, price, or distribution of securities inevitably was tempting bank officials to press their banking customers into investing in securities which the bank itself was under pressure to sell because of its own pecuniary stake in the transaction.

The Glass-Steagall Act helped restore American pubic confidence in the financial system by authorizing the formation of the Federal Deposit Insurance Corporation (FDIC) to provide deposit insurance for small savers. To reduce the danger of insurance losses, the law also restricted the speculative activities of insured banks.[29] Of course, in search of greater profits, banks have subsequently lobbied for a greater range of investment opportunities.

Several attempts since 1933 to repeal the commercial and investment banking sections of the Glass-Steagall Act have not been successful. As a result, the United States has been one of the world's few important nations to legally require the commercial and investment banking functions to be separate. In fact, the focus on investment provisions for commercial banks had become so widespread that the Glass-Steagall Act eventually came to be defined as only those sections of the Banking Act of 1933 that referred to the banks' securities operations (sections 16, 20, 21, and 32.)

SECURITIES EXCHANGE ACT OF 1934

Another major development in the regulation of securities markets was the creation of the Securities and Exchange Commission (SEC), as part of the Securities Exchange Act in 1934. The founding chairman of the SEC was Joseph P. Kennedy, father of future president John F. Kennedy and patriarch of the Kennedy clan. In his time Kennedy was widely known as a manipulator of financial markets. When asked why he chose Kennedy as the founding chair of SEC, President Franklin D. Roosevelt was inaccurately reported to have said, "you have to use a thief to catch a thief." However, according to Harold Ickes, Secretary of the Interior in the Roosevelt Administration, President Roosevelt said at a June 29, 1934 cabinet meeting: "The President has great confidence in him [Kennedy] because he has made his pile, has invested all his money in Government securities, and knows all the tricks of the trade."[30] Not surprisingly, when New Dealers learned of the Kennedy appointment to the SEC, Jerome Frank of the Department of Agriculture remarked: "Putting Joe Kennedy on the SEC is like setting a wolf to guard a flock of sheep."[31]

The Security Exchange Act of 1934 empowered the SEC with broad authority over all aspects of the securities industry, including the power to register, regulate, and oversee brokerage firms, transfer agents, and clearing agencies as well as the nation's securities self regulatory organizations. As such, the SEC designed the New York Stock Exchange (NYSE) as a self-regulatory organization whose oversight of the industry would be monitored by the SEC. That is, the NYSE took on the role of regulating itself. Similarly, the Investment Act of 1940 gave the SEC sole and total responsibility of the newly-emerging mutual fund industry in the 1940s. The Investment Act of 1940 was enacted to regulate the organization of companies that engage primarily in investing, reinvesting, and trading in securities and whose own securities are offered to the investing public. These regulations were designed to minimize conflicts of interest that easily arise in such complex operations.

More Scandals—McKesson & Robbins Company

By 1938, the Depression-era racehorse Sea Biscuit had just defeated Triple-Crown winner War Admiral at Pimlico and the U.S. was looking for a dramatic comeback in financial markets. Post-Depression scandals were not uncommon, however. The largest of these concerned fraud and a concealed identity: the story of Philip Musica, better known at the time as F. Donald Coster.

F. Donald Coster was president of the McKesson & Robbins Company, an $86 million drug commodity concern. With a Ph.D. and an M.D., Coster was a respected member of the business community. Apparently, F. Donald Coster was an alias for Philip Musica, who had been convicted for bribing customs officials in 1909 in connection with the importation of cheese. As Coster, in the 1920s, he was suspected of carrying on bootleg operations in connection with a hair tonic concern of Girard & Company, which later merged with McKesson & Robbins.

As president of McKesson & Robbins Company, Musica placed his brothers (two of whom had been implicated in previous scandals with him) in positions of trust in the company under assumed names. He then siphoned away the assets of the crude drug department of the McKesson & Robbins Company such that $18 million dollars in assets carried on the books were found to be non-existent. Coster's three brothers pleaded guilty to federal indictments for conspiracy to falsify financial statements filed with the SEC. They also were indicted by the New York County Grand Jury for larceny of moneys of the McKesson & Robbins Company and forgery of Dun & Bradstreet credit reports.

The crimes of Coster in connection with the McKesson & Robbins

Company were those of a confirmed swindler who pursued his criminal activities despite the fact that he had attained a position of eminence of the business world. Musica/Coster's story ended in suicide, like Ivar Kreuger's before him.

The accounting frauds at Kreuger & Toll (Ivar Kreuger) and McKesson & Robbins (Musica/Coster), gave rise to reforms that later proved to help the profession. The requirements for mandatory audits that followed the Kreuger & Toll fraud increased the market for accountants' services. Changes in audit procedures that followed the McKesson & Robbins fraud improved audit quality.

SAVINGS AND LOAN SCANDALS

Political inclinations toward bribery, dogmatic deregulation, and speculative opportunism combined explosively to produce the savings and loan scandal of the 1980s. Savings and loan associations, known colloquially as "thrifts" or "S&Ls," were local depository institutions originally created to provide mortgage loans to American homeowners. By the early 1980s, many of these institutions were in trouble. In particular, they suffered from the deregulation of interest rates, a situation which made it necessary for them to pay higher rates for short-term deposits when they had already lent their assets for long periods at low fixed rates. As a result, individual thrifts suffered very large losses. When such losses occurred in successive years, many of these institutions failed, with three possible consequences. The firms either had to be closed and liquidated (with depositors receiving insurance payoffs), merged with buyers who received assistance from thrift regulators, or put into conservatory, wherein the government installed new management that attempted to nurse the institution back to a healthy status. In 1989, the U.S. government created the Resolution Trust Corporation (RTC) to oversee many of these activities. At its peak, the RTC reached approximately $390 billion in size, and it was dissolved in 1993. By 1995, however, when the storm of scandal finally abated, the assistance to U.S. thrifts by the financial industry and the U.S. taxpayer had cost several hundred billion dollars.[32]

The thrifts' losses were the result of unmanaged asset/liability gaps that led to interest rate exposures, speculative investments in junk bonds, fraud, and, especially, massive losses from lending to and investing in the U.S. commercial real estate sector. Through deregulation of financial markets, President Ronald Reagan, in an attempt to stimulate these institutions, made it permissible for banks and savings and loan institutions to buy corporate bonds. Savings and loans were freed from dependence on local customer deposits and were permitted to borrow funds on a wholesale basis through Wall Street money brokers. At the same time, federal deposit insurance on individual S&L accounts had been raised to $100,000. In addition, S&Ls were encouraged to diversify their loan portfolios to reduce their reliance on the local housing market. The 1982 deregulation bill signed by President Reagan removed restrictions on thrift loan powers, allowing them to invest in junk bonds, property deals, and other speculative ventures.

Junk bonds take their name from the inferior quality of debt the bonds embody. The bonds are of less than investor-grade quality, as measured by ratios of debt to equity or debt to cash, and are generally issued to finance leverage buyouts (LBOs). Many of the thrifts bought junk bonds that soon went bankrupt. Between 1975 and 1986, some $71.5 billion of junk bonds were issued, with an average yield of 13.6 percent.[33] Yet about a third of the junk bonds issued from 1978 to 1983 had defaulted by 1988.

The premier issuer of junk bonds was Drexel Burham Lambert, a Wall Street investment banking firm. Michael Milken, Drexel's star managing director, became known as the "junk bond king" on Wall Street as he pioneered the widespread use of this new financial instrument. However, the quality of junk bonds declined progressively as the gap between an LBO company's earnings and the interest payments on its junk bonds was whittled away. As a result, a slight decline in income would send the junk bonds into default and the indebted company into bankruptcy. The collapse of the savings and loan industry and other missteps brought Drexel Burham Lambert into receivership. The firm quickly disappeared from the U.S. financial scene. In a plea bargain on his own charge of insider trading, Ivan Boesky, a merger arbitrageur, implicated Michael Milken in order to lighten his own sentence. Boesky received a three-and-a-half year prison sentence and a $100 million dollar fine after admitting to criminal charges. Milken also received a prison sentence, paid several hundred millions of dollars in fines, and was permanently barred from the securities industry.

The most notorious figure in the S&L scandals was Charles Keating, head of Lincoln Savings & Loan of Irvine, California. Keating purchased a large house-building company whose name he changed to American Continental. Years later, Drexel issued junk bonds and preferred stock for American Continental, enabling Keating to use the proceeds to purchase Lincoln Savings & Loan. Upon taking control of Lincoln, Keating fired the senior management and increased its supply of funds from investment bankers in order to grow the institution rapidly and speculate in risky securities and property deals. Keating put $100 million into Boesky's arbitrage partnership, then resorted to numerous accounting tricks to conceal his mounting losses. Among these was an unsecured bond that was distributed to Lincoln's customers, who assumed the bonds carried a federal guarantee. After the scheme was exposed Keating eventually was imprisoned. In just one civil action, he was assessed fines exceeding $3.6 billion.

Another factor contributing to the S&L scandal was the 1985 change in the tax status of real estate as investment property. This modification of the tax code caused a 20 percent drop in the value of some real estate properties overnight. Those institutions holding loans on such properties became financially distressed because the equity of the property, in many cases, became negative.

FINAL THOUGHTS

Our survey of classic speculators, financial bubbles, and business scandals highlights several similarities between the U.S. economic situation at the turn of the millennium and significant economic crises of the past. In both cases one finds a general lack of trust in commercial activity and/or confidence in the integrity of business leaders. Although the European financial markets were in their infancy in 1719, at the time when the Mississippi Company and the South Sea Company bubbles occurred, many parallels to the financial world of the late twentieth century can be observed:[34]

- The economic setting was one of rapid commercial expansion, facilitated by improvements in shipbuilding technology and growing overseas markets.
- Monetary expansion played a crucial role in inflating speculative bubbles.
- "Hot" foreign money helped both to inflate and deflate the Paris and London share markets.
- First-time and/or unsophisticated investors provided the "cannon-fodder" for the bubble.
- The management of the bubble companies had a vested interest in pushing up the company share prices.
- The future earnings of those firms were exaggerated on the assumption that they would be able to maintain monopolistic positions in their markets.
- A small number of very big firms dominated the stock market.
- The advent of an economic slowdown served to both expose and exacerbate the specific problems of the affected companies.

A similarity can be drawn between most of the schemes surveyed in this chapter which involved great economic opportunity deriving from new territories or new inventions such as the railroad, automobiles, electricity, and, in our time, the Internet and telecommunications. In the long run, these opportunities led to great leaps forward for civilization as a whole. Nevertheless, these same ventures also created large amounts of greed and speculation that inevitably were exploited by unscrupulous people.

Much can be learned from a review of the financial scandals that date back to the early eighteenth century. Three categories of theories about the causes of such business scandals exist. The first concerns the impact of fundamental conflicts of interest; the second involves the notion that economic "bubbles" generate corruption; and the third suggests that financial distress is often associated with fraud, wherein the burden of losses are passed on to others. In all cases, businessmen exclusively devoted to their own vested interests exploit the greed and credulity of their victims.

A relatively small number of companies can attract investors with implicit or explicit promises of high and prolonged monopoly profits. Further, it is always hard to argue against a bull market. Sir Isaac Newton, the scientific genius of his age, lost heavily on South Sea stock by buying, selling, and then re-entering the market on the eve of its collapse. Newton commented, "I can calculate the motions of the heavenly bodies, but not the madness of the people."[35]

One important outcome of the financial schemes of the early twentieth century were the efforts of government to protect investors. Beginning with the 1921 Martin Act in New York, and proceeding to the banking and securities acts of the 1930s and 1940s at the national level, laws were put into place to protect investors from fraud and financial ruin. Shareholders had the right to sue in cases where financial reports had been negligently prepared. Still, there remained a need for more reliable information to enable investors to judge both operating performance and the effectiveness of management. It is interesting that current wave of corporate and financial malfeasance has prompted similar efforts by government to increase investor protection with more accounting oversight and improved governance.

During the Great Depression, the New Deal administration of Franklin Roosevelt was eager to encourage the participation of business and professional groups in the process of corporate regulation for several good reasons. For one thing, a high degree of self-regulation by financial market participants would reduce the need for regulation that would increase the size and costs of government. Such self-monitoring also promised to win the political support of professionals like attorneys and public accountants, who had experienced a sharp falloff in the demand for their services during the Depression. Moreover, a self-regulatory approach was appealing to legislators because it seemed consistent with the traditional U.S. political ideal of "government by the governed." Business interests also favored this form of governance because it lessened the likelihood that corporate financial reporting would be commandeered by advocates of stronger government regulation of market competition. At the same time, these private regulatory groups knew that if they were perceived as being derelict in their duties, the public would pressure Congress for more objective oversight. So, the fear of losing autonomy to government and the potential for costly sanctions for malpractice would serve as a strong incentives for such private groups to establish monitoring arrangements that were effective in protecting the public interest.

The following chapters will chronicle the scandals and corruption that appeared on the national scene as an outgrowth of the 1990s financial bubble. Over time, despite all the abuse of investors, three factors have kept corporate firms from feeling a backlash from the public. First, big companies have continued to use politics in the same manner as forewarned long ago by the economist Adam Smith. A quote from Smith is appropriate here to highlight the efforts of business leaders to curry favor with and manipulate legislators and public officials:

> Merchants and master manufacturers are...the two classes of people who commonly employ the largest capital, and who by their wealth draw to themselves the greatest share of the public consideration. As during their whole lives they are engaged in plans and projects, they have frequently more acuteness of understanding than the greater part of country gentlemen. As their thoughts, however, are commonly exercised rather about the interest of their own particular branch of business, than about that of the society, their judgment, even when given with the greatest candor (which it has not been upon every occasion) is much more to be depended upon with regard to the former of those two objects than with regard to the latter. Their superiority over the country gentleman is not so much in their knowledge of the public interest, as in their having a better knowledge of their own interest than he has of his. It is by this superior knowledge of their own interest that they have frequently imposed upon his generosity, and persuaded him to give up both his

own interest and that of the public, from a very simple but honest conviction that their interest, and not his, was the interest of the public. The interest of the dealers, however, in any particular branch of trade or manufacturers, is always in some respects different from, and even opposite to, that of the public. To widen the market and to narrow the competition, is always the interest of the dealers. To widen the market may frequently be agreeable enough to the interest of the public; but to narrow the competition must always be against it, and can serve only to enable dealers, by raising their profits above what they naturally would be, to levy, for their own benefit, an absurd tax upon the rest of their fellow citizens. *The proposal of any new law or regulation of commerce which comes from this order ought always to be listened to with great precaution, and ought never to be adopted till after having been long and carefully examined, not only with the most scrupulous, but with the most suspicious attention. It comes from an order of men whose interest is never exactly the same with that of the public, who have generally an interest to deceive and even to oppress the public, and who accordingly have, upon many occasions, both deceived and oppressed it.*[36] (Emphasis added)

The second way in which public outcry over corporate scandals has been muted concerns the advent of corporate social responsibility. Here, corporations over time have begun to respond to calls for corporate citizenship, as the larger community demands that businesses have an increased concern for the broader social environment and an ever-changing social contract. Company executives are increasingly called upon to consider more seriously the impact of their company's actions on society.

Third, and most important, corporate America continues to create greater wealth and a rising standard of living. Although the stock market constantly fluctuates, the net result has been an ever-steady rise and continued dispersal of the wealth of the country. Especially with the advent of mutual funds, companies have experienced more dispersed ownership as workers in most segments of society reap some of the benefits of their growth. Government and corporate pension plans have in effect democratized the stock market. Today, the California Public Employees' Retirement System (CalPERS) is one of the most influential investors in the stock market.

In the next chapter, several of the prominent recent scandals such as Enron, WorldCom, and Tyco are examined. The reader will quickly note that the circumstances surrounding these scandals have parallels with the historical cases presented in this chapter. Specifically, these firms were all enjoying the economic boom of the 1990s and faced considerable pressure to keep their stock prices growing. Then, like the historical scandals, an economic downturn revealed inherent problems such as accounting fraud (WorldCom) management fraud and malfeasance (Enron), and management theft and greed (Tyco).

CHAPTER TWO QUESTIONS:
A SHORT HISTORY OF BUSINESS SCANDALS

1. What is a financial bubble and how does it cause a business scandal?
2. Before the twentieth century, what was the largest and most significant financial scandal in the history of business and what were the circumstances behind it?
3. What was the Bubble Act? How did it aid the South Sea Company?
4. Describe the kinds of scandals that took place within the railroad industry?
5. How does a Ponzi pyramid scheme work?
6. Explain why the Martin Act was ahead of its time?
7. What is the major significance of the Glass-Steagall Act?
8. What lessons can be learned from the financial scandals of history?

3

CORPORATE MALFEASANCE: FRAUD, THEFT, AND REGULATORY LAXITY

At the turn of the twenty-first century, the United States was transitioning from the Clinton presidency, which had just recovered from its own presidential scandal to the new Bush Administration. The country had enjoyed seven years of a bull market, and the Dow Jones Industrial Average stock index had reached a historic high of 11,722.98 on January 14, 2000 (See Figure 3-1). Progress in the economy had mirrored the stock market and one would have been hard pressed to find investors complaining about Wall Street, the New York Stock Exchange, the Securities and Exchange Commission, public accounting firms, or the largest companies in the U.S. It seemed that a capitalistic system characterized by private enterprise firms, well-developed financial markets, and government regulation was operating as it should. The Clinton Administration had achieved a record low unemployment level of three percent and, created over twenty million jobs, and national wealth soared to levels never imagined in the history of civilization. The twenty-first century seemed to promise further technological, social, and economic advance on both a national and global scale.

Fig. 3-1: Dow Jones Industrial Average, Dec 1998 to Mar 2004

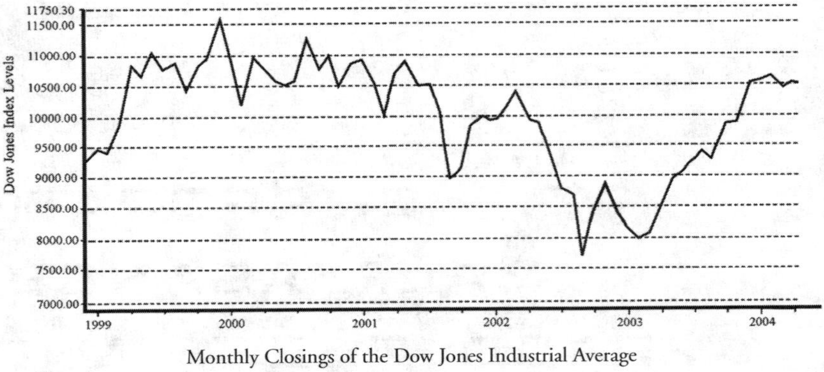

Monthly Closings of the Dow Jones Industrial Average

Source: Bloomberg

In mid-August of 2001, however, what was perceived by financial analysts as a minor fluctuation in the Dow Jones Industrial Average soon became recognized as a sign that an official recession was actually already underway. Soon, serious questions would be raised regarding the economy, market valuation, corporate malfeasance, and regulatory vigilance. The self-policing nature of such institutions as the New York Stock Exchange, public accounting firms, and corporate governing boards also became suspect, despite their long-held status as capitalistic safeguards. These factors represented important components of the subsequent sequence of economic and corporate collapse.

This chapter first discusses high profile U.S. corporate scandals such as Enron, WorldCom, and Tyco, though similar misconduct and a general breakdown in the corporate system were found to exist at several other companies—Global Crossing, Qwest, ImClone, Health-South, and Adelphia in the period between 1999 and 2002. About the same time scandals were exposed in several European firms, including Royal Ahold and Parmalat. These problems are discussed in a subsequent section. Beginning with Enron, this chapter examines these high profile companies in an effort to gain insight into how these problems came to be.

MAJOR AMERICAN CORPORATIONS LOSE THEIR WAY

ENRON

The first prominent firm to collapse under the pressures of the slowing economy of 2000-2001 was Enron. As the scandal at Enron unfolded, investors found themselves victimized by the combined forces of stock market pressures, corporate malfeasance, questionable oversight by the board of directors, and dubious conduct by the company's public auditors, law firms, and investment bankers.

Texas-based Enron, one of the largest energy-producing and trading organizations in the United States, quickly became the prototypical corporate example of the emerging "scandalous era." Enron managers used highly complicated financial engineering, convoluted partnerships, off-balance-sheet debt, and exotic hedging techniques to hide huge losses. When those losses emerged, the company managers sold millions of dollars in company stock while prohibiting their employees from selling theirs. All the corporate overseers employed to monitor Enron on behalf of its shareholders—the outside directors, auditors, regulators, and stock analysts—were eventually found to have not met their responsibilities.

The Enron story came alive in 1999 when the Enron Board of Directors allowed chief financial officer (CFO), Andrew S. Fastow, to set up and run two special partnerships—LJM Cayman L.P. and the much larger LJM2 Co-Investment LP—to purchase assets from Enron. These two partnerships known as special purpose entities were to engage in billions of dollars of complex hedging transactions with Enron, involving company assets and millions of shares of Enron stock. It is still not clear from Enron filings with the Securities and Exchange Commission (SEC) what Enron received in return for providing those assets and shares.

Fastow's lack of objectivity in his dual role as Special Purpose Entity (SPE) asset valuator and Enron CFO posed a serious problem, however. Fastow's explanation for heading both the financial operations of the LJMs and Enron was that this position enabled him to make sure the parties' interests "aligned" with investors. What he failed to mention was that his dual role as CFO and participant in the analysis of Enron assets from the partnership side put him in the perfect position to "cook the books" without detection.

The first sign of trouble came in the form of CEO Jeff Skilling's resignation as Enron president and chief executive in August 2001. Skilling attributed his decision to leave to the fall in Enron's stock price, (which had peaked several months earlier) and personal reasons. A day after Skilling resigned, Sherron Watkins, an Enron vice-president, sent an anonymous warning to Ken Lay, Skilling's replacement as CEO. Watkins wrote that questionable accounting practices would lead the company to "implode in a wave of accounting scandals."

In October 2001, Enron came under public scrutiny after becoming the subject of a criminal complaint in the U.S. District Court in Houston, Texas. The complaint alleged that Fastow and others used the SPEs to defraud Enron and its shareholders through transaction structures set up to make Enron appear more attractive to Wall Street investment analysts and credit rating agencies. The complaint alleged that Fastow and others at Enron used SPEs fraudulently to both manipulate Enron's financial results and to enrich themselves at Enron's expense. The complaint also brought to light Enron's enlistment of major financial institutions to assist in its financial statement manipulation.

As Enron's stock price rapidly plummeted to single digits and its cash position collapsed, the company's senior management became frantic. First, they attempted a merger with Dynegy, Inc., their power-trading rival, which was quickly aborted. Next, they attempted to sell assets for fast cash. Eventually, Enron did sell its world-class trading platform for approximately $1 billion, but this move proved to be too little, too late. Meanwhile, Enron officials attempted to use their contacts in the Bush Administration to seek some form of federal government support. Interestingly, Enron appeared to be very politically connected with numerous contacts and friends in the Bush Administration (see Table 3-1). The Bush Administration, including the president, exhibited wise political instincts during this period and appeared to stay completely disassociated from Enron by ignoring all of its requests.

Table 3-1: Enron's Political Contacts with the George W. Bush Administration

NAME	POSITION	CONNECTION	COMPENSATION
Thomas White	Secretary of the Army	Former Enron vice president	Owned $50 million in stock and options
Karl Rove	Senior adviser to the president	Shareholder	Owned at least $100,000 in stock, sold all shares in June 2001
Lawrence Lindsey	White House economic adviser	Consultant	Paid $50,000
Lewis "Scooter" Libby	Top Cheney aide	Shareholder	Sold tens of thousands of dollars in stock
Robert Zoellick	U.S. Trade Representative	Former Enron advisory-board member	Paid $50,000 per year
Marc Racicot	GOP chairman designate	Former Enron lobbyist	Amount of compensation not available

Source: Cummings, Jeanne & Hamburger, Tom "Enron's Pre-collapse Clout in WA Draws Fresh Scrutiny Amid Investigation" *Wall Street Journal* January 15, 2002.

One of the most in-depth and insightful analyses of the Enron scandal was written by the Department of Justice (DOJ) in its October 2002 press release covering the indictment of Fastow in October 2001. The DOJ summarized key factors contributing to the company's transgressions, creating a succinct review of the steps leading to Enron's financial crisis. Specifically, the complaint against Fastow alleged that in early 1997 Fastow, Michael J. Kopper (director of Enron's Global Finance unit), and others devised a scheme to defraud Enron and its shareholders through a series of transactions with certain Enron Special Purpose Entities (SPEs). The SPEs included:

LJM1: In June 1999, relying on false representations by Fastow and others, Enron's Board of Directors agreed to allow Fastow to create and serve as the managing partner of a new SPE called LJM1, and later a larger SPE called LJM2. Transactions entered into with LJM allowed Enron to manipulate its balance sheet by, among other things, moving poorly performing assets off their balance sheet by selling them to

LJM. Far from true sales of assets to a third party, however, Enron's "sales" to LJM were shams. At times, Enron even agreed in advance that it would repurchase the supposedly "sold" assets. Further, Fastow and Enron executives had a secret agreement that LJM would never lose money in its dealings with Enron, which was also able to manufacture needed earnings through sham transactions with LJM when it was having trouble meeting its financial goals. The LJM transactions allowed Fastow and others to personally earn huge sums of money in the form of management fees and skimmed deal profits.

LJM2: The complaint specified several instances in which Fastow allegedly engaged in illegal activities through LJM, including a sham transaction in which LJM "purchased" Enron's interest in a struggling company that was building a power plant in Cuiaba, Brazil and a transaction in which Enron, through Fastow and others, pressured a leading financial institution to buy a $28 million interest in a project involving electricity-generating power barges off the coast of Nigeria with a guarantee that Enron would repurchase the interest for an agreed-upon price within six months.

SOUTHAMPTON: The complaint alleged that Fastow and others defrauded Enron and National Westminster Bank by secretly investing in an Enron SPE, Southampton, and then siphoning off millions in income that rightfully belonged to others. Kopper pleaded guilty in connection with this scheme, and three British bankers were charged with wire fraud in connection with their roles in the scheme.

CHEWCO: According to the complaint, Fastow and others proposed the creation of an SPE known as Chewco in order to buy the limited partnership interest of the California Public Employees Retirement System in a venture known as the Joint Energy Development Investments, or JEDI. The complaint alleged that Fastow, Kopper and others at Enron arranged to fund Chewco through loans that were guaranteed by Enron. Since Fastow could not serve without triggering disclosure on Enron's books, Kopper was designated managing partner of Chewco. Kopper then allegedly paid several hundred thousand dollars in kickbacks to Fastow through transfers to Fastow's wife and other family members.

RADR: The complaint alleged that in May 1997, Kopper and Fastow created two SPEs, known collectively as RADR, to purchase a portion of Enron's interest in certain wind farms in California through supposedly independent third-party investors known as "Friends of Enron." The investments were actually funded by Fastow. According to Kopper, when the RADR investments became lucrative, Fastow demanded kickbacks and payments in the forms of annual $10,000 "gifts" to members of Fastow's family.[1]

As a result of the criminal complaint against Fastow in October 2001, Fastow's chief lieutenant, Michael J. Kopper, Director of Enron's Global Finance unit, pleaded guilty in August 2002 to conspiracy to commit wire fraud and money laundering. Kopper also agreed to cooperate with the government's ongoing Enron investigation. In June 2002, the SEC began an investigation of Enron. Soon after, a federal jury in Houston convicted accounting firm Arthur Andersen L.L.P. of obstruction of justice for destroying documents in order to prevent SEC review. Former Arthur Andersen auditor, David Duncan, pleaded guilty to obstruction of justice in connection with his role in the destruction of Enron-related documents.[2]

Other companies have sold corporate assets to SPEs. Since LJM was not a separate entity from Enron, however, Enron essentially was selling its assets to itself. All of the partnerships together were paid a reported $35 million for their "management fees." Fastow personally received $7 million for his role in negotiations in addition to the salary he was paid for his duties as CFO. It was through these partnerships and phony sales that Enron was able to continue to report growing revenues and profits to investors even though it was actually losing millions of dollars.

One of the stories most heavily covered by U.S. media in history, the Enron scandal involved a great many twists and turns that are too numerous to review here. However, Table 3-2 provides a timeline that includes some of the most important events and related dates.

Table 3-2: Enron Timeline

July 1985: Houston Natural Gas merges with InterNorth to form Enron, a natural gas pipeline company.

1989: Enron begins trading natural gas.

1990: Jeff Skilling joins Enron.

1996: Jeff Skilling becomes Enron's president and chief operating officer (COO).

November 1999: Launch of Enron Online, the first global commodity trading website.

September 2000: George Bush names Kenneth Lay as an adviser to his presidential transitional team. Lay, Enron chairman, contributes more than $290,000 to George Bush's election campaign.

August 2000: Enron stock shares hit all-time price high of $90.56.

February 2001: Arthur Andersen, Enron's auditor, discusses whether to retain Enron as a client amid concern over Enron's use of special partnerships to disguise debt. Jeff Skilling becomes chief executive officer (CEO) of Enron.

August 2001: Skilling resigns abruptly citing personal reasons. Lay returns to chief executive officer job and contends there are "no issues" behind the resignation.

August 2001: Sherron Watkins, an Enron vice president, sends an anonymous warning to Ken Lay. She says questionable accounting practices would lead the company to "implode in a wave of accounting scandals."

October 2001: Enron replaces Andrew Fastow and appoints as chief financial officer Jeffrey McMahon, the 40-year-old head of the company's industrial-markets division.

October 2001: The SEC elevates to a formal investigation its inquiry into Enron's financial dealings.

November 2001: Enron reduces its previously reported net income dating back to 1997 by $586 million, or twenty percent, mostly due to improper accounting for its dealings with the partnerships run by some company officers.

November 2001: The government seems unlikely to bail out Enron if it goes under, as Enron's political connections run silent during the firm's crisis. (See Table 3-1)

November 2001: The SEC investigates the actions of Arthur Andersen, Enron's auditor.

December 2001: Enron files Chapter 11 bankruptcy, the biggest in U.S. history at the time. The former energy giant also files a $10-billion lawsuit against Dynegy, alleging a breach of contract by Dynegy over its aborted $9-billion takeover of Enron. The lawsuit is also an attempt to halt Dynegy's takeover of Enron subsidiary Northern Natural Gas, a pipeline system that spans about 16,500 miles from Texas to the Great Lakes. Enron's highly questionable financial engineering, misstated earnings, and persistent efforts to keep investors in the dark were behind its collapse.

December 2001: Kenneth Lay, Enron's chief executive officer, declines to testify at a joint hearing of two House panels as Congress begins a painstaking investigation into the company's financial troubles. A handful of congressional panels and regulators investigate the causes of Enron's plunge into Chapter 11 bankruptcy protection, which may lead to new regulations spurring additional oversight of accounting firms.

January 2002: Senator Joseph Lieberman says the Senate Governmental Affairs Committee, which he heads, will hold hearings into Enron's collapse when Congress returns to work later that month.

January 2002: Internal Enron documents show top management and directors viewed controversial partnerships as integral to maintaining its rapid growth in recent years.

January 2002: The Justice Department says a task force has been formed to pursue a criminal investigation of Enron, confirming a probe that is expected to center on possible accounting fraud. Reports surface that Joseph Berardino, chief executive of Arthur Andersen, gave inaccurate information about Enron while testifying to Congress in December 2001. Former SEC Chairman Arthur Levitt says Enron's accounting problems offer more proof of a need for tighter controls of the accounting industry. Attorney General John Ashcroft recuses himself from the Justice Department's inquiry, citing a conflict of interest, and the Justice Department says much of the U.S. attorney's office in Houston will also be recused because many have family ties to the Houston company. Enron goes to great lengths to win assistance from the Bush administration as the company headed for bankruptcy court. House and Senate lawmakers return campaign contributions from Enron as the company's donations turn from political asset to liability. Several members of the Bush Administration also have connections to Enron. Table 3-1 shows some of Enron's Capitol Hill connections.

January 2002: Report emerges that an August 2001 letter to Enron CEO Kenneth Lay from whistleblower Sherron Watkins, a company vice president, detailed what she saw as the huge financial and public-relations risks facing the company. The SEC says it didn't do a thorough review of Enron's annual reports for at least three years prior to its collapse. Investigators sift through the complex financial structures of Enron's partnerships, which hid hundreds of millions of dollars of losses and debt from public view.

January 14, 2004: Wife of former Enron finance chief Andrew S. Fastow makes a plea agreement with a federal judge that could lead Fastow to make a similar deal. Andrew Fastow makes his plea agreement. (Fastow was unwilling to go ahead with his plea before he was satisfied that his wife's case was resolved as the family was aiming to ensure that both parents were not in prison at the same time.) Former chief accounting officer, Richard Causey, faces charges of fraud and conspiracy in the alleged manipulation of the fallen energy giant's finances. If he is convicted, Causey faces a maximum of 55 years in prison and could pay up to $5.25 million in fines.

July 7, 2004: Ken Lay indicted by a federal grand jury. Lay is the thirtieth person indicted or charged with crimes involving Enron and its collapse. Ten of the thirty people have plead guilty and are cooperating with the prosecution

---

Sources: "Enron: Timeline Key Dates Surrounding Enron Collapse" Staff and Agencies, *The Guardian Newspaper*, Feb. 4, 2002. John R. Emshwiller, and Kranhold, Kathryn "Highly Publicized Letter to Enron CEO Was Product of Internal Power Struggle" *Wall Street Journal*, Jan. 16, 2002. Laura Goldberg, "Enron seeks bankruptcy alternatives Company may sue Dynegy over termination of merger" *Houston Chronicle* Jan. 17, 2002, 2:03PM. Richard B. Schmitt, "Bankruptcy Judge for Enron Case Is Known as a Stickler for Detail" *The Wall Street Journal*, Dec. 7, 2001.

According to the terms of his plea bargain in 2004, former Enron CFO Andrew Fastow received an eye-popping 10-year prison term as well as the forfeiture of more than $29 million. To date, it is among the harshest penalties ever handed down for a white-collar crime. Fastow has admitted that "special-purpose entities" were at the heart of a "conspiracy" to commit fraud at Enron. If there is any evidence to be had about the complicity of former Enron CEO Jeffrey Skilling and Chairman Kenneth Lay, the 42-year-old Fastow is likely to have it.[3] In fact, shortly after Fastow's plea bargain, federal prosecutors arrested Jeff Skilling on numerous felony counts. Later, in July 2004, Ken Lay was arrested and charged with several crimes. Not surprisingly, the government's use of a plea bargain with lower level executives is a key tactic in pursuing prosecution of high-level executives.

TYCO

The Securities and Exchange Commission (SEC) began an investigation of Tyco's top executives and the accuracy of the company's books in 2002. Led by Dennis Kozlowski, the former Tyco CEO, the company had done very well for years. Just as in the case of Enron, however, when the economy began to slow, Tyco's cash flow shortages and accounting gimmicks became apparent and things began to fall apart quickly. In June 2001 the acquisition of CIT, a $50-billion commercial and consumer finance company, first drew attention to Tyco's merger and acquisition activities.[4] Under Kozlowski, Tyco had spent some $60 billion over a ten-year time span acquiring over 700 firms for external growth to meet investor performance expectations, CIT among them.[5] As one of the country's largest conglomerates, Tyco owned operations that spanned financial services, security services, medical supplies and devices, and industrial instrumentation.

In Kozlowski's view, mergers more readily enhanced earnings than organic growth.[6] He used accounting loopholes to prevent the acquisitions from negatively affecting Tyco earnings. Accounting rules in effect at the time allowed firms to adjust their purchase prices for an acquisition as long as such adjustments took place within one year after the acquisition took place. When Tyco bought CIT, it valued CIT's loans at fair market value and booked the loans in its accounts at par value (or face value of the loans). By the end of 2001, when Tyco found that the loans were not worth par, the company placed the difference into the goodwill category in its accounts rather than account for the adjustment through its profit-and-loss statement as a loan-loss charge.

In effect, Tyco, buried the loss where it would be difficult to find. The hidden amount, in this particular case, was $379 million.[7]

Later it was uncovered that Dennis Kozlowski, Mark Swartz (Tyco's former CFO), and Mark Belnick (the company's chief legal officer) had taken over $170 million in loans from Tyco for themselves without receiving appropriate approval from Tyco's compensation committee and/or notifying shareholders. The head of the board compensation committee was Frank Walsh, who had received $20 million in finder's fees for the CIT deal. For the most part, such loans to company officers were taken for little or no interest. As time passed, many of the loans were later converted to "bonuses" without appropriate approval, thereby absolving the executives of their responsibility to pay them back. Kozlowski and Swartz also sold seven and a half million shares of Tyco stock for $430 million without informing investors.[8]

Kozlowski's questionable activities at Tyco went well beyond tax avoidance. For a period of at least five years, while Kozlowski publicly claimed devotion to high standards of corporate governance, he regularly reached into Tyco's treasury to finance his extravagant lifestyle and enhance his personal image. All told, more than $135 million in Tyco funds went to benefit Kozlowski, largely in the form of forgiven loans, company payments for real estate, charitable donations and personal expenses over a period of five years. Further, Tyco secretly forgave an additional $25 million in loans to Kozlowski in 1999. More than $11 million of Tyco's cash was used to buy antiques, art and other expensive furnishings in Kozlowski's New York apartment, including the infamous $6,000 gold-and-burgundy floral patterned shower curtain. This huge decorating bill came on top of the $18 million Tyco paid for his Fifth Avenue duplex, which the company considered a corporate apartment. Later, Tyco picked up half the bill for a $2.1 million junket to the Italian island of Sardinia in 2001. The central event of the weeklong extravaganza was a 40th birthday party for Kozlowski's wife, Karen, complete with a performance by singer Jimmy Buffett. The combined force of these events resulted in the SEC filing of formal charges against Kozlowski in September 2002.[9]

In the course of the trial, experts estimated the losses to Tyco at

$600 million. Kozlowski and Swartz were charged with corruption, conspiracy, grand larceny, and falsifying records. Belnick was charged with falsifying business reports and failing to disclose to investors and Tyco's compensation committee loans he made to himself for the purchase of his Manhattan apartment and a Utah home.[10] At the trial's end, the SEC asked Kozlowski, Swartz, and Belnick to return to Tyco the funds taken from the company in various forms of undisclosed loans and compensation.

Another SEC complaint filed in a civil action concerned the registration statement that Tyco filed with the SEC in connection its $9.2 billion acquisition of The CIT Group Inc. in June, 2001. Tyco incorporated and attached to the registration statement an Agreement and Plan of Merger stating that no one other than Lehman Brothers and Goldman, Sachs & Company was entitled to an investment banking or finder's fee for representing Tyco in the transaction. At the time that Walsh signed the registration statement, he knew that Kozlowski, then Tyco CEO, had proposed that, if the transaction was successfully completed, Walsh would be paid a finder's fee for having arranged a meeting of the companies' CEOs to discuss a possible merger. In fact, after the transaction was consummated, Kozlowski had Tyco pay Walsh a $20 million "finder's fee" in the form of $10 million in cash and a $10 million charitable contribution to a foundation chosen by Walsh.

Thomas C. Newkirk, SEC Associate Director of Enforcement, said of Walsh: "Shareholders entrusted him with the responsibility of watching out for their interests in Tyco's boardroom and executive suite. Instead, Mr. Walsh himself took secret compensation and kept those same shareholders in the dark. Once again, the Tyco investigation has uncovered clandestine payments and hidden deals…. the evidence demonstrates that Tyco's top management viewed Tyco's assets as their own."[11]

Tyco's statement to the U.S. District Court in Manhattan stated that Walsh did not declare the finder's fee to the board. When the omission came to light, Walsh was asked to return it, and he refused. Walsh issued a statement saying the lawsuit "is clearly an overreaction to the recent and well-reported problems and management changes at

Tyco." He said he made the deal "at the direction of then CEO Dennis Kozlowski…I put more than 30 years of deal-making experience to work and helped to bring the transaction to a successful conclusion." Furthermore, he said, the fee consisted of two $10 million payments, one to himself which was disclosed, and one to a New Jersey charity to which he is an advisor, " but not a trustee with an active control on the funds."[12] Walsh pled guilty in December 2003 to charges that he failed to notify the board of a $20 million "finders fee" for brokering the acquisition of the CIT Group. Walsh avoided jail time by agreeing to repay $20 million, along with a $2.5 million fine as part of a settlement with the Manhattan District Attorney's Office.

Dennis Kozlowski, 56, and Mark H. Swartz, 43, were charged with grand larceny and enterprise corruption and each faced up to 30 years in prison time. Kozlowski and Swartz argued the $600 million in cash and loan forgiveness from Tyco was approved by board members and blessed by independent auditors. The two men's trial ended April 2, 2004 with the judge declaring a mistrial after a juror holding out for an acquittal received an intimidating letter and phone call. A retrial was expected to convene September 2004. Table 3-3 presents a time line for the various events and actions related to the Tyco case.

Table 3-3: Tyco Timeline

January 2002: Questions arise about the accuracy of Tyco's book keeping and accounting. Stock value drops 19 percent.

January 29, 2002: Kozlowski explains that the $20 million paid to Frank Walsh was a finder's fee for the acquisition of CIT.

January 30, 2002: Kozlowski announces that he and Mark Swartz (Tyco's then CFO) will each purchase five hundred thousand Tyco shares on the open market. This move is made as an assurance of the value of Tyco stock.

April 25, 2002: Kozlowski explains a loss of ninety-six cents per share for the quarter ending on March 31, 2002, and he outlines unusual costs that affected earnings and prospective strategic actions.

June 3, 2002: Kozlowski resigns as CEO of Tyco for personal reasons. John

Fort, former Tyco CEO, is named the temporary CEO.

June 4, 2002: Kozlowski receives his first indictment for attempted tax evasion.

June 10, 2002: Mark Belnick, hired by Tyco in 1998 as its chief legal officer, is fired.

June 17, 2002: Tyco, through the law firm of Boies, Schiller & Flexner, begins the process of suing Belnick for breach of fiduciary duty and fraud. Belnick maintains that he acted with integrity as Tyco's chief legal officer.

August 1, 2002: CFO Swartz resigns from Tyco.

September 12, 2002: New York District attorney Robert M. Morgenthau files civil charges against Kozlowski, Swartz, and Belnick for failure to disclose to shareholders information on the multi-million dollar loans they borrowed from Tyco.

Sept. 29, 2003: Kozlowski and Swartz trial begins.

Oct. 7, 2003: In the opening arguments of the trial, prosecutors assert that Kozlowski and Swartz stole $170 million by claiming unauthorized compensation and made another $430 million on their Tyco shares by lying about the conglomerate's financial condition from 1995 into 2002.

October 28, 2003: Jurors view the infamous videotape of the lavish birthday party for Kozlowski's wife in Sardinia.

January 8, 2004: Tyco's former-lead director, Frank Walsh, testifies that he and Kozlowski agreed to structure a $20 million payment to Walsh in the form of $10 million in cash and $10 million in charitable donations because they believed they would not have to disclose payments of that size.

April 2, 2004: Kozlowski and Swartz's trial ended with the judge declaring a mistrial after a juror holding out for an acquittal received an intimidating letter and phone call. A retrial is to convene in September 2004.

Sources: "Tyco Fraud," *Securities Fraud FYI (Online)*, "Tyco Timeline," *Washington Post News-week Interactive*, January 14, 2004.

WORLDCOM

One of the most sweeping bookkeeping deceptions in corporate history was uncovered in 2002 when telecom giant WorldCom was found to have overstated a key measure of earnings by more than $3.8 billion. Beginning in January 2001, WorldCom CEO Bernard Ebbers had apparently treated the company as his own bank account, borrowing hundreds of millions of dollars over a period of five quarters. When WorldCom's ruse was exposed, WorldCom stock, which had peaked at $64.50 in 1999, stopped trading at 83 cents, costing investors about $175 billion or nearly three times what was lost in the implosion of Enron.

WorldCom's problems began just as the firm's acquisition machine was grinding to a halt. WorldCom failed to get government approval for its purchase of Sprint, a buy that would have ranked WorldCom among the largest telecom firms in the world. Ebbers and Chief Financial Officer (CFO) Scott Sullivan had long worked in tandem in building WorldCom, originally known as LDDS. After acquiring dozens of companies and seemingly springing out of nowhere to buy MCI Communications in 1998, WorldCom had rapidly become known as a world-class telecom company. Most experts believed WorldCom would emerge as an ultimate survivor as the telecommunications industry consolidated. WorldCom's operations not only blanketed most of the U.S., but encompassed most of the industrial world.

WorldCom's collapse began when its internal auditor, Cynthia Cooper, began a routine investigation of accounting entries made by another employee. As she checked capital expenditures, Cooper discovered that quarter after quarter, beginning in 2001, Sullivan had been using an unorthodox technique to account for one of the long-distance company's biggest expenses: charges paid to local telephone networks to complete calls. Instead of marking them properly as operating expenses, Sullivan had classified a significant portion as capital expenditures. The maneuver had added hundreds of millions of dollars to WorldCom's bottom line and effectively turned a loss for all of 2001 and the first quarter of 2002 into a profit. Upon detecting the error, Cooper contacted Max Bobbitt, the head of WorldCom's auditing committee, and initiated a chain of events that resulted in Sullivan's firing in January 2002. At the time of Sullivan's dismissal, WorldCom publicly announced that it had turned up $3.8 billion of expenses that were improperly booked and would have to be restated.

The WorldCom scandal clearly warns how easily telecom companies can manipulate their books to inflate their earnings by using aggressive accounting practices or compromising accounting standards amidst huge speculative excesses. In fact, the WorldCom scandal, along with others, caused President George W. Bush to request a full investigation. He called the accounting irregularities surfacing at companies like WorldCom "outrageous" and promised that those responsible for such wrongdoing would be punished.

Just as with Enron and Tyco, the consequences of WorldCom's fiscal dishonesty have been immense. With respect to public confidence in corporate institutions, a profound loss of trust by investors, customers, and financial institutions occurred. More than five hundred thousand telecom workers lost their jobs since 2000. To WorldCom's relief, banks did not immediately re-call their loans, thus, allowing an effectively bankrupt WorldCom to continue operations. Nevertheless, the Nasdaq Stock Exchange halted trading in WorldCom stock, which, as indicated, had dropped in the course of three years from a high of $64.50 to less than one dollar.

In 2002, the SEC filed civil fraud charges against WorldCom, on the grounds that the firm "falsely portrayed itself as a profitable business." Soon after, the U.S. Justice Department launched a probe resulting in charges of securities fraud, bank fraud, and mail fraud. The board had fired long-time chief executive Ebbers, in part because of a controversy surrounding a $408 million loan WorldCom had extended to him to cover margin calls on loans secured by company stock. In 2004, Ebbers was indicted by federal authorities and was awaiting trial.

The federal government made a critical decision to allow the company to reorganize itself under bankruptcy protection. In 2004, World-Com emerged as a new publicly traded company under the name MCI. The federal judge overseeing class-action lawsuits dismissed thirty claims by WorldCom bondholders, including nine actions dismissed in their entirety. Among the claims forgiven were a $6 billion WorldCom public bond offering and a $2 billion bond offering. Not surprisingly, competitors, AT&T and Sprint, were outraged when the government allowed WorldCom to reorganize as MCI after the scandal, since both companies had suffered great losses as a result of the fraudulent book-keeping and accounting practices of their prime competitor.

The SEC's investigation into the accounting fraud at WorldCom turned up a number of key players. Table 3-4 lists several of these high-ranking WorldCom executives and other employees who were implicated in the scandal.

Table 3-4: Main Players in WorldCom Fraud

- *Bernard Ebbers*—former CEO of WorldCom, was charged in Oklahoma with 15 counts of violating the Oklahoma Securities Act. The Oklahoma charges were later dropped.
- *Scott Sullivan*—former CFO of WorldCom, was indicted on charges of securities fraud, conspiracy, and false statements to the SEC.
- *David Myers*—former controller of WorldCom, is charged with securities fraud, conspiracy, and false statements to the SEC. He is rumored to have accepted a plea bargain.
- *Buford Yates, Jr.*—former director of general accounting, pled guilty to charges of securities fraud and conspiracy.
- *Betty Vinson*—former director of management reporting, pled guilty to charges of conspiracy to commit securities fraud.
- *Troy Normand*—director of legal entity accounting, pled guilty to securities fraud and conspiracy charges.

Source: "WorldCom Fraud" Securities Fraud FYI (Online) (http://www.securitiesfraudfyi.com/worldcom_fraud.html)

GLOBAL CROSSING

Founded in 1997 by Gary Winnick, a former associate of junk bond king Michael Milken, Global Crossing set out to revolutionize the telecom industry by laying fiber-optic pipes below sea level to enable data to be transmitted worldwide. In a matter of five years, Winnick led employees and shareholders into financial ruin while pocketing hundreds of millions of dollars from Global Crossing before it filed for bankruptcy in January 2002.

In 1998, Global Crossing raised $397 million with an initial public offering. Riding the telecommunications hype of the 1990s, the company built the largest fiber-optic network in the world, transmitting text, data, video, and voice between twenty-seven nations. By 1999, Global Crossing's stock was valued at over thirty times its earnings. Soon the company purchased Frontier Communications, a large telecom entity, and later attempted, but failed, to take over U.S. West.

Yet by 2000 Global Crossing's debt, combined with increasing competition and a slowing economy, hit the company hard. About this time, Global Crossing was shown to have inflated earnings and cash flow to make its financial performance look better than it actually was. Most of Global Crossing's troubles stemmed from the more than $12 billion in debt the company had accumulated in the process of developing its global network of fiber optic cables.[13] In addition, they had used bogus transactions to book fictitious revenues and profits in order to meet Wall Street estimates. Using a mechanism known as "hollow swaps" the company had artificially inflated its sales by needlessly trading network capacity with other telecom companies, thus creating fictitious revenue-generating transactions.

Prior to Global Crossing's collapse, Winnick sold $734 million worth of company shares including $123 million in the weeks immediately preceding the implosion of its stock price. He also bought a $92 million estate abutting the Bel Air Country Club, spent hundreds of thousands of dollars redecorating the company's offices, and demanded that Global Crossing maintain a fleet of five jets, including a Boeing 737.[14] When the head of the company's Asia subsidiary, John Legere, was named CEO, he became the company's fifth chief executive in its four-year history. As Global Crossing sought to emerge from bankruptcy, Hutchison Telecommunications Limited and Singapore Technologies Telemedia paid $250 million for a 61.5 percent majority interest in the reorganized firm. Meanwhile, Congress began to examine the role of the company's accounting firms (Arthur Andersen, of Enron fame, among them) in its bankruptcy.

QWEST

Qwest built a global telephone, Internet, and data network in the 1990s and grew large enough to acquire the regional phone giant U.S. West in 2000. Soon after, the company's fortunes plummeted as its debt mounted and cash flows declined. In response, Qwest's strategy was to squeeze additional revenue from customers. Soon allegations began to surface that Qwest had artificially inflated its sales by needlessly trading network capacity with other telecom companies—a "hollow swap" strategy[15] creating fictitious revenue-generating transactions. These transactions were similar to the illegal transactions exposed in the demise of Global Crossing.

Four men were deeply involved in the scandal: Grant P. Graham, former senior vice-president for finance for Qwest's global business unit; Thomas W. Hall, former senior vice-president in the government and educational solutions group; John M. Walker, former vice-president in the government and educational solutions group; and Bryan K. Treadway, former assistant controller. These officials illegally booked revenue in an effort to hide the fact that Denver-based Qwest could not meet its target of double-digit revenue growth in the second quarter of 2001. Among other items, the four executives booked revenue from the sale of equipment to the Arizona School Facilities Board even though the equipment had not been delivered—a violation of generally accepted accounting principles.

In 2003, federal prosecutors charged these four Qwest executives with criminal fraud: Prosecutors claimed that the executives falsified documents and misled the regional telephone company's outside auditor in an attempt to illegally report $33.6 million in revenue. Other charges against the four executives included conspiring to commit securities fraud, filing false reports to the SEC, wire fraud, and making false statements to their accountants, including outside auditor Arthur Andersen. At the time, the maximum penalty for securities fraud was 10 years in prison and a $1 million fine, and the maximum penalty for making a false statement to the SEC was five years in prison and a $250,000 fine. At about the same time, the Securities and Exchange

Commission (SEC) brought civil fraud charges against eight Qwest executives, including the four charged by the Justice Department. Qwest was also charged with falsely claiming $109 million in sales of equipment and services before they were delivered to Genuity Inc., another telecommunications firm.

Qwest, the dominant provider of local telephone service in 14 western states, publicly disclosed that its accounting was under federal investigation. The company said it expected to restate approximately $2 billion because of improper accounting for the years 2000, 2001, and 2002. Qwest barely survived because its subsidiary, U.S. West, provided substantial assets and cash flows to arrest Qwest's operating decline and allow for its recovery. To raise funds, Qwest sold its phone-directory unit for $7 billion.

ADELPHIA

The story of Adelphia has been described as possibly "the most egregious instance of corporate self-dealing and financial chicanery in United States corporate history."[16] By 2001, Adelphia was the sixth largest cable operator in the United States, but it had been in trouble for some time, with regulators and investors voicing concerns about loans guaranteed by the company to its founders, the Rigas family. The family tried to head off some of these concerns by giving up four of the seven seats on the Adelphia board of directors and transferring $1 billion in assets to help cover the loans. Nevertheless, its faulty books attracted the attention of the SEC and Department of Justice.

In 2002, the Department of Justice (DOJ) alleged that the members of the Rigas family who essentially ran the business had systematically looted the corporation over a period of four years. According to Larry Thompson, Assistant Attorney General, "In less than four years... they stole hundreds of millions of dollars through their fraud and they caused losses to investors of more than $60 billion." The DOJ also alleged that the defendants had intentionally submitted false information to lenders and made false statements to the public in order to maintain their failing company's stock price. The defendants also were said to have concealed $2.3 billion in loans and misrepresented the company's financial performance and number of cable subscribers.

The DOJ characterized the Rigas' self-serving financial dealings as "brazen thefts": taking $252 million from the company to cover investments in the family's own brokerage accounts, and using fraudulent documents and accounting tricks to illegally obtain $420 million in Adelphia stock. Adelphia founder John Rigas was said to have lent himself $66 million from company funds without making required disclosures and to have spent $13 million of corporate funds to put a golf course on his own land.[17] The extravagance of the founding family included the expenditure of $6,000 every year for a jet to deliver a Christmas tree to the New York City home of one of Rigas' daughters. Unbelievably, when the first tree was deemed "too stubby" one year, a second one was delivered, also, by jet.

As a result of the firm's financial misdealings, five former Adelphia officials (including three of Rigas' family members) were arrested and charged with conspiracy to commit fraud. Founder John Rigas, and two of his sons were taken into custody by U.S. postal service police in Manhattan. Two other former executives, James Brown and Michael Mulcahey, were also arrested in Pennsylvania, where Adelphia's headquarters is located. Finally, Adephia sued the entire Rigas family for $1 billion for breach of fiduciary duties, in addition to several other infringements. Officials from the DOJ and the SEC said the actions of the former Adelphia officers led to tens of billions of dollars in losses to investors. In July 2004, federal prosecutors won convictions against John and Timothy Rigas. The jury remained deadlocked on charges against John Rigas' other son, Michael. The jury found Michael Mulcahey, former Adelphia assistant treasurer, not guilty on all 23 counts of conspiracy and fraud that he faced.

ImClone

In June 2003, Dr. Samuel Waksal, founder of biopharmaceutical company ImClone, was charged with insider trading for telling family and friends to sell their shares of ImClone stock a day before the Federal

Drug Administration (FDA) was to refuse to review ImClone's new cancer drug, Erbitux. The scandal widened as news emerged that "life-style guru" Martha Stewart, a close friend of Waksal, had also offloaded ImClone stock shares worth about $228,000 shortly before the FDA rejected the biotech firm's application. In Waksal's June 2003 trial, Prosecutor Michael Schachter told a packed Manhattan courtroom that Waksal had "violated a sacred trust with his shareholder and told numerous, separate and distinct sets of lies, surrounding his family's sale of the stock, sending out the message to investors that the game is rigged."[18]

In the criminal proceedings, Waksal pled guilty in March 2003 to six felony counts related to insider trading and charges of tax evasion regarding $15 million worth of art he purchased. Waksal was named in a 13-count indictment accusing him of bank and securities fraud and obstruction of justice.[19] He was sentenced to eighty-seven months in prison and ordered to pay $3 million in fines. He is serving his sentence at a federal prison in Pennsylvania.

Martha Stewart was indicted on charges of securities fraud, conspiracy and making false statements to federal agents. Although she claimed innocence, in 2004 Stewart was found guilty of making false statements to the SEC and FBI and of obstruction of justice. Stewart's Merrill Lynch stockbroker, Peter Bacanovic, was also found guilty of obstruction of justice and lying about Stewart's sale of ImClone stock. Martha Stewart resigned as chairman and chief executive officer of her company hours after being charged with securities fraud and obstruction of justice. She continued to serve on the company's board of directors until her conviction, however, and was named to the alternate position of chief creative officer.

Later, an investor in Martha Stewart's company filed a civil lawsuit against her as well. The lawsuit alleged that Stewart sold shares in her own company, Martha Stewart Living Omnimedia, because she knew she could be investigated on suspicion of insider trading in the ImClone case. The allegations of insider trading at ImClone caused shares in Martha Stewart Living Omnimedia to fall below half of their value at the time of the ImClone revelations. According to the investor bringing suit against Stewart, "Being a former stockbroker, Stewart knew that the suspicious timing of her ImClone stock sales would bring public, if not legal, scrutiny."[20] The charges against her, filed in Manhattan Federal Court in New York City, followed a separate suit by the SEC, for "illegal insider trading."[21]

Table 3-5 summarizes the legal and ethical violations of the companies reviewed in this chapter. Their CEO's and public auditors are also indicated.

Table 3-5: Corporate Legal and Ethical Violations

Company	CEO/CFO (unless otherwise noted, if charged)	Industry	Accountant/ Auditor	Legal and/or Ethical Violations
Enron	Ken Lay: Chairman Jeff Skilling: CEO Andrew Fastow: CFO	Energy	Arthur Andersen L.L.P.	• Concealed debt and massive losses • Arthur Andersen was convicted of obstruction of justice
Tyco	Dennis Kozlowski: CEO Mark Swartz: CFO Mark Belnick: General Counsel	Financial Services; Medical Supplies	Price/ Waterhouse/ Coopers (PwC)	• Improperly adjusted losses • Used accounting loopholes to prevent Tyco's acquisitions from negatively impacting earnings
WorldCom	Bernard Ebbers: CEO Scott Sullivan: CFO David Myers: Controller	Telecommun-ication	Arthur Andersen L.L.P.	• Turned a loss into a profit by improperly classifying expenses
Global Crossing	CEO not indicted	Telecommun-ication	Arthur Andersen L.L.P.	• Inflated earnings and cash flow to make its financial performance look better
Qwest	CEO not indicted	Telecommun-ication	Arthur Andersen L.L.P.	• Created fictitious revenue-generating transactions by inflating sales
Adelphia	John Rigas: Founder Timothy Rigas: CFO	Cable	Deloitte & Touche	• Concealed loans • Misrepresented the company's financial performance and the company's number of cable subscribers
ImClone	Sam Waksal: CEO	Pharmaceuticals	Arthur Andersen L.L.P.	• Insider trading

Source: Author's compilations, company annual reports

SCANDALS APPEAR IN EUROPE

MISSING OIL RESERVES AT SHELL

In January 2004, oil company Royal Dutch/Shell Group, one of the world's largest publicly traded oil concerns, disclosed that it had overstated its proven oil and natural gas reserves by 20 percent, or the equivalent of 3.9 billion barrels of oil. The oil portion alone, representing about two-thirds of the revision, involved some $67.5 billion in potential future revenue, assuming moderate oil prices of $25 a barrel. The overstatement was significant because reserve calculations, though technical and arcane, drive an oil company's prospects, much like research pipelines and patents drive a pharmaceutical company's forecasting model. The size of the overstatement also raised the prospect of more regulatory scrutiny of Shell, including SEC enforcement action. Initially the SEC declined to comment on the reclassification of reserves at Shell or reserve issues concerning any other oil company. However, former SEC chief accountant Lynn Turner did say in January 2004 that the revision looked like more than a mistake. "A 20 percent restatement of proven reserves is a humongous error," said Turner. "For a company like Shell to have missed its proven reserves by that much is not an oversight. It's an intentional misapplication of the SEC's rules."[22]

Shell's then Chairman and CEO, Sir Phillip Watts, was fired over this incident. Before rising to the position of chairman, Watts was the head of the firm's exploration and production division. This unit posted the overly aggressive oil reserve bookings, thus putting Watts at the center of the scandal.

Shell maintained that the reclassification would not have a material effect on its financial statements. The company said the reclassification did not materially change the estimated total volume of oil and gas that it believed it could extract ultimately or its production over the next two years. Nevertheless, this "re-classification" and the accompanying stock market reaction to the Shell overstatement has caused shareholders to suffer billions of dollars in losses. Such consequences highlight the on-going capital market "jitters" in response to any disclosure of possible wrong-doing by corporate entities. The possibility of high market losses as a result of the disclosures of relatively minor missteps reflects the fear of investors that such blunders may reflect deeper, more fundamental problems within companies. As the investigation continued, the SEC issued a damning report into Shell's overstatement of its oil reserves, which finds that the cover-up was older and more widespread than the company had previously acknowledged. The SEC and British regulators have also jointly fined Shell $150 million.[23]

ROYAL AHOLD

By 2003 Royal Ahold, a Dutch food retailer and distributor, had grown to become the world's third-largest grocer. Using an aggressive acquisition strategy, the 115-year-old Dutch company was operating in twenty-seven countries around the world. In 2003, the company had $60.9 billion in revenues, 59 percent from the U.S., where it owned the Giant and Stop & Shop grocery store chains. Yet in a pattern all-too-familiar to Wall Street, Ahold surprised investors in 2003 when it announced that it had overstated earnings by at least $500 million in 2001 and 2002. Ahold's disclosures followed promises of 15 percent growth—a goal that had proved to be unattainable—and prompted an immediate sixty percent decrease in its stock market value and the resignations of its chief executive and chief financial officers.

Ahold's accounting irregularities were disclosed in the context of its U.S. Foodservice division, the nation's second largest wholesale supplier to restaurants and institutional dining systems. Ahold's books reflected inflated promotional allowances provided by food manufacturers and, in many cases, payments documented without the manufacturers' permission.

Questions have been raised with respect to Ahold's Global business practices and the company is currently being investigated by the U.S. Department of Justice and the SEC, as well as regulators in the Netherlands. Even if the roots of Ahold's financial problems were to be found in the U.S., they would naturally extend directly to headquarters in Holland and point to serious questions about Ahold's financial controls worldwide. Ahold's ultimate restatements reached $1 billion. By the time the scandal ended in 2003, Ahold remained afloat with a $3.35 billion line of credit from a syndicate of banks, including ABN AMRO, Goldman Sachs, ING, and JP Morgan.[24]

PARMALAT

Parmalat is a long-lasting milk and cookie-making company headquartered in Italy. Its shares (depository receipts) trade in the over-the-counter market in the United States. The company maintains an American headquarters in New Jersey and has other operations across the country. Near the end of 2003, the SEC sued Parmalat Finanziaria SpA, accusing the company of defrauding U.S. investors in what regulators called one of the largest and most brazen corporate financial frauds in history. Trouble at Parmalat was initially disclosed when the company revealed that a U.S. bank had no record of a $4.9 billion account allegedly maintained by a Parmalat subsidiary based in the Cayman Islands. Italian authorities soon followed the lead of U.S. investigators and widened their probe. Thus far, seven Parmalat executives have been arrested, including former finance director Fausto Tonna; Parmalat founder, Calisto Tanzi; and other senior Parmalat executives. An eighth warrant is still being considered. In the interim, the company was run by an Italian government-appointed rescue administrator, and eleven people were held by investigators. Police have also questioned auditors for the two accountancy firms responsible for the company's books—the Italian arms of Grant Thornton and Deloitte & Touche.

Those arrested have been portrayed by prosecutors as the operations center for a conspiracy in which Parmalat's finance department allegedly fashioned bogus documents showing assets the company never had and sales it never made. Prosecutors are now probing the shortfall of more than $8 billion on Parmalat's balance sheet in a scandal that has riled Europe much the way that Enron, Tyco, and World-Com battered confidence in business in the United States.[25] A source close to the company has said that the accounting irregularities have surpassed at least $14 billion and could grow to over $15 billion when all their transgressions are discovered. Table 3-6 presents a timeline of key events in the Parmalat scandal.

Table 3-6: Parmalat Timeline

1961: Calisto Tanzi forms Parmalat at the age of 22.

1990: Parmalat is listed on the Milan stock exchange.

1999: The company sets up subsidiary Bonlat in the Cayman Islands.

2003

27 February: Parmalat gives up trying to sell as much as 500m euros of bonds, raising questions about how the company was planning to pay back its existing debt.

28 March: Chief Financial Officer Fausto Tonna resigns and is replaced by Alberto Ferraris.

11 November: The company's shares decline amid questions regarding transactions with the Epicurum fund in the Cayman Islands.

14 November: Ferraris resigns and is replaced by Luciano Del Soldato.

9 December: The company misses a 150 million euros bond payment and Del Soldato quits. Enrico Bondi is called in as a consultant to help turn the company around.

15 December: Tanzi resigns as chairman and chief executive officer of Parmalat, later replaced by Bondi.

19 December: Bank of America claims a document showing 3.9 billion euros in Bonlat's bank account is forged.

20 December: Fraud investigation is started as Prime Minister Silvio Berlusconi promises to safeguard jobs.

24 December: Parmalat goes into administration.

27 December: Tanzi is taken into police custody as he returns to Italy from Spain.

30 December: Tanzi admits that the hole in Parmalat's accounts is about 8 billion euros, though he denies ordering any cover up. He says top managers acted of their own accord, but does admit siphoning off about 500m euros from other Parmalat-owned companies.

31 December: Police arrest five former Parmalat executives including Fausto Tonna and Luciano Del Soldato.

2004

4 January: Senior officials from the US Securities and Exchange Commission

are reported to be investigating the way Bank of America and other banks sold billions of euros worth of Parmalat bonds.

5 January: Police question Fausto Tonna in Parma, alleging he helped construct a web of offshore bank accounts and holding.

8 January: Accountants Grant Thornton expel their Italian partner firm because of its involvement in auditing Parmalat. Italian officials investigate accountants at Deloitte & Touche.

17 January: Bank of America says it can find no trace of an account, which a creditors' group had said, contained about 7 billion euros.

19 January: Franco Gorreri, finance director until 1992 is arrested. (This makes number 11.)

23 January: Alessandro Bassi, former aide to Fausto Tonna, commits suicide.

26 January: Auditors determine that as of September 2003 Parmalat had debt of 14.3 billion euros, almost eight times what management had claimed at the time.

Source: http://news.bbc.co.uk/go/pr/fr/-/1/hi/business/3369079.stm

OTHER EUROPEAN SCANDALS

In the late 1990s, Belgium-based speech and language software maker Lernout & Hauspie was hailed as one of the brightest stars in Europe's tech sector. The maker of speech-recognition software fell into a financial crisis in 2000 after being accused of overstating revenue from its Asian operations. The company, which at one time had a market capitalization of more than $10 billion, later went out of business.

Belgian authorities are pursuing criminal charges against Lernout's founders. In January 2004, Etienne de Callatay, head of equity research at Bank de Groof in Brussels, noted, "What would be good would be to have a first major case of a company and its management being sued for wrong practices. That would clearly set the tone for change."[26]

Ireland experienced its own scandal in 2002 after *The Wall Street Journal* reported that Elan, a pharmaceuticals company, had used deceptive accounting practices to inflate revenues. The company's shares lost more than 95 percent of their value amid an SEC investigation, which is continuing. Recent changes to financial regulation in

Ireland include the establishment of an accounting supervisory authority, as well as the unification of regulators covering banking, insurance, mortgages and credit unions. But the U.S.'s SEC, rather than the Irish Stock Exchange, is dominating the dialogue over compliance issues, especially in the pharmaceuticals sector, said Ian Hunter, senior equity analyst at Goodbody Stockbrokers in Dublin.[27]

Table 3-7 Prominent European Corporate Ethical Violations

Company	Country	Ethical Violations	Restatement/Stock Market Reaction
Royal Dutch/Shell Group	Holland	• Overstated reserves by the equivalent of 3.9 billion barrels of oil	• 20 percent restatement of proven reserves
Royal Ahold	Holland	• Overstated earnings by at least $500 million in 2001 & 2002 • Inflated promotional allowances provided by food manufacturers' and documented payments without the manufacturers' permission • U. S. distributors found to have been manipulating various margins and inflating firm financial reports	• $ 1 billion • 60 percent decrease in stock value
Parmalat	Italy	• Accounting irregularities surpassing $14 billion (possibly closer to $15 billion) • Allegedly held $4.9 billion in U. S. bank but account did not actually exist • Fashioned bogus documents showing assets that did not exist and sales that were never made • $8 billion shortfall on balance sheet • Seven executives arrested, 11 being held by investigators	• $500 million in 2001 and 2002
Lernout and Hauspie	Belgium	• Overstated revenue from Asian operations	• Out of business
Elan	Ireland	• Used deceptive accounting practices to inflate revenues	• Company share value dropped 95 percent

INTERNATIONAL REACTIONS

Various reactions to U.S. corporate wrongdoing such as that seen at Enron, WorldCom, and Tyco, occurred across the globe in the years following the scandals. On July 5, 2002, for example, U.K. Trade and Industry Secretary Patricia Hewitt announced that her agency would take action to prevent similar types of scandals from occurring in the United Kingdom.[28] Historically, the U.K. has allowed executive directors to appoint company auditors, creating the same type of environment conducive to inaccurate accounting practices seen in the United States. In an effort to prevent accounting scandals however, the U.K. Trade and Industry office stripped executives of the power to appoint company auditors.

According to Secretary Hewitt, the U.S. scandals have shown a "much too cozy relationship between finance officers or chief executives and their auditors [such that] there is clearly a case for the audit committee to appoint auditors on behalf of the shareholders." U.K companies may also be required to rotate auditing firms. "There are obvious attractions to the idea that you should rotate the auditors rather than potentially having an audit company serve the company for a very, very long time."[29] Hewitt later said, "Action is also needed to be taken to restore confidence. Confidence has been lost in the independence of auditors as a result of Enron. The relationship between the company and the auditor was blurred, to put the point kindly. Big auditing firms could also be barred from providing other, lucrative services to companies they are auditing."[30] Further government action will depend on the report of the review body's findings to Hewitt.

Italy's Parmalat scandal, and doubts over internal controls at the Netherlands' Ahold Corporation, have caused the investment world to focus on the ability of European regulators to respond to problems with decisive investigations and sustainable reforms. Europe's approach to corporate governance has typically consisted of a tightening of government regulatory control through the gathering of disparate oversight functions under one roof. By working more closely during the past two years with the European Commission, national regulators in the European Union's (EU's) fifteen member states are speeding the adoption of commission directives that cover everything from accounting practices to the role of independent company directors.

Although Europe may be scoring corporate-governance victories on paper, observers say its regulators have had significantly less success than the U.S. Securities and Exchange Commission when it comes to influencing day-to-day behavior on trading floors and in corporate boardrooms. In Europe, most regulators have preferred a principles-based system in which companies subscribe to a code of conduct and must explain themselves in areas where they do not comply. This approach is different from that of the U.S., which has attempted to legislate good corporate governance. Neither approach has proven to be superior to the other, since financial scandals continue to unfold in both places.

The Committee of European Securities Regulators (CESR) has held that U.S.-style legislation is unnecessary. The Committee has called for broader powers for European regulators, but has stopped short of recommending the establishment of a single industry regulator. The European Commission's financial-services action plan has identified its priorities and is trying to harmonize the rules and powers of national regulatory authorities.

CONCLUSION

The litany of scandals described in this chapter give rise to a number of implications concerning corporate governance and the world economy. These implications are addressed in the Sarbanes-Oxley Act legislation, the subject of the next chapter. We glean several lessons from the U.S. and European financial misdeeds described in this chapter.

1. The dependence of corporations on rising stock prices, along with their connection to executive stock options, pressured companies to demonstrate continuous short-term earnings growth.

2. The relationship between chief executive or financial officers and their auditors has been much too close. A strong argument can be made for the audit committee of the board to appoint auditors on behalf of the shareholders. Even more, companies should consider rotating the auditors rather than having an audit company continuously serve the company over the long term.

3. Accounting firms face conflicts of interest in providing good and reliable information. Thus, auditors should be barred from providing other services, particularly consulting, to the company with which they are engaged.

4. Controversy exits over the best approach to regulation. European regulators have pushed a principle-based system while U.S. regulators have attempted to legislate better corporate governance.

5. The burst of the technology bubble of the 1990s affected the telecom industry in a way that made it particularly vulnerable to the pressure to issue exaggerated financial statements and conceal company information.

6. Companies that used myriad financial innovations developed in the past decade such as special purpose entities (SPEs), derivatives, and stock options were prone to manipulate financial statements.

In a country and, indeed, a world that is undergoing massive economic consolidation, restructuring, and globalization, it is critical that economic regulations, governance, and policing/enforcement be effective. Upon review of the widespread scandals that occurred in both the U.S. and Europe at the turn of this century's business downturn, a number of observations appear appropriate. Specifically, several venerable U.S. institutions seem to be malfunctioning and deserving of serious review and change.

The health of the U.S. and/or world economy is the essential backdrop of the quality and effectiveness of a country's economic regime. That is, it is no accident that the breakdown in our corporate governance systems, financial market regulation, and institutional behavior occurred in the midst of an economic recession that quickly vitiated corporate revenues and cash flows. The pressures and stresses resulting from the slowdown were exacerbated by the fact that it followed one the greatest economic booms in U.S. history.

The boom clearly added to an aggressive, overly competitive and greed stricken corporate culture wherein all economic players sought ever-increasing profits, mega-deals, and exorbitant salaries. In this type of turbulent and complex environment, various problems and issues can be hidden or not addressed because resources (cash flows) are abundant. Yet, as an economic downturn dampens cash flows, it soon becomes difficult, if not impossible, to meet profit expectations. This results in the pressures which give rise to the various examples of corporate malfeasance, regulatory inadequacy and laxity, and unethical behavior of those professionals that serve our economic system—public auditors, lawyers, and bankers.

Perhaps, no other profession was more tainted than public accounting during this scandalous era. Indeed, Arthur Andersen (AA) acted more like a co-conspirator and partner of Enron than its arms-length public auditor. And, of course, as a result of its actions, this once prestigious firm has vanished from existence. It is probably no accident that only AA has disappeared as a result of the scandals given its disproportionate association with indicted corporations. Nevertheless, the other major accounting firms were not pristine. They, too, participated with various tainted companies and have suffered financially as a result of their misdeeds.

Litigants in the Enron case have taken action related to the financing and advisory aspects of SPEs against large financial institutions such as J.P. Morgan Chase and Citigroup. The legal exposure of such companies is not surprising either, since they are very large, highly visible, and have "deep pockets." Further, their fiduciary role and due diligence requirements suggest that they are also culpable in this case.

The goal of the SEC and other federal authorities is to deter crimes. The rationale is that corporate officers will violate the law when the expected benefits outweigh the costs. Accordingly, prosecutors need to increase the costs. It is important that prosecutors show they understand complex schemes and can actually prove crimes were committed.

Several legal pursuits of corporations include charges of obstruction of justice. This was the basis for the cases against Martha Stewart as well as Arthur Andersen. In Stewart's case, even though civil authorities alleged she had sold shares on inside information, she was not charged criminally with insider trading. Instead, she was convicted of obstructing justice. The message: lying to federal authorities will be prosecuted.

For prosecutorial pursuits to be effective, top-ranking executives engaged in complex, fraudulent schemes must know that authorities will not only bring charges, but also have the skills to win cases. The indictment of Bernie Ebbers of WorldCom is very complex with allegations involving how he and others manipulated revenue-recognition policies to meet analysts' expectations. The cases against Dennis Kozlowski of Tyco and John Rigas of Adelphia are similarly complex. Thus far, it appears that the government can meet the challenge and, if so, an important message is being delivered.

CHAPTER THREE QUESTIONS:

CORPORATE MALFEASANCE:
FRAUD, REGULATORY LAXITY, AND THEFT

1. Does splitting the role of Chairman of the Board and Chief Executive Officer (CEO) lessen the potential problems in corporate governance?

2. When you think of American business scandals of recent years, what infamous names come to mind? Why those names?

3. Do you believe that CEOs are entitled to the amounts of money that they receive in their compensation packages?

4. Should corporations give expensive personal benefits (country club memberships, personal jets, company loans, fully furnished Park Avenue apartments, etc.) to their key executives, in addition to their multi-million dollar salaries?

5. Given the kinds of scandals that have occurred in America and Europe, why do you think there have not been as many scandals reported out of Asia?

6. Do you think that there is a correlation between an economic boom and the propensity for a culture of corporate greed?

4

ADDRESSING CORPORATE SCANDALS: THE SARBANES-OXLEY ACT AS A PANACEA?

When president George W. Bush signed the Sarbanes-Oxley Act (SOA) in August of 2002, the nation instituted the most radical and comprehensive redesign of its federal securities laws since the 1930s. Although the Sarbanes-Oxley Act is too broad to review in its entirety, this chapter reviews the portions of the Act that should prove most significant for the corporate world. The SOA makes it abundantly clear to all players that there will be consequences for malfeasance in the corporate environment.

The SOA comprises four parts, and this analysis covers three. The first looks at the creation of the Public Company Accounting Oversight Board (PCAOB), which has the power to set rules that give independence to auditors and ban accounting firms from doing certain consulting work for their clients. Such oversight is central to efforts to restore investor confidence. The second discusses how firms will govern themselves. The third examines those provisions of the SOA that address how auditing committees will assist in the governance of corporations. The rest of the chapter offers a case study of early usefulness of the SOA, then explores implications of the Act.

THE PUBLIC COMPANY ACCOUNTING OVERSIGHT BOARD (PCAOB)

The Public Company Accounting Oversight Board (PCAOB) was created with a mandate to guard against accounting abuses such as those that have plagued the nation in the last twenty years. During the 1980s and 1990s, the public accounting firms enjoyed double-digit income growth by creating management consulting operations and developing sophisticated systems for tax planning, mergers, and acquisitions. Opponents of this kind of diversification, called the "multidisciplinary model," argued that it badly distracted accountants from auditing, their core work. The primary role of the PCAOB is to ensure that the independence of auditors is not undermined by other fee-generating activities. Accounting firms still do auditing, consulting, and tax work for clients, but the SOA now bans them from doing these functions at the same firm. In addition, corporate audit committees must give prior approval to any non-audit work done by audit firms, such as planning or legal advice.

The creation of this brand new entity results from the widely publicized failure of the audit profession to police itself and marks an end to the era of self-regulation by the U.S. accounting profession. The previous system, which depended on peer review, has been scrapped. PCAOB's main task is to independently inspect of the work of audit firms, with the largest audit firms being examined annually.

This new accounting regulator obtains some of its funding from the Securities and Exchange Commission (SEC). Other funds for its activities come from listed companies, who pay on a sliding scale according to their market capitalization. The ten largest companies are expected to annually contribute about $1 million each.[1]

CORPORATE SELF-REGULATION

CEO/CFO REPORT CERTIFICATION

The SOA contains two provisions requiring firms' officers to personally certify the periodic reports that must be filed with the SEC.[2] A section of the Act requires CEOs and CFOs to declare in each periodic financial statement that the report fully complies with the requirements of the Securities Exchange Act of 1934 and that the information contained in the report fairly presents, in all material respects, the company's financial condition and results of operations. Certifying officers of domestic public companies will face charges for false certification of financial information, with penalties of $1 million and/or up to ten years imprisonment if the violation was "knowing" and $5 million and/or up to twenty years imprisonment if the violation was "willful."[3]

In addition to verifying the financial statements, CEOs and CFOs must certify in each annual and quarterly report filed with the SEC that they have reviewed the report. Based on their knowledge, they are certifying that the report does not contain any material misstatements or omissions in the financial information. This is to say that the report fairly presents, in all material respects, the company's financial condition and results of operations. In addition, they are certifying that they have designed and reviewed the effectiveness of internal controls to ensure that they receive material information and they have disclosed to the audit committee any fraud and all significant deficiencies in the design or operation of the internal controls.

DISGORGEMENT OF CEO AND CFO COMPENSATION AND PROFITS

A company is required to repair its financial statements when there is material noncompliance with any financial reporting requirement. If that noncompliance resulted from misconduct, a penalty may be imposed: The CEO and CFO must immediately reimburse the company for any bonus or other incentive- or equity-based compensation they received during the twelve-month period preceding the relevant filing. However, it is not specified whose misconduct will be relevant or what level of misconduct (e.g., negligent, knowing, or willful) is required to impose this penalty.

Ban on Personal Loans to Executive Officers and Directors

No public company may make, extend, modify or renew any personal loan to its executive officers or directors. There will be limited exceptions for loans made in the ordinary course of the company's business, on market terms, for home improvement and manufactured home loans, consumer credit, or extension of credit under an open-end credit plan or charge card. Companies may maintain currently outstanding loans to executive officers and directors provided that the terms of the loans are not materially modified.[4]

Accelerated Reporting of Trades by Insiders

The deadline for insiders (including executive officers, directors, and ten-percent shareholders) to file a report on any trading in their company's securities has been shortened. The report is due within two business days after the execution date of the transaction, rather than prior to the tenth day of the month following the transaction, which was the deadline under previous rules. The SEC may extend this deadline if it determines the two-day period is not feasible.[5]

Insiders are required to make the filing of the transaction report available electronically. Also, each issuer who maintains a corporate website is required to post a copy of the filing on its website by the end of the business day following the filing, and the SEC will be required to make the filing available electronically within the same time frame.

Prohibition on Insider Trades During Pension Fund Blackout Periods

Directors and executive officers normally may trade any of a company's equity securities obtained as compensation for their services. There is a prohibition, however, on such trading during any blackout period imposed under a company's 401(k) plan or other profit-sharing or retirement plan, except for certain regularly scheduled no-trade periods. Any profits realized by an officer or director in violation of this provision, regardless of that person's intent, may be recovered by the company. This can be accomplished in several ways, including through a shareholder derivative suit.

NEW AUDIT COMMITTEE STANDARDS

The SEC has adopted rules that direct the national securities exchanges and Nasdaq to adopt the following criteria for companies listed on their exchanges:

• The audit committee directors are independent.

The audit committee must be composed entirely of independent directors. To be considered "independent," members may not accept any consulting, advisory, or other compensatory fee from the company, except in his or her capacity as a board or board committee member, and may not own or control 5 percent or more of the voting securities of the company or be an officer, director, partner, or employee of the company.

• The audit committee has authority to engage advisors.

The audit committee must have the authority, and any funding it finds appropriate, to engage an outside auditing firm, independent counsel, or other advisers it determines necessary to the execution of its duties.

• The audit committee has employee complaint ("whistle blowing") procedures in place.

Audit committees must establish procedures for the receipt, retention, and treatment of complaints regarding accounting, internal accounting controls, or auditing matters, and for the confidential, anonymous submission by employees of concerns regarding questionable accounting or auditing matters.

The importance of whistle blowing to a healthy business system cannot be overemphasized. Without Sherron Watkins at Enron, Cynthia Cooper at WorldCom (both discussed in chapter 3), and Noreen Harrington at Canary Capital (discussed in Chapters 6), it is doubtful whether those scandals would have been exposed as quickly and as precisely as they were. Nor is it likely that such beneficial public policy, regulatory, and legislative responses would have resulted.

On the subject of whistle blowing, Ralph Nader, a leading consumer advocate, commented that the former Soviet totalitarian regime, with all its prisons and enforcement against free speech, seemed to generate more whistle blowers than the United States. Somehow many of our businessmen, lawyers, accountants, regulators, and even business school professors have become so entwined with our corporate system that few venture to give criticism or expose wrongdoing. The SOA promises to provide a means whereby information and complaints may reach company boards without bringing retribution to the informant.

The SOA was clearly written in the light of all the scandals that have taken place, with Enron, WorldCom, and Tyco in mind. The cause-and-effect relationship is so clear that one is bound to conclude that the SOA was in essence molded by the same firms that it intended to regulate.

HEALTHSOUTH: AN EARLY TEST OF THE SARBANES-OXLEY ACT

In 1984 Richard M. Scrushy, along with four partners, pooled $50,000 to create the HealthSouth Corporation. Its first purchase was an outpatient rehabilitation center in Little Rock, Arkansas. By the year 2000, HealthSouth became the official sports medicine provider for the National Football League's New England Patriots and Washington Redskins, as well as for Major League Soccer's New England Revolution. Interestingly, its equity was a top five performer within Standard and Poor's 500 index. In short, Scrushy had apparently built a major growth company, believed to be the largest U.S. provider of outpatient surgery, diagnostic imaging, and rehabilitation services. The company had nearly 1,700 facilities and 51,000 employees in every state and abroad.

Scrushy had to step down as CEO amid reorganization that included spinning off the company's surgery centers into a new public company. In September 2002, the SEC launched an investigation into Scrushy's selling of HealthSouth securities. The SEC later suspended trading of HealthSouth stock alleging that HealthSouth and CEO Scrushy committed accounting fraud and overstated earnings by $1.4 billion beginning in 1999. This was followed by the first of eleven guilty pleas of other HealthSouth executives that would surface with the unfolding of the scandal. The Board of Directors placed Scrushy on administrative leave and appointed Joel Gordon to perform as interim chairman.

On the same day that the HealthSouth board of directors fired Scrushy, another HealthSouth financial officer, Emery Harris, pled guilty to fraud charges and questions began to emerge concerning possible insider trading. Harris was sentenced to a five-month prison term for his role in the company's accounting-fraud scandal.[6]

The SEC eventually charged two former executives, William T. Owens and Weston Smith (a former CFO), with insider trading and securities fraud as well as false certification of financial records. Later, five more HealthSouth executives would admit taking part in the alleged financial scandal and would be charged: Angela C. Ayers, Cathy C. Edwards, Kenneth Livesay, Rebecca Kay Morgan, and Virginia B. Valentine. It was later discovered that HealthSouth executives faked some $2.5 billion in earnings, or almost twice as much as the previously alleged amount. Michael Martin, another former CFO, agreed to plead guilty to fraud charges. However, a federal judge has rejected his plea and scheduled a hearing for a later date.

HealthSouth's chief information officer and former assistant controller, Ken Livesay, pled guilty to federal fraud charges and related allegations. His admissions raised the total of the healthcare chain's overstated profit to nearly $2.5 billion since 1997. In 2003, documents filed with Livesay's plea agreement said that HealthSouth also overstated its pretax income in 1997 by $440 million and in 1998 by $635 million

Former HealthSouth vice presidents Ayers, Edwards, and Morgan and former assistant vice president Valentine each received four years probation. They were ordered to spend six months in house arrest and fined $2,000 by U.S. District Court Judge Inge Johnson. Morgan was ordered to surrender $235,000 she received in tainted income. Each could have received up to five years in prison. These four and Harris entered plea agreements in April 2003, and pledged to cooperate with the government's investigation, which resulted in an indictment charging company founder and former chairman and chief executive Scrushy with eighty-five criminal counts, including fraud, conspiracy, and money laundering. Scrushy also was charged with violating the Sarbanes-Oxley Act. His attorneys said they intended to challenge the law's validity. Scrushy has pleaded innocent to all charges and is free on $10 million bond.

Another former HealthSouth treasurer and CFO, Malcolm McVay agreed to plea guilty to fraud. With the fourth former CFO pleading guilty, the House Energy and Commerce Committee announced an investigation into HealthSouth. The committee requested financial documents from the Birmingham-based rehabilitation giant and its longtime auditor, Ernst & Young.

HealthSouth terminated rights to severance pay and benefits for Scrushy, its chairman and CEO, when the firm fired him following the 2003 indictment. However, prosecutors alleged he used money gained by the HealthSouth fraud to buy assets including diamond jewelry, a plane, a yacht, Cadillacs, cuff links, works of art by famous painters, land and an armor-plated sport-utility vehicle.

Informed individuals indicate HealthSouth will seek additional compensation from its fired leader if he is convicted. Under a new corporate crime law that took effect in 2002, CEOs and finance chiefs must forfeit certain bonuses and stock-sale gains made in connection with an earnings restatement that results from misconduct. HealthSouth is a test case for this new federal statute. Scrushy collected about $11.5 million in bonus money during 2002, according to HealthSouth.[7]

William Curtis Miller, an executive with Ernst & Young, testified that his firm relied on too few people for information about how HealthSouth was managed and did not properly check some accounts.[8]

The HealthSouth scandal is a model case for using the Sarbanes-Oxley Act to federally prosecute corporate fraud. In addition to DOJ's criminal prosecution of Scrushy, the SEC is pursuing him in a civil lawsuit for accounting fraud. The SEC issued new documents against Scrushy estimating that, if he is found guilty of insider trading, the agency could seek as much as $700 million from him. This figure includes recovery of treble damages and disgorgement of his trading profits.

SARBANES-OXLEY PAYING DIVIDENDS

Armed with the severe criminal penalties provided by the Sarbanes-Oxley Act, the government has relied on plea bargains to prosecute corporate executives. The HealthSouth inquiry has already netted eight criminal convictions, accomplishing in just weeks what might have stretched across months or even years in the past. The prosecutions were the first ever under Sarbanes-Oxley.

The HealthSouth case has already produced a greater number of convictions than most of the other high-profile scandals that began the twenty-first century. The closest to it is Enron, where a total of seven former executives have faced criminal charges. In the investigation of WorldCom, five former executives have been charged with felony counts. At Adelphia Communications, six former executives have been indicted. Additional charges against other executives are still expected in some of these cases, just as they are in HealthSouth.

One reason the HealthSouth case moved so quickly is the number of executives who came forward to cooperate with the government. Investigators said the legal ramifications of the Sarbanes-Oxley Act have prompted some defendants to come forward, as has as the realization that the chances of getting a good deal diminish with every person who agrees to cooperate with the government.

With the passage of the SOA, top U.S. officials announced the intent to speed up and intensify corporate-fraud prosecutions. The Department of Justice and the Securities and Exchange Commission collaborated closely on the HealthSouth case, and local U.S. attorneys and Federal Bureau of Investigation offices in cities around the country have adopted a range of new measures aimed at prosecuting corporate fraud.

William Donaldson, the present SEC Chairman, said in an interview that the HealthSouth prosecution moved quickly in part because the agencies "really have been working closely" to coordinate the case. "Tougher criminal sanctions make it much more likely that midlevel executives are going to come in rather than take a chance on a long prison term," said Donaldson. He said the SEC plans to keep a "sharp focus" on enforcing corporate-fraud cases, but added that the agency also wants to be balanced in its efforts. "We want to be strong and prompt but fair," he said.

The Sarbanes-Oxley Act, "focused the responsibility of some of these executives squarely on the fact that if you make fraudulent or false statements, you are going to be held criminally responsible," said Deputy Attorney General Larry Thompson, chair of the president's task force on corporate crime. Before the task force focused federal resources on white-collar crime, "these types of investigations sometimes took three or four years to complete," Mr. Thompson added.

With the stringent new provisions of Sarbanes-Oxley available, prosecutors say there is less reason to dig back years in time to prove further crimes and add additional counts. "If they're willing to admit to what they did in the most recent quarters, and there is fraud, we do not really care what they did in 1994 or 1995," said Alice H. Martin, the U.S. attorney in Birmingham. Richard C. Smith, deputy chief of the Justice Department's fraud section, said the approach "is sort of like taking a rifle shot to the head," rather than a shotgun.[9]

DEMISE OF ARTHUR ANDERSEN

The accounting firm Arthur Andersen L.L.P. was involved in many of the corporate scandals of the 1990s. WorldCom and Enron were the most notorious. Yet the list is quite extensive, including prosecutions involving Sunbeam, Waste Management, Global Crossing, Dynegy, Haliburton, Colonial Realty, and Qwest.

Mr. Arthur Andersen should be turning over in his grave after the conviction of the company that has borne his name for over sixty years. Andersen himself was something of a rising star back in the boom days of 1920s accounting. At age 23, he was the youngest certified public accountant in the state of Illinois—and one of only 2,200 CPAs in the country—and at the age of 27, he became the head of the Department of Accounting at Northwestern University. By the following year, he became the first university professor to move into public accounting, although he continued to teach at Northwestern for nearly a decade. Andersen is noted for saying "The thoroughly trained accountant must have a sound understanding of the principles of economics, of finance and of organization." He is also credited with saying, "It has been the view of accountants up to this time that their responsibility begins and ends with the certification of the balance sheet and statement of earnings. I maintain that the responsibility of the public accountant begins, rather than ends, at this point." Challenging standard practices and taking a business approach to auditing, Andersen was known for encouraging his employees to "think straight and talk straight."[10] Arthur Andersen died in 1947. His disciple, Leonard Spacek, took the helm of the firm that year and remained in charge until 1963, by which time the firm had grown into a worldwide giant.

Arthur Andersen LLP participated in the Waste Management fraud, which resulted in a recovery of millions of dollars for victim investors. It also participated in the Colonial Realty fraud that ultimately led to penalty payments by that firm and bans on certain activities. Critics of Waste Management and Sunbeam Corporation alleged aggressive accounting to disguise poor earnings growth. The firms had to restate their earnings for the previous five years. Without admitting guilt, Andersen paid a $7 million fine and agreed to an injunction that prohibited the accounting firm from auditing government accounts. That settlement would serve as Andersen's undoing after the meltdown of Enron.

Andersen gave its approval to Enron accountants for a variety of illegal propositions. However, the most hideous action taken by Andersen officials was the deliberate destruction of evidence in order to hide Andersen's role in the Enron scandal.

The jury delivered a guilty charge against Andersen after five weeks of hearing evidence and ten days of deliberations. A few hours after the verdict, Andersen announced it would cease auditing public companies—the mainstay of its business. With the verdict the company lost its license to audit listed firms because, by law, the SEC cannot accept corporate financial statements audited by a convicted felon. The guilty charge was the final blow to a professional reputation that was already in tatters. The threat of lawsuits by investors still hang over individual partners involved in Andersen's misdeeds.

Andersen's fate has created a new caution in the wider industry. The accounting industry is expected to become much more cautious and rigorous in the aftermath of this landmark trial. "If you were a partner and you observed this verdict, you would surely increase the steps in every audit you were involved in, spend more time on the documentation," said Randolph Beatty, Dean of the Leventhal School of Accounting at the Marshall School of Business in California. "All of that leads to very severe increases in the time and fees for doing auditing."[11] Following the guilty verdict handed to Arthur Andersen, the four major accounting firms that remained were set to become significantly larger, and to charge higher fees.

Despite the threat of higher fees, experts agree the turmoil facing the industry will result in better accounting practices. "There should be an improvement in the quality of audits, which means an improvement in the financial reporting by companies," said Sharav. "We must continue to focus laser-like on rebuilding the profession's reputation and on restoring investor confidence in our capital markets," said James Turley, chairman of Ernst & Young.[12]

Arthur Andersen LLP was the egregious auditor (and/or consultant) for five of the seven companies that we summarized earlier in Table 3-5. Andersen paid the ultimate price: the death of its auditing operations in mid-2002. However, it was not the only firm involved in "aggressive" accounting practices.

THE PLIGHT OF OTHER ACCOUNTING FIRMS

Ernst and Young has been charged by the U.S. Internal Revenue Service (IRS) for promoting aggressive and perhaps illegal tax avoidance schemes. The firm paid over $300 million to settle a lawsuit filed by investors for its alleged role in Cendant Corporation's accounting fraud during the 1990s. The firm, however, denied wrongdoing. Understand, however, that, as part of any plea bargain, the SEC and other authorities allow financial companies to deny guilt in any subsequent legal actions taken by shareholders or other aggrieved parties. In this case, a guilty plea would have put the company out of business.

Cendant has tried for almost five years to recover a $47.5 million severance package from former Chairman Walter A. Forbes. The New York residential real estate and travel-services concern has been struggling to rebuild its reputation after a huge accounting scandal in the late 1990s.

Forbes resigned under pressure in July 1998. Cendant subsequently alleged that he improperly charged the company for personal use of a leased jet, personal American Express charges and about $100,000 in cash advances. While insisting "there were no improprieties" in his travel-and-entertainment expenses, Forbes wrote Cendant a personal check for $2.3 million in February 2000 to repay the disputed outlays.

Cendant decided those expenses provided grounds for dismissing its chairman for cause and denying him severance. But an arbitration case that the company brought to recover the exit payments has been stalled at Forbes request.

The accounting firm KPMG found itself in trouble over a restatement by the Xerox Corporation for five years of earnings. KPMG signed-off on the company's books, and was subsequently fired. Xerox agreed to pay a record $10 million in civil penalties.

Price-Waterhouse-Coopers (PwC) had a role in the Allied Irish Banks scandal, in which currency trader John Rusnak pleaded innocent to U.S. charges that he fraudulently hid $691 million in losses. Separately, PwC had two of its accountants barred from auditing because of the Tyco scandal. Richard Scalzo, the former PwC engagement partner responsible for the firm's audits of Tyco, was found to have recklessly violated the antifraud provisions of the federal securities laws and to have engaged in improper professional conduct. Apparently, Scalzo did not perform appropriate audit procedures for Tyco. He should have explored certain executive benefits, executive compensation, and related party transactions. Scalzo was confronted with numerous warning signs about Tyco management's integrity and hints that the company was being looted. Scalzo was convicted not because he failed to discover the looting but because he did not look for transgressions despite the warnings. As a result, the SEC barred the one-time auditor of Tyco from practicing as an accountant.

In another case, PwC partner Warren Martin was barred from auditing the books of publicly traded companies because of his poor auditing of MicroStrategy Inc., a company that announced a massive financial restatement in 2000. Martin failed to develop adequate audit evidence for MicroStrategy's revenue recognition, and he failed to properly consider language and dates in MicroStrategy's contracts that conflicted with the company's revenue recognition. He also failed to consider concerns raised by PwC personnel that should have alerted Martin to the audit failures. PwC paid $55 million to settle a class-action shareholder lawsuit related to its MicroStrategy audits. Additionally, PwC agreed to pay a $5 million fine to settle SEC charges that its independence as an auditor firm was compromised.

The cases against accounting firms are numerous. The fact that the public depends on reliable figures from audited statements draws great attention to misstatements and failed audits. The syndicated radio program *Marketplace* reports it found that in more than half of seven hundred corporate bankruptcies over six years, auditors gave the companies a clean bill of health—in some cases just months before they went under.[13]

FREDDIE MAC SUPPRESSES PROFITS

The "Freddie Mac" case is especially notable because this accounting scandal involved a government sponsored enterprise (GSE). The scandal centered on the way former Freddie executives "adjusted" gains on many derivatives trades. "A derivative instrument (or simply a derivative) is a financial instrument that derives its value from the value of some other financial instrument or variable. For example, a stock option is a derivative because it derives its value from the value of a stock."[14]

With steady earnings growth projected, Freddie Mac orchestrated the deferral of profits to future years. The resulting crisis led to the replacement of three senior executives, including long time chairman and chief executive Leland Brendsel, whom the Freddie Mac Board replaced with Gregory Parseghian. Shortly thereafter, Freddie Mac's regulation body, the Office of Federal Housing Enterprises Oversight (OFHEO), became concerned about Parseghian's involvement in the firm's scandalous accounting practices related to derivatives and requested that he step down. Subsequently, Freddie's Board selected Richard Syron, ex-president of the American Stock Exchange and former Chairman of the Federal Reserve Bank of Boston, as its CEO. A federal regulatory agency filed administrative charges seeking to force Brendsel to relinquish about $34 million for his involvement in accounting abuses before relinquishing his CEO position. The sum included a civil penalty of $5.8 million, $24.4 million in severance and benefits, and $3.8 million in past bonuses.

Freddie's executives estimated that accounting errors of $4.5 to $4.7 billion would require significant restatement of earlier years' financial statements. Richard Baker, the head of the House Finance Services sub-committee, raised questions concerning Freddie Mac's accounting practices. He noted that Freddie Mac and Fannie Mae had a combined outstanding debt of $1,499 billion at the end of 2002. Their combined assets at the same date were estimated at $1,600 billion. These assets were nearly 45 percent more than those at Citigroup, the largest U.S. bank. Freddie Mac and Fannie Mae had such high leverage because they operated with an implied government guarantee, making it cheaper for them to sell their debt securities than other private sector mortgage lenders. This advantage lowered their borrowing costs, theoretically making it easier for them to invest in or guarantee home mortgages.

However, senior Federal officials noted that the implied government guarantee, which resulted in the market's belief that the government (or the U.S. taxpayer) would bail out such debt-laden firms in a crisis, could be catastrophic if the two firms actually did need assistance. As Freddie Mac and Fannie Mae mortgage portfolios rose to $1,300 billion in 2003, the budget of their regulator (OFHEO) only rose by $32 million. The bottom line was that Freddie Mac's regulating body could not afford to fix either of the two firms if they became financially distressed.

In late 2003, the Federal Reserve published a staff study that concluded that the vast majority of the federal government's multi-billion dollar subsidy to Freddie Mac and Fannie Mae was intended to benefit U.S. homeowners with more credit availability and lower interest costs.[15] It found, though, that in fact, those billions of dollars actually go to benefit of the two firms' stockholders. These research findings coupled with the constant pressure applied by private sector "watch groups" and by congressional oversight hearings ensure that government sponsored enterprises will remain among the most politically visible institutions in the country for many years to come. The OFHEO is increasing capital, risk management, and supervisory standards for the GSEs. Moreover, Congress is seriously considering increasing its oversight by moving responsibility for them from OFHEO to the U.S. Treasury. Other policy advocates are suggesting that a new, autonomous regulator be established, instead of placing Fannie and Freddie under direct Treasury control.

BROAD EFFECTS OF CORPORATE MALFEASANCE

These corporate scandals visibly affected the national economy. Conventional measures of both business and consumer spending remained disappointing despite aggressive measures by the Bush Administration and the Federal Reserve to stimulate the economy. On the fiscal policy front, President Bush led a major tax cut through Congress. The Federal

Reserve cut interest rates numerous times down to until they reached post-World War II lows of 1 percent on the federal funds rate.

After enduring the recession that began in Spring 2001 and the economic shutdown in the third quarter of 2001 that arose from the September 11, 2001 terrorist attacks, the economy was poised for a rebound. In fact, there was a bounce up in the fourth quarter of 2001 and the first quarter of 2002. Economists anticipated a steady positive response to the fiscal and monetary stimulus. Yet, to much chagrin, the economy failed to continue upward as the gross domestic product (GDP) slowed and unemployment worsened. Adding to America's woes was the weakness of financial markets. Although stock market pundits expected a serious rebound because the market "always" appreciated significantly in advance of economic rebounds from recession, equities either muddled or declined. Debt markets began to take on more deflationary characteristics as opposed to the modest inflation that would normally accompany a true recovery.

During intense testimony and cross-examination before the U.S. Congress in the summer of 2002, Dr. Alan Greenspan, Chairman of the Federal Reserve, said "corporate malfeasance" caused the economy's failure to respond to stimulus. Under such circumstances, he said, diminishing trust in U.S. corporations forestalled world economic growth. A number of steps were under way to address this dilemma. First, the SEC leadership and budget were changed: Harvey Pitt resigned under pressure and was replaced by William Donaldson. Congress appropriated a 45 percent increase in the budget of the Securities and Exchange Commission budget. Second, Congress passed the Sarbanes-Oxley Act. Third, Congress held extensive public hearings, effectively using the national media to publicize its efforts.

ASSESSMENT AND FINAL THOUGHTS

It is clear that our economic and political system chooses not to take a hard line on directors of corporate boards. Even though such people effectively occupy the top spots in our governance system, the recent scandals resulted in little punishment for board directors. One could argue that they are, indeed, a protected and elite class. Enron's Board actually waived the firm's code of conduct. Tyco's Board, on the other hand, did take action against Frank Walsh, the head of its own compensation committee. Despite the "protected class" treatment that may exist for directors, one can be encouraged by the Sarbanes-Oxley Act's requirements regarding director independence and audit committee requirements.

The SOA's goal is to clean up the auditing process. It creates the Public Company Accounting Oversight Board (PCAOB) to oversee auditors and to strengthen auditor's independence by rotating audit partners every five years. This Board is led by a nationally credible individual, William J. McDonough, the former President of the Federal Reserve Bank in New York. The Act also requires executive certification of financial statements, expands rules governing conflicts of interest and heightens criminal penalties. In addition, it imposes tougher penalties on directors and restrictions on auditors providing non-audit services. The importance of providing accurate and reliable financial information is paramount in developing stakeholders' sense of trust toward corporate entities.

Freddie Mac, a government-sponsored enterprise, had weaknesses in accounting controls as well as deliberate mismanagement of earnings. Policies at the company encouraged improper accounting because executives' bonuses were tied to meeting specific earnings targets.

Our economic and regulatory systems' reliance on self-regulation and self-policing has been dealt a serious blow. Although U.S. public accounting standards legally fall under the purview of the SEC, the SEC has until recently generally deferred to the convention of self-governance in public accounting.

The SOA was the major federal legislative result of our era of scandal. Its final form appears to have been very closely written to address the specific, outrageous conduct exhibited in the Enron, Tyco, and WorldCom cases. The early evidence suggests that it will be successful. The HealthSouth case illustrates that the SOA is timely, rigorous, and effective.

Other Wall Street entities, notably the New York Stock Exchange, the mutual fund industry, and the investment banking community have endured self-regulation problems similar to those of the accounting industry. As a result they, too, have been unable to maintain sufficient public trust. The next chapter examines the financial community.

CHAPTER FOUR QUESTIONS:
ADDRESSING CORPORATE SCANDALS:
THE SARBANES-OXLEY ACT AS A PANACEA?

1. What are the major concerns of the Sarbanes-Oxley Act?
2. What are the goals of the Sarbanes-Oxley Act?
3. What are the fundamental assumptions behind the Sarbanes-Oxley Act?
4. What causes the wrongdoings of a corporation to mushroom into a scandal?
5. How can public corporations be made accountable to their investors? Accountable to the general public?
6. How does the unethical behavior of a corporation affect economic activity of the firm, the region, the nation and/or the world?

5

SCANDAL SPREADS TO
WALL STREET

The decline of the U.S. economy in 2001 and the concurrent downward spiral of the U.S. stock market not only gave rise to corporate sector pressures and resulting scandals, but also exposed wrongdoings on Wall Street. Human greed and ethical collapse lay at the root of the scandals, both in the corporate and financial sectors. During this time, the Securities and Exchange Commission (SEC) seemed unwilling or unable to regulate the financial marketplace.

This chapter begins with a discussion of the SEC and its embattled Chairman, Harvey Pitt, and the events leading to Pitt's ultimate resignation. Next, the chapter examines the unfolding Wall Street scandal and New York State Attorney General Eliot Spitzer's efforts to address it. This section reviews the major settlements with ten major investment banks as well as high profile investigations of investment analysts Henry Blodgett, Jack Grubman, and Mary Meeker, as well as investment banker Frank Quattrone.

Third, the chapter explores the breakdown of the New York Stock Exchange (NYSE) by reviewing the roles of its celebrated CEO, Richard Grasso, its Board of Directors, the SEC, and its new chief administrator, John Reed. The NYSE breakdown illustrates the challenges arising from self-regulated organizations.

PRESSURES MOUNT IN WASHINGTON: SEC CHAIRMAN HARVEY PITT AT CENTER OF CONTROVERSY

In 2002, SEC Chairman Harvey Pitt proposed "a new body, dominated by public members," that would have power to discipline and control quality of accounting firms and their employees. In addition, this body would perform investigations, bring disciplinary actions, and bar individuals and firms from performing audits. Many in the investment community thought such a new body should definitely choose its members from outside the industry and should have power to set auditing standards.[1]

Pitt's proposal came after he faced criticism over his handling of the SEC's investigation of Enron, including the actions of its auditor, Arthur Andersen LLP. Critics of Pitt could not see how the SEC under Pitt could oversee all the nation's big accounting firms, including Andersen, because of his prior role as a private lawyer defending the accounting industry. A wholly different system seemed necessary to successfully oversee what promised to be a massive inquiry into the huge and spreading accounting scandal.

Pitt also turned his attention to the National Association of Securities Dealers (NASD). There were numerous faults in the NASD's past operations. The most notable was that the organization was hesitant to go after the industry's biggest players in tough cases. An SEC crackdown in the mid-1990s, required the NASD to spend an additional $100 million to upgrade its regulatory unit. The crackdown followed allegations that NASD dealers had colluded to keep "spreads"—this is, the difference between bids and asking prices—artificially high, thereby fattening the coffers of Wall Street firms at the expense of individual investors. In 2001, the NASD beefed up its enforcement staff and in 2002 pursued cases against major Wall Street firms, including Morgan Stanley's former Dean Witter Reynolds unit for the selling of unsuitable funds to retirees. The NASD, along with the SEC, also contested the way Credit Suisse First Boston (CSFB), a unit of Credit Suisse Group, charged unusually high commissions to some hedge funds in exchange for shares of initial public offerings (IPOs) in 1999 and 2000. Although CSFB had said its allocations were in line with industry practice, the firm agreed to pay $100 million to regulators to settle the issue with no admission of guilt.[2]

On November 6, 2002, Harvey Pitt resigned. Appointed in 2001, he had been under heavy pressure to respond more vigorously to the numerous corporate financial scandals of 2002. Pitt resigned in part because his choice to head the new Public Company Accounting Oversight Board (PCAOB), William Webster, appeared to be drastically unsuitable. Pitt failed to disclose to fellow SEC board members sensitive information about Webster. Just days after Webster's appointment, the public discovered that he had been the audit committee chairman of U.S. Technology, a company facing charges of fraud.

Many observers regarded Pitt's troubles as a distraction for the SEC at a time when the market was reeling from corporate scandals—including Enron and WorldCom—and the economy was becoming increasingly fragile. Many considered Pitt's resignation to be an absolute necessity for tougher, more effective reform.[3]

BUSH'S REACTION: STATUS QUO?

During the Summer of 2002, President George W. Bush gave a speech to business leaders on Wall Street which addressed corporate fraud and laid out a plan for reforms that his administration thought would reinstill confidence in financial markets. The administration believed that loss of trust within many segments of the corporate environment was furthering the market downturn. Bush said, "At this moment, America's greatest economic need is higher ethical standards—standards enforced by strict laws and upheld by responsible leaders."[4]

Many of the president's proposals were not new. From strengthening laws to requiring independence of company directors and equity analysts, Bush reiterated themes he and Harvey Pitt had earlier introduced in the wake of Enron's accounting irregularities. "A lot of what the president discussed is already in place," said Thomas Ajamie, a Houston attorney who represented corporate clients involved in Enron actions. "When you talk about lengthening a prison sentence from 5 years to 10 years, that's not the degree of change we need to change the 'club' system."[5]

The idea that corporate executives are a privileged group of good old boys was a theme hit on time and again during the Congressional hearings on WorldCom. Lawmakers attacked former executives of WorldCom during their appearance before a committee of the House of Representatives. During that hearing, California Democrat Maxine Waters said the spate of scandals was the product of "the shameful corporate culture of old-boy relationships."[6]

Given these perceptions by the committee, it is no wonder that those critical of President Bush's speech say his proposal relied too heavily on corporate America policing itself, a policy that had clearly failed. Securities lawyer Christopher Bebel, of law firm Shepherd Smith & Bebel, said, "His [Bush's] words have a hollow ring when there's a substantial question as to whether he himself may be an offender of the very issues he is discussing."[7] On this point, many unanswered questions still remained surrounding the President's selling of stock in Harken Energy in 1990. Bush himself brushed the issue aside. The White House had previously acknowledged that he failed to follow the law and disclose details of shares he sold when he was a company director. However, this omission was blamed on clerical mistakes made by company lawyers and the issue was not further investigated.

THE MARTIN ACT ADDRESSES WALL STREET WRONGDOING

New York State Attorney General Eliot Spitzer and Manhattan District Attorney Robert Morgenthau made well-publicized use of New York's 1921 Martin Act, a state "blue sky" law, a measure to control bogus sale of stock (see Chapter 2). The Martin Act became a sleeping giant in 1955, when legislators added criminal penalties. These penalties were very severe when joined with the law's extremely broad "fraud" provisions. In 1986, intentional violations were made felonies. So, in several key respects, the Martin Act arguably is more than a fraud statute because it inflicts criminal and civil liability if designated acts occur.

Following the financial scandals at Enron, WorldCom, and elsewhere, prosecutors at both the federal and state levels had been under intense public pressure to punish the individuals believed responsible for the scandals and to improve the overall regulatory scheme in order to prevent them from being repeated. The Martin Act proved invaluable.

In the 1970s, the New York State Attorney General at the time, Louis Lefkowitz, brought Martin Act actions against a handful of improper securities offerings and brokerage firms with inaccurate accounting. Even then, most of the New York cases were eventually passed on to the SEC for enforcement or regulatory action. When the SEC and the NASD assumed more active involvement with broker regulation and enforcement, the Martin Act went dormant until Spitzer chose to resurrect the law. A series of high-profile Martin Act proceedings[8] have resolved a potpourri of financial and non-financial-problems:

- A $100-million settlement with Merrill Lynch in 2002, based on alleged undisclosed analysts' conflicts of interest
- District Attorney Morgenthau's cases against Tyco executives
- The civil lawsuits against five executives of WorldCom and Qwest alleging bribes in the form of "spinning" shares in highly-sought IPOs in exchange for steering business to a broker and where analysts allegedly received de facto payouts by issuing flattering research reports
- A $15-million fine paid by Citigroup's Jack Grubman to avoid criminal fraud charges
- In a negotiated settlement New York's major brokerage firms agreed to pay more than $1.4 billion for allegedly biased ratings on stocks to help win investment banking business. The ten firms would pay fines, sever links between research and investment banking, and fund independent stock research for investors. Regulators in California, Massachusetts, Alabama, Texas, New Jersey, Illinois and Utah all took part in the investigation, and each state will take part of the recovery.

Under the authority of the Martin Act, Spitzer pursued other financial misdeeds. This Act has been such a powerful tool in the hands of Spitzer because it was written in a day when defendants' rights were not defined.

ELIOT SPITZER—THE PUBLIC'S HERO

Eliot Spitzer became New York's sixty-third State Attorney General on January 1, 1999. Spitzer brought considerable experience to the office of State Attorney General. He was a clerk to United States District Court Judge Robert W. Sweet, and, later, an associate at the law firm of Paul, Weiss, Rifkind, Wharton, and Garrison. He served as an Assistant District Attorney in Manhattan from 1986-1992, rising to become Chief of the Labor Racketeering Unit, where he successfully prosecuted organized crime and political corruption cases. Spitzer is building a reputation as "the People's lawyer."

Spitzer's initiatives make New York a national leader in environmental stewardship, labor rights, personal privacy, public safety, criminal law enforcement, and investor protection. His investigations of the Midwest and Mid-Atlantic power plants have helped reduce air pollution responsible for acid rain and smog in the Northeast. His efforts to curtail abuses in the green grocery industry have been hailed as landmark labor rights cases. His investigations of Internet companies and direct marketers have resulted in new privacy protections for consumers throughout the nation. His "code of conduct" was the foundation for a settlement that reformed the way the largest gun manufacturer in the United States designs and distributes handguns. His prosecutions of sophisticated white-collar crimes have resulted in some of the nation's largest fraud recoveries. Spitzer's investigations of conflicts of interest on Wall Street have been the catalyst for dramatic reform in the nation's financial services industry.

REFORMS START: THE GLOBAL SETTLEMENT
FOR INVESTMENT BANKS

In 2003, Spitzer's investigations led ten of the U.S. top investment firms to settle enforcement actions involving flagrant conflicts of interest between research and investment banking. The SEC, NYSE, NASD, and Elliot Spitzer's historic settlement with these investment banks required payments of penalties of $487.5 million, disgorgement of $387.5 million, payments of $432.5 million to fund independent research, payments of $80 million to fund investor education, as well as mandating sweeping structural reforms. The total of all payments approximated $1.4 billion.[9]

The ten firms are:

- Bear, Stearns & Co. Inc. (Bear Stearns)
- Credit Suisse First Boston LLC (CSFB)
- Goldman, Sachs & Co. (Goldman)
- Lehman Brothers Inc. (Lehman)
- J.P. Morgan Securities Inc. (J.P. Morgan)
- Merrill Lynch, Pierce, Fenner & Smith, Incorporated (Merrill Lynch)
- Morgan Stanley & Co. Incorporated (Morgan Stanley)
- Citigroup Global Markets Inc., formerly known as Salomon Smith Barney Inc. (SSB)
- UBS Warburg LLC (UBS)
- U.S. Bancorp Piper Jaffray Inc. (Piper Jaffray)[10]

Settlement details for all ten investment firms appear in Table 5-1. Current SEC Chairman William H. Donaldson, New York State Attorney General Eliot Spitzer, North American Securities Administrators Association President Christine Bruenn, NASD Chairman and CEO Robert Glauber, former New York Stock Exchange Chairman and CEO Richard Grasso, and state securities regulators publicly announced these enforcement actions, thereby finalizing in principle the global settlement that had been announced by these regulators in

December 2002. The settlement followed the regulators' joint investigation of allegations about investment banks exercising undue influence over securities research at brokerage firms.

Regulators said that all ten entities failed to maintain appropriate supervision over their research and investment banking operations in violation of NASD and NYSE rules. The charges were as follows:

- CSFB, Merrill Lynch, and Citigroup issued fraudulent research reports in violation of the Securities exchange Act of 1934 and of various state statutes.

- Bear Stearns, CSFB, Goldman, Lehman, Merrill Lynch, Piper Jaffray, Citigroup, and UBS issued research reports that were not based on principles of fair dealing, and did not provide a sound basis for evaluating facts while containing exaggerated claims.

- UBS and Piper Jaffray were paid for research but did not disclose the payments, a violation of the Securities Act of 1933 and of NYSE rules.

- Those two companies, as well as Bear Stearns, JP Morgan and Morgan Stanley also made undisclosed payments to others for research.

- CSFB and Citigroup engaged in inappropriate "spinning" of hot IPO allocations and had broken record-keeping rules.

None were required to admit guilt as part of their settlements, but all of the banks agreed to stop giving clients shares of IPOs with the aim of winning investment-banking business.

To understand the likely impact of the global settlement, we review how analyst practices changed during the 1990s and then turn to what the settlement put into place. An illuminating statistic was presented to Congress during the hearings leading up to the passage of the Sarbanes-Oxley Act: The ratio of "buy" to "sell" recommendations by securities analysts employed by brokerage firms rose from 6 to 1 in 1991 to an eventual high of 100 to 1 in 2000. During the 1990s, analysts moved from being neutral or objective referees to becoming overt supporters of their firms' underwriting clients.

Table 5-1: Specific Settlement Payments (in $ millions)

Firm	Penalty	Disgorgement	Independent Research	Investor Education	Total
Bear Stearns	25.0	25	25	5	**80**
CSFB	75.0	75	50	0	**200**
Goldman Sachs	25.0	25	50	10	**110**
J.P. Morgan	25.0	25	25	5	**80**
Lehman Brothers	25.0	25	25	5	**80**
Merrill Lynch	100.0*	0	75	25	**200**
Morgan Stanley	25.0	25	75	0	**125**
Piper Jaffray	12.5	12.5	7.5	0	**32.5**
Citigroup (SSB Unit)	150.0	150	75	25	**400**
UBS – Warburg	25.0	25	25	5	**80**
Total ($ millions)	**487.5**	**387.5**	**432.5**	**80**	**$1,387.50**

*Payment made in prior settlement of research analyst conflicts of interest with the states' securities regulators.
Source: "SEC, NYSE, NASD and Eliot Spitzer settle with U.S. Investment Banks" SRI Media Apr 28, 2003.

PENALTIES, DISGORGEMENT, FUNDS FOR INDEPENDENT RESEARCH, AND INVESTOR EDUCATION

As mentioned, the ten firms were ordered to make payment for penalties and disgorgement (see Table 5-1). The government sought to force firms to return funds acquired illegally and to discourage further violation of conflicts of interest. The individual penalties include some of the highest penalties ever imposed in civil enforcement actions under the securities laws. Under the terms of the settlement, the firms were not to seek reimbursement or indemnification for any penalties that they paid, nor would they seek a tax deduction or tax credit with regard to any federal, state, or local tax for any penalty amounts that they paid under the settlement.

SUMMARY OF THE ENFORCEMENT ACTIONS

In addition to the monetary payments, the firms were also required to comply with significant stipulations that would dramatically reform their future practices, including separating the research and investment banking departments at the firms, changing how their research is reviewed and supervised, and making independent research available to investors.

Under the terms of the settlement, an injunction was entered against each of the firms, enjoining it from violating the statutes and rules that it allegedly violated. It is now believed that these enforcement actions will reform industry practices regarding the relationship between investment banking and research and will bolster the integrity of equity research.

To ensure that stock recommendations are not tainted by efforts to obtain investment banking fees, research analysts are insulated from investment banking pressure. The firms are required to sever the links between research and investment banking. Important reforms in the settlement include:

- The firms are to physically separate their research and investment banking departments to prevent a flow of information between the two groups.

- The firms are to create and enforce "firewalls" restricting interaction between research and investment banking, except in specifically designated circumstances.

- The firms' senior management members are to determine the research department's budget without input from the investment banking section and without regard to specific revenues derived from investment banking.

- Research analysts' compensation must not be based, directly or indirectly, on investment banking revenues or input from investment banking personnel, and investment bankers are not to have a role in evaluating analysts' job performance.

- Research management personnel are to make all company-specific decisions to terminate coverage, and investment bankers are not to have a role in company-specific coverage decisions.
- Research analysts are prohibited from participating in efforts to solicit investment banking business, including pitches and road shows. During the offering period for an investment banking transaction, research analysts are not to participate in road shows or other efforts to market the transaction.

To ensure that individual investors get access to objective investment advice, the firms were obligated to furnish independent research. For a five-year period, each of the firms are required to contract with no fewer than three independent research firms that would provide reliable information for the firm's customers. An independent consultant for each firm would have final authority to procure this outside research.

To enable investors to evaluate and compare the performance of analysts, research analysts' historical ratings had to be disclosed. Each firm was to make its analysts' historical ratings and price target forecasts publicly available.

Seven firms collectively paid $80 million for investor education. These funds are intended to support the development of programs designed to equip investors with the knowledge and skills necessary to make informed decisions. The remainder of the funds are to be paid to state securities regulators for investor education purposes.[11]

In addition to the other restrictions and requirements imposed by the enforcement actions, the ten firms collectively entered into a voluntary agreement restricting the practice known as "spinning." This is the allocation of securities in hot IPOs—which are initial public offerings that begin trading in the aftermarket at a premium—to certain company executive officers and directors. The idea is to promote fairness in the allocation of IPO shares and to prevent firms from using these shares to attract investment banking business from executive officers.

SUMMARY OF GLOBAL SETTLEMENT

The global settlement tries to eliminate the influence of underwriters on securities analysts. The settlement stipulates that underwriters and analysts must be separated by firewalls and analysts' compensation must be determined without input or influence from underwriters. Both underwriters and analysts may remain within the same firm and deal with the same clients. Ultimately, regulators recognized that securities research is not a profit center. Separating analysts from broker-dealer firms that underwrite stocks would lead to far fewer analysts employed in the industry.

The global settlement may prevent egregious abuses, but because securities research cannot support itself in an era of declining commissions, it must depend on subsidies from other divisions. These subsidies may not be forthcoming unless analysts "assist" or add value to those other divisions.

The most innovative and creative feature of the global settlement is its requirement that the defendant firms subsidize, for a limited time, independent research by so-called "research boutiques." Under the settlement, any time that an underwriting firm provides its own research to a retail client, it must also provide independent research reports on the same topic.

Independent firms' research may not be any more accurate than the analysis it supplements, but at least those firms are more neutral or objective. The client can then see a set of views and, perhaps, better understand the subjectivity of the process.

CELEBRITY INVESTMENT ANALYSTS INVESTIGATED

A brief review of the misdeeds of some celebrated analysts reveals how subjective research can be subverted into a self-serving process.

HENRY BLODGET'S RESIGNATION

Henry Blodget is a former managing director at Merrill Lynch, Pierce, Fenner & Smith and senior research analyst and group head for the

Internet sector at the firm. In 2003, the NASD audited him and found that he was issuing fraudulent research under Merrill Lynch's name. Specifically, he expressed positive research opinions that were inconsistent with privately expressed negative views. Blodget's conduct constituted violations of the federal securities laws as well as NASD and NYSE rules, which require that published research reports have a reasonable basis, present a fair picture of the investment risks and benefits, and not make exaggerated or unwarranted claims. The SEC, NASD, and the NYSE assessed $4 million in payments and fines. Of Blodget's $4 million in total payments, $2 million constituted a penalty and $2 million constituted disgorgement. The entire $4 million was put into a distribution fund for the benefit of Merrill Lynch customers. In reaching this settlement, Blodget neither admitted nor denied these allegations, but he was censured and permanently barred from the securities industry[12]

MARY MEEKER NEVER INDICTED

Mary Meeker, a Managing Director for Morgan Stanley ranked number 40 among *Time's* Top 50 Digital Cyber Elite. At age 38, she was one of Wall Street's star technology-stock analysts and ranked among the most powerful women in the world by *Fortune* magazine. Meeker is perhaps best known for recommending Microsoft, America Online, Compaq, and Dell as strong buys when they were in their infancy, making clients millions of dollars. Her influential Internet Report, Internet Advertising Report, Internet Retailing Report, and The Technology IPO Yearbook helped cement her reputation as an authority on one of the fastest growing—if volatile and bizarrely valued—sectors in the history of the stock market. More than 150,000 copies of her reports are in circulation.

A longtime booster of Amazon.com, Meeker helped secure a high-yield debt deal for the online bookseller. Meeker was instrumental in numerous IPOs such as Broadcast.com. This company, whose website offers streaming audio and video, made stock market history with an initial stock-price rise of 248 percent in its first four hours of trading. When making investment decisions, Meeker had a mantra: With Internet stocks, there will be only a few huge winners and hundreds of losers, but the gains in wealth created by the winners would more than make up for the losers.

Meeker was suspected of having kept ratings high for companies she helped bring public. She assisted Morgan Stanley in deciding which IPOs it would underwrite. Her research had a history of being reliable and exclusive (she only covered companies with strong fundamentals); however, as Internet stock values began to fall, her ratings stayed incongruously high when compared to the actual value of the stocks.

Morgan Stanley's correspondence records were scrutinized during various 2002 investigations for evidence of conflict of interest. During the Internet bust, Meeker had published ratings that, according to the task force, were influenced by her role in Morgan Stanley's investment banking business. Companies that wanted to offer stock publicly desired Meeker's approval because of the reputation of her analysis. However, as the boom grew, her approval became less exclusive. Eventually, she began co-authoring research reports with colleagues so that Morgan Stanley could offer the weight of her approving signature more frequently to potential investment banking clients.

As Meeker's ratings remained high through the boom and late into the bust, she refused to downgrade stocks that were falling in market value. Investigators reviewing her high ratings wondered if she had legitimately believed the stocks were bound for recovery, or if she simply kept ratings high for the benefit of Morgan Stanley's investment banking clients.

Ultimately, Morgan Stanley finalized two research-related settlements with regulators of the securities industry and was fined $1.65 million. The investment firm also agreed to a separate $125 million securities fraud settlement that was its part of the total $1.4 billion industry settlement required by regulators (discussed earlier). Meeker, however, emerged from all these investigations unindicted and remains an analyst at Morgan Stanley.

JACK GRUBMAN: PERMANENTLY BARRED FROM THE SECURITIES INDUSTRY

Jack Grubman, a former managing director of Soloman Smith Barney Inc. (SSB), led research for SSB's telecommunications (telecom) sector and was the linchpin for the SSB's investment banking efforts in the sector. A coordinated investigation conducted by the SEC, the New York Attorney General's Office, the NASD, and the NYSE found that Grubman's behaviors exemplified the undue influence that existed between investment banking interests and research analysts at brokerage firms. Grubman issued fraudulent, misleading, and otherwise flawed research reports under the SSB name. As such, he aided and abetted SSB's violations of antifraud provisions of the federal securities laws, of NASD and NYSE rules, and of New York state law. Grubman was consequently censured and permanently barred from the securities industry. He paid a total of $15 million to settle charges.

During 1999-2001, Grubman issued several fraudulent research reports on the stocks Focal Communications and Metromedia Fiber. These reports contained misstatements and omissions of material facts about the companies, contained recommendations contrary to the actual views regarding the companies, overlooked or minimized the risk of investing in these companies, and predicted substantial growth in the companies' revenues and earnings without a reasonable basis. Grubman also issued numerous research reports on six telecom stocks—Focal Communications, RCN Communications, Level 3 Communications, XO Communications, Adelphia Business Solutions, and Williams Communications Group—that were not based on principles regarding these companies' actual business prospects. These reports contained exaggerated and unwarranted claims about these companies, and/or contained opinions for which there was no reasonable basis. In November 1999 Grubman published a misleading research report upgrading AT&T. The report contained omissions of material facts. Grubman neither admitted nor denied these findings.[13]

Grubman's AT&T analyses came under particular scrutiny because the CEO of Citigroup, Sanford Weill, apparently urged him to review his AT&T stock rating. Weill was an AT&T director. Simultaneously, Michael Armstrong, AT&T CEO, was a Citigroup director. Shortly after Grubman upgraded his AT&T rating, AT&T chose SSB to manage a spin-off that earned them $45 million in banking fees. A few months later, Grubman reduced his rating to "hold."

During this period, Grubman boasted in emails that Weill pushed him to gain favor with Armstrong and he even helped to discredit Citigroup co-CEO John Reed. Grubman later declared that his emails were fabrications based on "zero reality" and that he invented the story to inflate his professional importance and to make an impression on a friend.

Grubman was also a key figure in the WorldCom saga. He strongly recommended the company's stock while earning millions of dollars in banking fees. He was a key advisor to the CEO of WorldCom, Bernard Ebbers. His "strong buy" recommendations remained in place almost to WorldCom's point of bankruptcy. In July, 2002 a congressional committee investigating the collapse of WorldCom questioned Grubman.

FRANK QUATTRONE: THE MASTER OF TECHNOLOGY IPOS

Frank Quattrone, one of the nation's most powerful investment bankers, transformed Credit Suisse First Boston (CSFB) from a run-of-the mill firm in IPOs into the nation's second-largest IPO underwriter. The 45-year-old Quattrone was earning as much as $100 million a year. This was in addition to the wealth he had accumulated through personal investments in technology stocks, which included groundfloor investments in companies his banking group later took public.

Working first at Deutsche Bank and later as head of CSFB's Technology Group in Palo Alto, California, Quattrone straddled the worlds of Wall Street and Silicon Valley. He took public some of the biggest names of the Internet era, including Amazon.com, Netscape, Cisco Systems, and VA Linux.

On April 23, 2003, Frank Quattrone was indicted on criminal

charges of obstruction of justice and witness tampering as part of an ongoing investigation into malpractice surrounding the offering of new equity shares. The charges relate to alleged attempts by Quattrone to hide evidence of his investment banking transactions, despite apparently knowing that his activities were being investigated. Quattrone's department, one of the hottest on Wall Street during the hi-tech boom, was accused by federal prosecutors of issuing biased research and unfairly allocating shares in sought-after flotations. This latter behavior is called "spinning."

These charges followed the NASD accusing Quattrone of corruption. Credit Suisse had also been among those investment banks accused of blurring the divide between investment banking and supposedly impartial equity research. Here, CSFB would use their own evaluation techniques to determine analysts' compensation, calling on bankers to rank the analyst from one to three.[14] This way, analysts had to issue glowing reports of companies that may normally be evaluated as poor or lackluster. This angered many investors who suffered large losses in the stock market slump. Unsurprisingly CFSB paid a significant part of the $1.4 billion settlement eached with Eliot Spitzer, New York State Attorney General.

Some believe that Quattrone was prosecuted merely because of his prominence during the tech boom. Others say it was to send a message to Wall Street executives to comply with government probes or face charges. At his Fall 2003 trial, a sharply divided, eleven-member federal jury struggled to determine if Quattrone had tampered with witnesses, or whether he obstructed grand jury and SEC inquiries by telling CSFB subordinates in an e-mail to "clean" records. After five days, the jury admitted that it was hopelessly deadlocked and a mistrial was declared. The case was rescheduled and decided in April 2004. Quattrone was convicted on two counts of obstruction of justice and one count of witness tampering and was sentenced to eighteen months in prison.

Table 5.2 summarizes the alleged activities of the investment analysts and bankers discussed above.

Table 5-2: Investment Bankers and Analysts

Analyst and Position	Alleged Activities
Henry Blodget, Former managing director of Merrill Lynch	expressed positive opinions about stocks that he privately expressed negative views on and issued fraudulent research
Mary Meeker, Managing director for Morgan Stanley	gave high ratings on stocks that she helped bring public and continued to give high ratings to falling stocks; never indicted
Jack Grubman, Telecom stock analyst and managing director for the Saloman Smith Barney (SSB) Unit of Citigroup	issued fraudulent, misleading, and flawed research reports
Frank Quattrone, Company Head of CSFB's Technology Group	convicted of criminal charges of obstruction of justice and witness tampering, April,2004

THE NEW YORK STOCK EXCHANGE: ANOTHER SELF-REGULATION FAILURE

The NYSE's role as a regulator dates to Congress' creation of the SEC in 1934 to police securities markets. The public increasingly needed protection from a variety of abuses. Congress granted the SEC authority to delegate frontline regulation to the NYSE itself, thereby designating the NYSE as a self-regulatory organization (SRO) monitored by the SEC. Unfortunately, self-regulation is often insufficient.

RICHARD GRASSO: FROM HERO TO GOAT

Wall Street rewards ambition and Richard Grasso had plenty of it. A man of action from an early age, Grasso dropped out of college to join the army. In 1968, he went to work at the NYSE. In 1977, he became NYSE vice-president. In 1995, he became the first NYSE chairman and CEO to rise from the ranks. He quickly turned the NYSE on its head, in a relentless effort to shape it for future challenges. Grasso did not believe NYSE was well-positioned to confront Nasdaq, the automated marketplace of the internet age, and other electronic trading systems. As of 2002, Grasso was regarded by the investment community as nothing short of a hero. As CEO of the NYSE, he led the successful reopening of the U.S. stock market only six days after the terrorist bombings of September 11, 2001. Many financial-industry executives did not believe reopening the exchange would be possible in such a short period of time. Despite the negative sentiment of the investment community, Grasso would not take no for an answer. For this he received America's praise.

With that prompt opening in September 2001, he successfully sent two messages to the American people and to investors. First, Grasso wanted to rebuild morale among the wounded American public by quickly restoring a stock exchange that was and still is an important symbol of the American free-market capitalist system. Second, he believed it was important to show that terrorism could not disable or incapacitate the American economy.

When the NYSE resumed trading later in September 2001, equity prices temporarily plunged with daily share volumes averaging 2 billion. Soon after that, however, the market experienced a remarkable rebound. Grasso's performance undoubtedly helped restore investor confidence in the future of the U.S. economy and American business.

This was the context in which the NYSE Board announced its unanimous approval for a one-time payment of almost $140 million to Grasso as part of a new contract that would also pay him at least $2.4 million a year in salary and bonuses through May 2007. The $140 million included retirement funds and savings he had vested in the NYSE during his 35 years at the firm. Grasso would earn $1.4 million in base salary, and a minimum bonus of $1 million annually, according to the NYSE. The new agreement tacked two years on to his existing contract, first signed in 1999. The NYSE would, also pay off and close out Grasso's retirement and deferred compensation accounts. Grasso had $40 million in savings, $51 million in accrued retirement benefits, and $47.9 million in incentive awards. The NYSE announcement came a day after the not-for-profit NYSE reported that earnings had risen 30 percent for the first half of 2003. The exchange had $27 million in net income for the period, while revenue totaled $540 million.[15] Figure 5-4 compares Grasso's compensation to the NYSE's net profit.

Figure 5-3: Richard Grasso's Compensation

NYSE profit vs. Grasso's Compensation, in millions

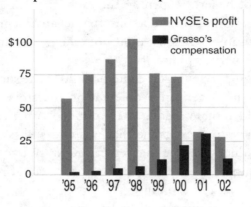

Source: NYSE

The compensation committee of the NYSE's Board set Grasso's pay. Most of these committee members represent securities firms that the NYSE regulates. Board members who did not sit on the compensation committee have said they did not know how much the chairman was earning.

Despite the impressive NYSE earnings results and Grasso's heroic performance in 2001, the former CEO was criticized for his sizable pay package and lack of transparency at the exchange. According to several reports, the SEC, run by Grasso's predecessor, William Donaldson, expressed surprise at the scale of the compensation. The *Wall Street Journal* quoted an unnamed SEC official as saying, "The commission will fully review this issue and compensation practices very carefully." Another commission official said. "Given that we expect to set the example for all the listed companies, there's some concern here."[16]

The Grasso case sparked an examination of the value of executives in any firm throughout the nation. "This is an SRO [self-regulated organization] and he's [Grasso] making more than the president [of the United States]," said Ann Yerger, deputy director of the investors' council. "The big issue is how do you benchmark someone like him."[17]

In Grasso's defense, Carl McCall, Chairman of the NYSE's human resources and compensation committee, commented that "Under Dick's leadership, the NYSE has experienced tremendous growth and success. Dick's leadership has been outstanding."[18]

It seems that the Grasso pay package amplified previous complaints about the NYSE and the composition of its 27-member board, which included executives from Wall Street brokerages, listed companies, and specialist firms. "The NYSE board is not serious about changing for the better," said T. Sheridan O'Keefe, president of the National Association of Investment Professionals. "They know they can get away with it and no one can do anything about it, whether it's good for the country or not."[19] However, the exchange would soon face intense pressure from shareholder groups and larger institutional investors to radically alter its structure.

On September 17, 2003, after Grasso's official resignation, H. Carl McCall was named lead director by the NYSE board and emerged as the new public face of the exchange. The board voted thirteen to seven in a conference call to accept Grasso's resignation. Grasso offered to resign at the outset of the call if the board members felt it was the right thing for him to do.

After McCall was appointed, he made it clear that the board would move quickly to find a successor to Grasso and to address concerns that had been raised about conflicts between NYSE's regulatory and business roles. The names that came up most frequently included some of the financial world's elder statesmen: former SEC Chairman Arthur Levitt, former Federal Reserve Chairman Paul Volcker, and billionaire investor Warren Buffett, Chairman of Berkshire Hathaway.

As the search for Grasso's successor began, McCall said the board was still discussing whether Grasso would receive severance pay in addition to the $139.5 million lump sum paid to him in September 2003. The issue depended in large part on whether Grasso left for "good reason." His contract said that if he left for "good reason" he was entitled to receive close to $9 million through May 2007, when his contract would expire.

Grasso's contract also included about $48 million due him over the next four years. Grasso had said on September 9, 2003, that he would pass up this additional amount, even though legal experts had said he could legitimately argue his entitlement to it. His decision to forego the $48 million could have been perceived as an admission of his being overpaid. Alternately, he may have waived it to soften criticism in hopes that he could continue as chairman.

The troubles at the NYSE proved to be an opening for the rival Nasdaq stock market, which had historically aspired to be an equal to the NYSE. The National Association of Securities Dealers (NASD) split off its regulatory function from Nasdaq in 1996, under the threat of an SEC lawsuit, and sold the exchange in 2000. Since the divestiture, the Nasdaq has long marketed itself as more modern and technologically advanced than the NYSE. Nasdaq officials said that up until 2003, they enjoyed 60 percent of initial public offerings versus the NYSE's 40 percent. Nasdaq companies were smaller, however.

The controversy has led to a great deal of speculation regarding the future of the NYSE and investment exchanges as a whole. While some thought that the NYSE would spin off its regulatory body, others felt that all regulation should be left up to either the NASD or the SEC. The idea was that having one group oversee traders at multiple exchanges might help insulate the regulators from competitive pressures.[20]

Continuing their fence-mending campaign, McCall and Co-Chief Operating Officers Robert Britz and Catherine Kinney met with representatives from the NYSE trading floor. Many floor traders and brokers were outraged over Grasso's pay and the board's performance, saying the chairman earned his large paychecks while their profits were being squeezed by lower trading volume and higher fees imposed by the NYSE. Many wanted to see major changes.

State and local pension fund officials, who collectively managed more than $500 billion in 2003, demanded that the NYSE make broad reforms. Specifically, the group of pension fund officials led by California Treasurer Phil Angelides, and New York State Comptroller Alan G. Hevesi, met with ten NYSE directors at the exchange. The officials told the directors they wanted the exchange to separate its business side from its regulatory side, separate the jobs of chairman and chief executive, and increase representation on the board for institutional investors such as pension funds and mutual funds.

In addition the group called on the SEC to name an independent panel to investigate the NYSE board's approval of former chairman Richard Grasso's pay. The last request was deemed important because Grasso's pay was approved, in large part, by board members from brokerage firms that the exchange regulated. "We're not talking about just rearranging chairs in the boardroom," Angelides said at a news conference after the meeting. Angelides also reiterated his view that Grasso should return a large portion of a $139.5 million payment made to him by the exchange. The pension fund officials stopped short of urging that members of the NYSE board who had approved Grasso's compensation should resign as some other shareholder advocates had done. But the officials said they expected the makeup of the board to be radically different in the near future. Denise L. Nappier, Connecticut's treasurer, said the exchange needed a major shake-up. "From my perspective, the culture at the Big Board is like a private club with an old-boy network very much in place, and that has got to change," she said.[21]

The SEC did not directly respond to the request at the time but said in a statement: "Chairman Donaldson is committed to working with John Reed," who would assume the position as interim head of the NYSE on September 29, 2003—"toward a process that will ensure the highest standards of governance at the exchange." Reed, the former Co-CEO of Citigroup brought instant creditability and competence to the NYSE. He agreed to work for $1 a year.[22]

Reed, as new interim chairman, told Bloomberg News that he wanted to reshape the culture of the exchange, reduce the size of its board by at least half and bring "fresh blood" into the 211-year-old organization. "You can't run the NYSE like a club or you won't have the confidence of the public."[23]

Grasso's $140 million payday cost him his job. It is easy to attribute Grasso's downfall to the evils of greed, but there is much more to the story. Grasso was playing by the old "high pay okay" rules,[24] and the game had changed when the stock market bubble burst and corporate scandals erupted. Although known for his public relations skills,

Grasso did not apologize. The board had insisted on disclosing his pay immediately rather than waiting until the NYSE annual report came out early in the next year. However, they created for themselves the dilemma of having to explain why they forced out their CEO for taking the money that they had approved for his compensation.

The whole argument over Grasso has presented a spectacle of rationalization and bickering. Grasso and his defenders say he did nothing wrong—he was only cashing the checks the NYSE board gave him. Others respond, sure, the directors should be criticized but Grasso cannot be so innocent. Some argue that he "cashed out" to take advantage of the sharp cuts in the top federal income tax bracket. Low interest rates would allow him get a huge payout for his pension rights.

It has been reported that the NYSE, relying on a report prepared by a former federal prosecutor, may insist that deposed chief executive Dick Grasso return as much as $100 million of his hefty compensation. Exchange directors are expected to decide soon about whether to sue their former leader. Grasso is compiling his own lawsuit to secure $48 million in future retirement pay he earlier agreed to forgo as well as $9.7 million in severance.

In May 2004, Eliot Spitzer filed suit with the New York Supreme Court requesting that Grasso return more than $100 million of his $200 million in salary to the not-for-profit NYSE. His suit claimed that the pay package was so huge that it violated state law governing not-for-profit groups and resulted from Grasso's manipulation and intimidation of the exchange's "unwitting and uncurious board of directors."

The Spitzer lawsuit also alleged that investment banker Kenneth Lagone who had headed the NYSE compensation committee in 1999-2003, misled exchange directors about the size of Grasso's compensation package.

CARL McCALL ADVOCATES SEPARATING TRADING AND REGULATION

H. Carl McCall, the former comptroller of New York State and 2002

Democratic nominee for governor, joined the NYSE board in June 1999. He became co-chair of the exchange's governance committee when it was formed.

McCall, who as indicated above had strongly defended the pay of ousted NYSE Chairman Grasso, announced his resignation from the exchange's board on September 25, 2003, to give interim chairman John S. Reed a free hand to remake the NYSE.

McCall listed a number of reforms he hoped the NYSE would enact, including electing directors every year, evaluating directors each year, and making sure new board members would be picked by independent directors and not by the chairman. Previously, directors were elected every two years and most were nominated by Grasso.

McCall also called for "an immediate examination to identify and evaluate ways to separate the regulatory and trading functions to ensure that they are effective, independent and beneficial to the investing public."[25]

JOHN REED BEGINS WORK

John S. Reed made his first visit to the exchange in September 2003 and said in a letter to NYSE members that he would "embrace and make appropriately transparent new governance procedures."[26] He, also, said the exchange would "install a permanent senior management." The letter was Reed's first formal communication with NYSE members. Reed was expected to play a major role in shaping reform proposals that the NYSE would be submitting to the SEC later that year.

In his new role as interim chairman and chief executive, he could apply his analytical skills but lacked colleagues with whom he could consult. He was essentially alone, working with a board that he did not know well and whose judgment had been called into question by the outcry over Grasso's $187.5 million compensation package. To compound that challenge, he had to work with NYSE member firms with divergent interests, as well as with various outside parties who were putting intense pressure on the exchange to make major changes.

The first task asked of Reed was to dismiss Kenneth G. Langone,

Chairman of investment firm Invemed Associates, from the NYSE board. The AFL-CIO, which represents unions managing $400 billion in pension plan funds, requested the action because Langone had chaired compensation committees in prior years that approved much of Grasso's pay. He also had resisted calls to leave the board and maintained that Grasso's pay was appropriate.

Reed's closest adviser was SEC Chairman William H. Donaldson. The two men served together on the board of Philip Morris. People who know both men said they have a deep mutual respect, if not a close friendship. Donaldson and Reed spoke almost immediately after Reed agreed to take the NYSE job and have been in regular contact ever since.[27]

Reed's first major challenge was to turn his full attention to designing a set of governance reforms that would satisfy the SEC, Congress, the NYSE's 1,366 members, and institutional as well as individual investors. He met with officials from large state pension funds and traveled to Washington to testify before the House Financial Services Committee.

Admirers of Reed said that if anyone could devise a NYSE reform plan that satisfied everyone, it was he. Reed was known to be fascinated by management flow charts and corporate governance dilemmas. This fascination stretched beyond business to a wide range of other issues. NYSE members argued that maintaining the exchange's regulatory function was just such an issue and that losing it could threaten the viability of the institution. However, big institutional investors and shareholder advocates wanted to see the exchange stripped of its regulatory authority over firms that conduct business on the floor.

After initial meetings with directors and the brokers and traders who own the exchange, Reed described the regulatory function as critical to the exchange's success in attracting new listings and increasing trading volume. But he also promised to come up with an innovative governance structure that would remove conflicts of interest and restore confidence in the NYSE.

Sources familiar with Reed's thinking said that he wanted to radically reduce the size of the NYSE's board and fill it with people from outside the securities industry. The traders and brokers who own the exchange would sit on a committee with a voice in how the NYSE operates but with no say on executive pay or other governance issues.

In addition to favoring smaller boards with sharply defined responsibilities, Reed was believed to be zealous about corporate disclosure, a fact demonstrated by his insistence that the exchange disclose publicly the compensation of all its top executives. Any final governance changes at the exchange were expected to include disclosure rules that at least meet—and more likely exceeded—what was required of companies whose shares trade on the exchange.

Reed, meanwhile, was careful to keep expectations low. He planned to stay only a few months. And he said his only responsibilities were to find a permanent replacement and to push through governance changes that would eliminate conflicts of interest. He would not address ongoing investigations into possible anti-investor practices by the specialist firms that conduct trading on the NYSE floor.

VIOLATIONS OF "TRADE-THROUGH RULES"

The NYSE disciplined five of the biggest "specialist" firms that conduct trading on the exchange floor for practices benefiting themselves at investors' expense. Specialists are supposed to match buyers and sellers at a given price whenever possible. However, some investors, notably Fidelity Investments, have complained that some specialists step in between orders, by buying from a seller and then selling to a buyer at a slightly higher price, then pocketing the difference. This practice violates securities law known as the "trade-through rules." The trade-through rules require trades to be channeled to the market offering the best price, even if a trader wants to transact business elsewhere more quickly. Disciplinary fines to the firms amounted to $240 million.[28] The firms involved were:

- LaBranche & Co.
- Spear, Leeds & Kellogg
- Fleet Specialist

- Van der Moolen Specialist
- Bear Wagner Specialists

Reports of the NYSE imposing fines refueled the critics of the exchange who say it should be stripped of its regulatory authority. Major investors, such as Fidelity Investments, were already pushing for the specialist system to be scrapped. They wanted to see the exchange convert to a system that, like the Nasdaq and most others globally, electronically matches buyers and sellers.[29]

Big mutual funds are putting renewed pressure on the SEC to change the rules governing the NYSE. Officials at these funds say the specialist system is outmoded and costs investors money but is protected by SEC rules. "In my opinion the political clout of the NYSE has kept [the SEC] from doing good work on market structure issues," said Harold S. Bradley, senior vice president at American Century Investments. "Now it's time for the NYSE to give up its 25-year-old framework and join the computer age." SEC officials said in Senate testimony that the agency's review of securities markets, and its recommendations for how their structure should change in light of new technology and competition, would not be ready for months. SEC Chairman William H. Donaldson said the agency is "pretty much at the end of fact gathering," knows the arguments on all sides and now "must sort it out."[30]

John Thain took over as chief executive of the New York Stock Exchange at the beginning of 2004 for $4 million a year, a third of the $12 million Mr. Grasso received in 2002. John Reed, who had been acting as both chief executive and chairman, remains as chairman. Thain, a former Goldman Sachs president, in his first board meeting as chief executive of the New York Stock Exchange, appointed a new finance officer, Amy Butte. Butte immediately laid out plans for a new trading technology that would reduce the need for human intervention in stock trading. Thain's trading proposal would soon reshape the way stocks are traded on the floor of the NYSE, one of the last exchanges to still use floor traders to match buyers and sellers.

FINAL THOUGHTS AND CONCLUSION

The cross-section of corporate scandals described in the last three chapters reflects an unmistakable fact: that two linchpins meant to bear the weight of overseeing our economic system were in serious need of repair. First, the SEC was found to be wholly ineffective as a prime regulator. In response, the SEC complained that it lacked anything near the budgetary resources needed to staff and prosecute the broad array of corporate and regulatory issues under its purview. Fortunately on this score, the scandals armed SEC Chairman Harvey Pitt with the ammunition needed to wrestle more resources from the Bush Administration and Congress. However, it is still not clear if enough resources are in place to address their regulatory challenges. Perhaps, the most egregious failing of the SEC concerned its performance in regulating the financial sector. Specifically, it is clear that it was Eliot Spitzer's efforts that exposed and cleaned up the various problems on Wall Street. Effectively using New York's blue sky law, the Martin Act, his very small staff reached a $1.4 billion settlement and far reaching agreements with ten of the nation's largest investment banks.

Although there are no assurances, it is to be hoped that the SEC will continue to fight for adequate resources and will keep moving forward toward greater oversight effectiveness. The SEC aggressively argues that we must keep a vigilant watch over the corporate and financial sectors at the federal level, thereby limiting the involvement of various states in these matters. Yet where would the United States be today if Eliot Spitzer, armed with New York's blue sky law, the Martin Act, was not allowed to take action?

A second linchpin of public oversight system is that of self-regulation. The reader will recall our discussions in chapter four of the total breakdown of our public accounting sector which the SEC had primarily allowed to police itself. We hope the new Public Company Accounting Oversight Board and the Sarbanes-Oxley Act will effectively fix this problem.

The self-policing of regulatory and business practices at the nation's securities exchanges appear to be improving. The new governance frameworks of both the NYSE and NASD may prove effective. The SEC must in the end be active in guiding the self-regulatory process to assure compliance.

CHAPTER FIVE QUESTIONS:
SCANDAL SPREADS TO WALL STREET

1. What are some of the major contributions of Eliot Spitzer in the Wall Street investigations?
2. How was the Martin Act used to inflict civil liability on the investment banks involved in the Wall Street scandals/ wrongdoings?
3. How did the Martin Act address the Wall Street scandals?
4. What role did Elliot Spitzer play in the infamous Wall Street scandals?
5. What types of settlements were made with the major investment banks?
6. Who were some of the major investment banks that were involved in the allegations of undue influence of investment banking interest on securities research at brokerage firms? Who were some of the individuals?
7. What were the reasons behind the resignation of Richard Grasso as Chairman and CEO of the New York Stock Exchange?

6

MUTUAL FUND
SCANDAL:
MORE THAN A FEW
BAD APPLES

Mutual funds (a slang term for Investment Company) are the
financial marketplace equivalent of motherhood and apple pie.
No other pure investment vehicle affects more American households
than mutual funds. During the period 1970-2000, this industry grew
140 fold. The industry's assets under management rose from approximately $50 billion to over $7 trillion. Mutual fund firms offer several
types of equity, fixed income (bond), and money market funds. Over
53.3 million households are invested in mutual funds, either directly or
indirectly, through their pension plans. No other American institution
held such great promise of meeting the various savings and investing
needs of so many. The important investment functions of portfolio
management, security analysis, diversification, and financial record
keeping, coupled with fiduciary trust standards are all easily available
to American families, regardless of wealth.

The discovery of widespread corruption by so many prestigious
investment companies is especially despicable because of the innocent,

trusting people that were greatly harmed. This corruption and immorality encompassed almost every facet of the business.

This chapter discusses the various types of wrongs committed by mutual funds including: illegal late trading, improper market timing, illegal sales practices, questionable fee schedules, and lax Boards of Trustee governance. We also consider Eliot Spitzer's leadership role in addressing the scandals. The chapter records the misdeeds of specific funds and their punitive settlements with Spitzer and/or the SEC. Finally, various reforms either considered or adopted by the SEC are presented.

MUTUAL FUND "LATE TRADING" AND "MARKET TIMING" SCANDALS

From April 2001 until the summer of 2002, Noreen Harrington worked for a division of Stern Asset Management that managed a pool of assets for hedge funds. She became aware of questionable trading at Canary Capital Partners LLC, a multi-million dollar hedge fund managed by Stern Asset Management. Harrington asked her boss, Ed Stern, to take action but he refused. On another occasion, when co-workers came to her complaining about an under-performing mutual fund in their 401k that had a "special relationship"[1] with Canary, she reported that Stern would not drop the fund because the fund company permitted him to "market time" its funds. After Harrington left the firm, she was looking over her sister's 401k pension plan one day and realized that there would not be enough money for retirement. It was then she realized the significant impact these improper trading activities could have on ordinary investors and felt compelled to come forward. In light of the "whistle blowing" conditions under which corporate scandals of past years had been uncovered, it came as no surprise that this new Wall Street humiliation which surfaced early in June 2003 was the result of a woman who went to the New York State's attorney general's office and told them "you guys need to look at this."[2]

On September 9, 2003, New York Attorney General (NYAG) Eliot Spitzer announced that his office had gathered evidence that improper trading schemes, which potentially cost investors billions annually, were pervasive in the mutual fund industry. Following the tip received from Harrington, the NYAG office launched an investigation into the allegations of unethical and illegal trading practices in the industry. That probe would ultimately lead to numerous criminal and civil actions against several high-profile firms. The trading schemes are called late trading and "market timing."

Late trading involves buying shares at a given day's price after the usual 4 P.M. closing, typically in collusion with a broker or fund processor. It is illegal, prohibited by the Martin Act and by SEC regulations because it allows certain investors to profit from information not available to the public. Spitzer characterized late trading as "allowing betting on a horse race after the horses have crossed the finish line."

Market timing occurs when rapid short-term trades are made of mutual fund shares in order to take advantage of a market inefficiency in adjusting value over time. The method is used when the net asset value price assigned to a mutual find's shares, at the 4 p.m. close or at hourly intervals during the day, does not reflect the current market value. Buying at that price and selling at market can bring a quick profit.

Both late trading and market timing damage long-term investors, for whom mutual funds were created. Market timers sell the shares the next day and realize a profit, thereby diluting the value of shares held by long-term investors. While market timing itself is not illegal, most funds discourage it, so arrangements made to permit timing may be a violation of the funds' policies. Often, however, funds permitted these actions; in exchange they would request a cut of the profit or require that the other institution keep a certain amount of assets under their management. According to Spitzer, permitting timing in this way is "like a casino saying it prohibits loaded dice, but then allowing favored gamblers to use them in return for a piece of the action."[3] We now turn to some key firms involved in this drama.

CANARY CAPITAL PARTNERS

The New York State Attorney General (NYAG) announced in September of 2003 that Canary Capital Partners LLC, two Canary-related entities, and Edward Stern, the entities' managing principal, were willing to settle their illegal trading claims for $40 million. Many who believed that these timing piracies were practiced by just a few rogue traders felt satisfied by the settlement, which consisted of a $10 million penalty, restitution of $30 million in illegal profits, and a requirement that Canary's officers and employees assist in the investigation of the mutual fund industry. However, the settlement revealed the tip of an iceberg. Soon Eliot Spitzer's office, with Stern's cooperation, uncovered evidence of widespread malfeasance throughout the mutual fund industry.

Stern had orchestrated a complex network that exploited the mutual fund trading system and ordinary investors. With the assistance of Security Trust Co. N.A., a Phoenix, Arizona firm, Stern executed orders after the 4 p.m. close. Security Trust, which processes mutual fund trade orders for over 2,300 pension plans and retirement systems, processed these late trades as if they were timely. Security Trust masked the illegal trades as orders placed by one of their many pension plan clients. This accomplished two things: (1) it concealed the trades placed with funds that Canary had arrangements with, which included the Bank of America's "Nations Funds" family, Invesco, Banc One, Janus, and Strong funds; (2) it gave Canary the ability to trade with the hundreds of funds offered in the pension plan systems for which Security acted as the order processor.[4]

Market timing strategies, heretofore, could only work in up markets since there had been no way to short mutual funds. Stern and his trading technician Andrew Goodwin developed a synthetic derivative for shorting mutual funds that allowed them to profit when the market was falling as well as when it rose. This derivative worked by getting access to current lists of fund holdings. While most investors only had access to these lists twice a year, and even then the information would be several months old, Stern was able to get virtually real-time lists from fund managers because of the millions of dollars that his market timing arrangements brought to these companies.[5]

By most accounts, Canary and Stern received a light punishment for their transgressions, especially when compared to the settlements with other entities that would come later in the investigation. David Brown, chief of the NYAG's Investment Protection Bureau who led the investigation for Spitzer, saw Canary as a key asset to their investigation. "The truth is that we picked the absolute best person to bring in as our cooperator," said Brown. "He's given us 20 or 30 names of mutual funds, 20 or 30 names of hedge funds, ten late-trading vehicles." Said Spitzer, "He did get a good deal. People who are there early get good deals. We did the right thing."

BANK OF AMERICA'S—NATIONS FUNDS FAMILY

In early 2002, portfolio manager Jim Gendelman noticed an odd pattern of money flowing into and out of Nations International Equity Fund, a portion of which he managed for Bank of America's (BofA) Nations Funds unit.

When Gendelman asked the bank, through a co-worker, where that money was coming from, he was told that BofA gave an investor the green light to perform frequent trades in the fund. Gendelman says the flow of money was not hurting his ability to manage the fund, but even so, he was disturbed to hear about the approval given the trader's activities. He asked BofA to place a two percent redemption fee on rapid sales involving Nations International Equity Fund, which it did in August 2002.

Even so, it was up to the bank to actually impose that fee on the rapidly trading investor and this appeared not to happen. Gendelman said that the odd money-flow pattern persisted. In late 2002, a bank official approached him to ask whether the investor could move more assets in and out of the fund, a request Gendelman refused. The investor was later revealed to be Edward Stern. Gendelman's experience indicates the role that some fund managers played in late trading and market timing schemes that later came under investigation.

Perhaps most scandalous is how Bank of America leveraged its broad platform of financial services to advance market timing of its funds. The bank provided a $300 million credit line and derivative facilities that were used to time the firm's own funds. Bank of America also provided Canary its own trading terminal that it could use to trade fund shares as late as 6:30 p.m.—two and a half hours after the close of the market.

Robert H. Gordon, chief executive of Bank of America's mutual fund business, left the company in mid-September 2003. Gordon was named in the complaint that Spitzer's office filed later in that month against Canary Capital Partners. Two days later, two other Bank of America employees were named in the complaint: Charles Bryceland, who had run the bank's brokerage and private-banking office, which catered to wealthy clients in New York; and Theodore C. Sihpol III, a broker who reported to Bryceland. They were both fired. Several unnamed lower level employees were fired as well. However, Richard DeMartini, the bank's head of asset management, also named in Spitzer's complaint, was not among them.[6]

Bank of America and FleetBoston Financial Corp (Fleet), also embroiled in the scandal, agreed to a $675 million joint settlement in March 2004. Bank of America announced a definitive agreement to acquire Fleet earlier in the year, and the two firms were eager to settle in order to prevent delays in gaining final approval of their merger. Bank of America agreed to payments of $250 million in restitution to investors and another $125 million in penalties. The settlement with NYAG required eight members of the Board of Directors of Nations Funds, Bank of America's mutual fund complex, to resign for approving the market timing measures. Fleet was required to pay $70 million in restitution and $70 million in penalties.[7] Together, the two firms agreed to reduce the fees it charged investors by $160 million.

Spitzer did not stop there. Armed with recordings of phone conversations indicating Sihpol knowingly participated in highly questionable if not illegal activity related to market timing and late trading, Spitzer unsealed an indictment against Sihpol in April 2004 on 40 criminal counts. The indictment alleged grand larceny, fraud, and violations of securities law.[8]

PUTNAM INVESTMENTS

When Peter Scannell of Putnam Investment caught onto market timing activities by outside investors, he blew the whistle to the SEC. The SEC did not act. He then took his story to Massachusetts' state regulators, who did. What they heard led them to file State civil fraud charges against Putnam. During his time at the firm, Scannell created a spreadsheet to track market timing at Putnam, which shows that from July 2000 to January 2003, ten investors made 5,340, trades involving $657 million. Their gains were close to $2 million. Scannell's allegations, first reported in *The Boston Globe*, so embarrassed the SEC that the head of their Boston office, Juan Marcelino, resigned.[9] Putnam Investments, a unit of Marsh and McLennan Company, was the first mutual fund to be charged in the ensuing scandal.

In October 2003, Putnam became aware that several employees, including two senior fund managers, had been involved in market timing. Putnam officials had first discovered the activity in 2000 and ordered it stopped. However, the employees involved were not punished at the time, and the directors of the Putnam funds were not notified. When that information was later made public, Putnam, one of the nations oldest and largest fund firms, suffered large losses. Assets dropped by more than $30 billion in November 2003 as investors fled the Boston firm, leaving Putnam with $245 billion in assets as of November 30, 2003. The firm fired fifteen employees for improper trading and Chief Executive Lawrence Lasser resigned in November 2003, after eighteen years in that post.

The settlement with the SEC agreed to in principle in November 2003 and finalized in April 2004, required Putnam to pay a $100 million penalty and another $10 million in restitution.[10] Putnam also agreed to apply "significant and far-reaching corporate governance, compliance, and ethics reforms." Putnam settled without admitting or denying guilt. The SEC decided to retain an independent consultant to calculate the cost to Putnam's shareholders of improper trading at the firm. Under the settlement, Putnam agreed to require that all employees who invest in Putnam funds hold those investments for at least 90 days, and employees who are responsible for managing money must hold their investments for at least one year. Putnam chairman John Hill attributed the break down in compliance to four reasons. First, he identified widespread ignorance of the impact of market timing. Second, the firm's bifurcation of responsibilities for enforcing compliance enabled individuals to slip through the cracks. Third, the fact that the compliance department and the General Counsel were several layers down in the organization prevented upper management from being fully knowledgeable about the transgressions. Fourth, Putnam had provided inadequate employee training in ethics and compliance.[11] In addition to all the other reforms, Putnam agreed to have a compliance review by an independent third party once every other year starting in 2005.[12]

THE STRONG FUNDS

Over three decades Richard Strong built Strong Financial into a major mutual fund complex that, at its peak in early 2001, oversaw $40 billion in assets. It managed more than sixty stock and bond mutual funds, plus billions of dollars more in pension-fund and private accounts. The self-styled poor boy from rural North Dakota vaulted onto the Forbes 400 list as one of the richest Americans. In its most recent estimate, the magazine valued his assets at $800 million.

In December 2003, Strong stepped down from his position as Chairman of both the Strong Funds and Strong Financial when he came under investigation by state and federal agencies. He resigned in part to try to staunch the flow of assets pulled out of his company by concerned investors. Soon thereafter, the firm was rumored to be on the auction block. Among the firms expressing interest to Goldman Sachs, the investment bank conducting the sale, were Wells Fargo, KeyCorp, Bank One, Lehman Brothers, Wachovia, New York Life, and Delaware Investments, a unit of Lincoln National Group.[13] The price to buy the Strong Funds was initially rumored to be about $900 million. Wells Fargo ultimately bought Strong, although the sales price was not disclosed; it was believed to be materially below $900 million. However, it took several months to sell the Strong Funds. Apparently, one of Strong's bond funds proved to be an obstacle to finding an acquirer.

After struggling for years with bond defaults, dismal performance, and investor defections, Strong High-Yield Municipal Bond Fund held 68 percent of its assets in securities that would be hard to unload quickly at reasonable prices, according to one of the fund's reports to shareholders and company officials. Large holdings of so-called illiquid securities are problems for funds because a rush of redemption requests from fund investors can force portfolio managers to quickly sell securities. As a result, funds with 15 percent or more of their assets in illiquid holdings generally are barred under federal guidelines from purchasing additional illiquid instruments. Even though it had sold some illiquid bonds, however, Strong High-Yield Municipal Bond Fund had not been able to bring the percentage of illiquid holdings below 68 percent, the October 2003 level. This was because, although the absolute amount of dollars invested in illiquid bonds had fallen, shareholder redemptions had reduced the fund's total assets significantly.[14]

Richard Strong's public agony began in September 2003 when Eliot Spitzer alleged that Strong Capital Management, a wholly owned subsidiary of Strong Financial, and three other companies had let the Canary Capital Partners hedge-fund group exploit their mutual funds for profit at the expense of other fund holders. In the civil complaint filed against Canary in New York State Supreme Court, Spitzer alleged that Strong Capital had, among other things, let Canary make rapid-fire trades in four Strong funds, even though the company discouraged other investors from doing this. In return, Canary allegedly agreed to add $18 million to assets it had under management with Strong's mutual funds and to invest $400,000 in a high-fee hedge fund run by Strong Management.[15]

Being named, but not charged, in the Canary affair was embarrassing enough to Strong Capital Management, but after Canary Capital began to fall—the first domino in line—things began to get much worse for Strong himself. Strong Fund directors declared that an internal investigation had found evidence that Richard Strong had personally "market-timed" Strong funds, and for a longer time period than Canary had done. In the preceding six years or so, they estimated he had made in some $600,000 in profits from timed trading. [16] Later, regulators determined that he had actually made $1.8 million in timing profits.

Spitzer now had a smoking gun, pointing at the top officer of a major fund company, and he made the most of it. In congressional testimony he branded Richard Strong and the Strong Fund directors as "Exhibit A" in "corporate malfeasance" and "dereliction of duty." He further claimed that there were two sets of rules at Strong regarding fast, in-and-out market-timing trades. Strong fund prospectuses clearly discouraged such trades for regular fund holders, reserving the right to impose a one percent redemption penalty on them or even to refuse to execute them. The Spitzer complaint added that internal e-mails indicated that Strong Capital Management alerted its transfer agent and clearing broker about its arrangement with Canary, so that its transactions would not be rejected for "flipping," that is, for the rapid in-and-out trades that the company had long preached publicly against. [17]

Spitzer's complaint alleged that an agreement existed between Strong Capital Management and Canary in late 2002, which stipulated that the hedge-fund group would have to be invested in any fund on the last day of each month if it had a position in that fund at the beginning of the month. In this way, investigators suspected, Strong tried to mask the fact that timing was allowed at its funds by ensuring that outfits like Morningstar, which tracks monthly investment flows, would not pick up any tell-tale swings in assets. [18]

In May 2004, Strong agreed to pay $60 million and was barred from the securities industry for life. Additionally, he issued a two-paragraph apology that concluded, "my personal behavior in this regard was wrong and at odds with the obligations I owed my shareholders, and for this I am deeply sorry." Spitzer commented, "he made a profit and violated the trust of thousands of investors and now has suffered a public humiliation." Strong Financial agreed to pay $80 million in fines and restitution as well as reduce its fees by at least $35 million over five years, pushing the total settlement to $175 million, including Strong's personal payment of $60 million.

JANUS CAPITAL GROUP

Richard Garland, CEO of Janus International, gave e-mail approval to rapid trading of Janus mutual-fund shares. Garland's e-mails were featured prominently in the complaint the NYAG's office filed against hedge fund Canary Capital, and he subsequently stepped down as head of the firm's international business section. However, the market-timing agreement with Canary Capital was one of about a dozen that Janus discovered in its ranks. Like many other funds, Janus sales documents say that they discourage market-timing activity in their funds.[19]

In the e-mails contained in NYAG's initial complaint, Garland indicated he was willing to take in money from market-timers such as Canary in order to boost assets under management on which Janus received management fees. Another Janus employee expressed concern in an e-mail about doing business with market-timers because their buying and selling of shares could hamper portfolio managers in overseeing their mutual funds. Garland replied, "I have no interest in building a business around market timers, but at the same time I do not want to turn away $10-$20m! How big is the [Canary] deal...?" According to the complaint, Garland gave the "go ahead" for Canary's additional timing capacity on April 3, 2003, after learning that the assets involved could amount to between $10 million and $50 million.[20] Neither Janus nor Garland were charged with any wrongdoing, as technically, nothing illegal was done.[21]

Erich Gerth, who joined Janus in July 2003 from Goldman Sachs Asset Management, succeeded Garland. Like Garland, he would report to Janus Chief Executive Mark Whiston, overseeing the distribution of Janus funds overseas. At the same time, however, the firm said Whiston would not become chairman on Jan. 1, as his employment contract had previously stipulated. Instead, Steve Scheid, an independent director on Janus Capital Group's board, succeeded Landon H. Rowland as chairman.[22]

The company said the formula was changed to reduce Whiston's payout on his 2003 bonus, which was paid entirely in company stock. The contract was also extended by a year through 2006. Janus said that if Whiston had not waived his right to become chairman and instead chose to leave the company at this time, he would have received a cash severance payment of between $20 million and $23 million. [23]

Whiston was not implicated in the trading scandal. However, he and Janus have yet to answer the question of whether the CEO knew about the timing arrangements that Janus allowed in its funds. The company said that the few employees "central to the decisions" to accept fund traders' money left the company. Garland had reported directly to Whiston. The chief executive was asked during an October conference call between Janus and analysts whether he knew about the trading arrangements. Whiston replied, "I'd love to be able to answer that question, but given the obvious sensitivities of the situation, it's not advisable and not something I can do today."[24]

Janus Capital became the first mutual-fund company to calculate a dollar value of losses suffered by investors because of improper trading in Janus funds. A review by Ernst & Young determined that the payment to shareholders amounted to one cent or more per share for each of the seven funds affected. Those funds are Janus Enterprise, High Yield, Mercury, Overseas and Worldwide, and Janus Adviser International Growth and Adviser Worldwide. [25]

In April 2004, Janus agreed to a $225 million joint settlement with the attorneys general of New York and Colorado. The company will pay $50 million in restitution, $50 million in penalties, and reduce its fees $125 million over five years. Janus had earlier agreed to make a $31.5 million payment to investors, including a return of the $22.8 million gains the frequent traders made. Another $2.7 million was paid for the opportunity cost forfeited because money was not available to the funds. Janus said it would repay $1 million in fees it earned on the trading arrangements and $5 million in redemption fees it had inappropriately waived for the market-timing traders. [26]

In the end, Janus announced a series of measures to protect its fund shareholders and improve corporate governance. The company said fund prospectuses would include clearer language to discourage frequent trading and the company would increase redemption fees from 1 percent to 2 percent on funds that currently impose such fees. Janus reiterated that it found no evidence that investors did any late trading in its funds, which, unlike market-timing, is illegal.[27]

MASSACHUSETTS FINANCIAL SERVICES COMPANY

An investigation into trading practices at Massachusetts Financial Services (MFS) Company revealed that from at least late 1999 to 2003, some MFS funds were open to market-timers and were being heavily timed. MFS operates approximately 140 mutual funds. As of August 2003, assets of MFS funds totaled approximately $94 billion, of which some $44 billion was held in "unrestricted" funds that MFS secretly permitted to be timed. Timing activity accounted for an estimated five percent of these unrestricted funds.[28]

In February 2004, MFS made a $350 million settlement with Spitzer's office. It simultaneously announced agreements with the SEC and the New Hampshire Bureau of Securities Regulation. The agreements required the company to pay $175 million in restitution to injured investors, cut its management fees by an estimated $125 million over the next five years, and pay a penalty of $50 million. In addition, MFS agreed to hire a senior executive to ensure that management fees charged to the funds are reasonable and are negotiated at arms length.[29]

MFS's Chief Executive, John Ballen, and its President and Chief Equity Officer, Kevin Parke, agreed to pay $300,000 each to settle claims that they knew about market timing in eleven of the firm's funds.[30] Both, under the settlement with federal regulators, are barred from serving as an officer or director of any mutual-fund firm for three years.[31] Ballen was given a nine-month suspension from working in the securities industry, while Parke was suspended for three months. Under Sarbanes-Oxley Act regulations, all of the misappropriated funds will be returned to MFS shareholders.[32] Ballen and Parke also received bonuses from MFS based on fund assets under management and were rewarded for attracting market timers. The settlement ordered the executives to return $50,000, representing the portion of bonuses derived from market timing activity.[33]

MFS also agreed to beef up compliance and strengthen the independence of its board of directors to address late trading at MFS which the SEC said generated substantial profits for timers at the expense of shareholders.[34] In a move to regain creditability amidst the scandal, MFS hired former Fidelity Investments' mutual fund chief Robert C. Pozen as non-executive chairman.

ALLIANCE CAPITAL MANAGEMENT

Alliance Capital Management was also involved with market timers. The company had approved over $600 million in timing capacity to various hedge funds, and maintained a "top ten timers" list. The list involved timers so large that Canary Capital did not make the list! The top market timer was Daniel Calugar, a Las Vegas attorney, to whom Alliance had granted $220 million in timing capacity. From 2001 to 2003, he pocketed $64 million in profits, according to the SEC. Similar to the other arrangements discussed, Calugar compensated Alliance by investing large amounts of capital into their various funds.

In December 2003, Alliance agreed to a hefty $600 million settlement, consisting of $150 million in restitution, $100 million in penalties, and an additional $350 million in fee reductions for investors over 5 years. The company adopted a new governance rule stating that 75 percent of the fund's board of directors must be independent, including an independent chairman.[35]

OTHER PROMINENT FIRMS

Many other prominent firms have also been connected to scandal.

Pilgram, Baxter & Associates

- Co-founder Gary Pilgram allowed a hedge fund in which he invested to market time the firm's PBHG funds with the approval of CEO and co-founder Harold Baxter

- Pilgrim and Baxter charged with civil fraud and breach of fiduciary duty
- Fund parent Old Mutual rebrands the firm's fund "Old Mutual"

Bear Stearns

- Bear fired three clearing house employees and places a senior managing director on voluntary leave in connection with allegedly improper mutual fund trading[36]
- James Delvecchio, the head of operations in Bear's mutual fund clearing unit, is a person of interest to regulators because of his knowledge of Bear's possible involvement in improper clearing activities benefiting late traders[37]
- Regulators are investigating whether Bear Stearns officials helped Canary engage in late trading and whether Bear actually marketed its platform to market timers

Canadian Imperial Bank of Commerce

- Arranged more than $1 billion in financing to market timers
- Spitzer and the SEC filed criminal and civil charges, respectively, against Canadian Imperial Bank of Commerce's former managing director, Paul Flynn, in February 2004, alleging he had knowledge of two clients engaging in late trading activities

Franklin Resources

- In February 2004, Massachusetts regulators charged Franklin Resources with allowing Las Vegas investor Daniel Calugar to make short term trades in exchange for a $10 million investment[38]
- Likely to settle charges by the SEC

- Under investigation by regulators in New York and Florida for market timing-related offenses
- Found evidence of market timing by a few employees in their 401(k)
- In December 2003, placed two unnamed officers and an unnamed trader on leave

Federated Investors

- As a result of an internal investigation, the company established a $7.6 million fund to compensate investors harmed by market timing and late trading activities[39]

Security Trust

- Provided Canary with "one-stop shopping" for both market timing and late trading.

Pimco Advisors

- Provided Canary with more than $4 billion worth of trades and lists of fund holdings in exchange for more stable fund investments

Fred Alger and Co.

- Vice President James Connelly resigned, was fined $400,000, and pled guilty to attempting to erase e-mails authorizing employees to allow market timing by defunct hedge fund Veras Investment Partners[40]

Invesco

- The Invesco Dynamics fund allowed Canary $10.4 billion— twice the size of the fund— in trading volume in two years
- CEO Raymond Cunningham personally negotiated capacity arrangements for Canary
- Solicited market timers under its "special situations" program
- Michael Legoski, Invesco's top timing officer, stated in an October 2001 memo, "If done correctly, this kind of business can be very profitable."

Prudential Securities

- Five brokers charged in November 2003 with market timing fraud by Massachusetts regulators
- Martin Druffner, head of the group of brokers, charged by Massachusetts regulators in November 2003 of using 62 different aliases to make repeated mutual fund trades

Charles Schwab

- Fired two U.S. Trust sales staffers in November 2003 for allegedly trying to destroy documents related to regulatory inquiries
- In November 2003, Schwab announced it had found a "limited number of instances" of possible late trading[41]

Citigroup's Smith Barney

- Fired four unnamed brokers in October 2003 for "inappropriate behavior related to "market timing" mutual funds.

Merrill Lynch

- Fired three brokers in October 2003 in connection with market timing activities involving Millennium Partners, a $3 billion Manhattan hedge fund[42]

UBS AG

- In November 2003, fired two brokers and disciplined nine from its former PaineWebber unit in connection with market timing issues

A.G. Edwards

- Fired two brokers, Charles Sacco and Joshua Boyle Jr., in October 2003 over market-timing allegations[43]

Bank One

- In October 2003, Mark Beeson, head of the mutual fund group, and John AbuNassar, head of the institutional investment group, resigned amid an internal investigation
- Anticipates enforcement action from the SEC for allowing Canary Capital to time its funds.

MUTUAL FUND FEES QUESTIONED

As the mutual fund scandal unraveled, NYAG Spitzer turned his attention to fees charged by mutual funds. In a landmark agreement, Alliance Capital Management agreed to reduce its mutual fund fees by twenty percent, equaling approximately $350 million over the next five years. In addition they would pay $250 million in penalties and restitution. Spitzer's office believes that these penalties will shift the company's focus from the managers' to the shareholders' interest. The

SEC, which also participated in the Alliance Capital negotiations, declined to accept a portion of the settlement stating, "this is a case of illegal market timing and not fees."[44]

It was understandable that the SEC was apprehensive about commenting on the legitimacy of fees charged by mutual fund firms. Having a governmental unit put restrictions on fees is the equivalent of price setting, which violates a central principle of a free enterprise marketplace.

Mutual fund fees have long been considered irrational. They appear to benefit from economies of scale, meaning that the size of the funds' assets does not proportionately increase the cost of managing a fund. Because large funds do not cost much more to run than small or medium sized funds, the variance in fees charged between funds should not be as great as observed.

The Putnam settlement initially negotiated by the SEC was void of fee reductions and was criticized by Spitzer as too lenient.[45] Putnam later negotiated fee reductions with Spitzer's office.

Nonetheless, according to Spitzer, "Improper trading and the exorbitant fees charged are both consequences of a governance structure that permitted managers to enrich themselves at the expense of investors...and desire for increased fees led managers and directors to abandon their duty to investors and to condone improper and illegal activity." [46] Spitzer also believes a firm breaches its responsibility to investors when it charges mutual fund investors significantly more than institutional investors for similar services. On the contrary, the Investment Company Institute (ICI) suggests mutual fund fees encompass a package of services provided by firms. According to Matthew Fink, ICI president, the management fees of mutual funds support the costs of shareholder communications, fund pricing, fund accounting and bookkeeping, costs of building and office equipment, and compliance with state and federal laws and regulations. Fink seemed to suggest that Spitzer was comparing the fees of pension funds with those of mutual funds on the basis that the fees cover basic asset allocation and portfolio management expenses. However, he asserted that aside from the basic asset allocation and portfolio management costs, mutual fund fees also cover the record-keeping costs associated with tracking capital-gains distributions, preparing account statements for individual shareholders, issuing proxy statements and shareholder reports, as well as the various compliance costs that "go well beyond the costs associated with pension funds."[47]

While arguments have arisen regarding how rational fees are in the mutual fund industry, all parties seem to agree that there is certainly a need for better fee disclosure. Rather than pursue fee reductions, the SEC implemented a policy requiring more disclosure of fee structures, including placing a dollar and cents value on fees applied to a $1,000 fund investment in the semiannual shareholder report.[48] This requirement was designed to ease comparison of fee structures between funds, better enabling the investor to choose funds with lower fee structures.

ILLEGAL SALES PRACTICES—DIRECTED BROKERAGE BUSINESSES

The investigation of the mutual-fund industry has focused largely on abusive trading that allowed speculators to profit at the expense of long-term investors. However, as the probe of the $7 trillion industry broadened, regulators increasingly turned their attention to the murky world of mutual-fund sales practices. Some fund companies paid brokerage firms for a spot on the "preferred lists" of brokerage firms or for access to the firms' brokers.[49]

The industry calls this "paying for shelf space," just as cereal makers or soap companies frequently pay to get on grocery store shelves. The problem involves the fact that few investors realize their brokerage firm may have a financial incentive to recommend certain funds over others with similar, or even better, performance. Thus, investors are "steered" to funds because of payments made to brokerages. This steering is known as "directed brokerage." The SEC indicates that these arrangements are widespread. Federal regulators examined fifteen unnamed broker-dealers and found that fourteen of them received cash payments from particular mutual-fund groups or received higher commissions from those to which the funds were directed. This action provoked the SEC to consider new rules that would require brokerage firms to more clearly spell out potential conflicts. Currently, brokerage firms are required to disclose revenue-sharing payments. However, the SEC has allowed firms to meet this requirement by providing investors with a fund prospectus that indicated that "substantial amounts" are paid to the broker in connection with the sale of fund shares.

Brokerage-firm practices vary widely as to whether they have preferred lists and, if so, how many funds are on them. A.G. Edwards Inc., for example, has no formal preferred list of funds. UBS AG has roughly 20 fund families, each of which offers many funds, on its "primary" list. Citigroup Inc.'s Smith Barney unit groups mutual funds into three tiers. The fund companies in the first tier have an easier time getting access to Smith Barney brokers.

Mutual-fund executives say that a spot on a preferred list does not guarantee sales of a particular fund or fund family. However, it does mean higher visibility, making it more likely that brokers will recommend the company's funds. Brokerage firms, for example, often invite fund companies on their preferred lists to speak to top producers, help train rookie brokers, and sometimes set up conference calls between brokers and portfolio managers.

While the specifics vary, fund companies typically pay brokers for shelf space in two main ways. Some give the brokerage firm a percentage of the annual sales of the fund or a percentage of the fund assets held by the brokerage, or some combination of the two. Others compensate brokers by directing trading business to firms that sell more of their funds. The money involved can be substantial. The nation's 50 largest fund companies make roughly $1.5 billion in revenue-sharing payments a year. Even small banks and broker-dealers charge fund companies $40,000 to $50,000 a year for shelf space.

Some brokers provide favored treatment to a small group of fund companies that provide revenue sharing. At Edward Jones & Co., just seven fund companies account for 90 percent to 95 percent of the firm's mutual-fund sales. Edward Jones received $90 million from revenue sharing agreements in 2003, prompting the SEC to launch an investigation that could lead to enforcement action against the company.[50]

A spokesman for Edward Jones said that its brokers "have absolute freedom to sell thousands of mutual funds in addition to those offered by the preferred fund families."[51]

Other firms have arrangements with a much bigger universe of funds. Wachovia Securities, a unit of Wachovia Corp. has special revenue-sharing arrangements with 65 out of the 100 fund families its brokers sell. Wachovia says that revenue-sharing payments used for marketing purposes tend to give certain funds higher visibility. Merrill Lynch & Co., meanwhile, charges at least 100 different fund companies a fee for access to the firm's 13,400 brokers. "Funds are not favored or disfavored on the basis of economic relationships," a Merrill spokeswoman says.[52]

Problems with these arrangements were highlighted in November 2003 when the SEC and the National Association of Securities Dealers (NASD) charged Morgan Stanley with failing to tell clients that it gave preferential treatment to certain mutual-fund companies in return for millions of dollars in brokerage commissions and cash payments. Morgan Stanley settled the case without admitting or denying guilt. Among other things, the settlement requires Morgan Stanley to distribute $50 million among investors and to provide more disclosure of its financial arrangements with fund companies. Similarly, the SEC put mutual funds on notice in March 2003 when it charged MFS with fraud in failing to properly disclose its use of brokerage commissions generated by trading to reward brokers for selling its family of funds. MFS also settled for $50 million, all of which will go to fund shareholders. The fund had already discontinued its directed brokerage program.[53]

Morgan Stanley states that thirteen fund companies, including Fidelity Investments, Franklin Templeton Investments and PIMCO—currently pay the brokerage firm up to 0.20 percent of sales and 0.05 percent of assets annually on funds sold by Morgan Stanley brokers. They also pay up to $19 a year for each fund held in a Morgan Stanley account to cover administration and record keeping.[54]

FUND TRUSTEES AS CHIHUAHUAS

Amid the burgeoning scandals, observers have questioned the accountability and responsibilities of mutual fund officials and regulators. Traditionally governance of mutual funds has been fairly lax. Some individuals sit on the board of trustees of over 60 different funds simultaneously. Most fund boards meet two to four times annually and even then only for a few hours, and often by teleconferences. Some observers suggest that boards select chairmen on the basis of personal relationships, bringing into question the extent of their independence and objectivity.[55] NYAG Spitzer stated that board trustees often "did not live up to the standard of care they were obligated to." During his congressional testimony, billionaire investor Warren Buffett, notoriously critical of the industry, likened the supposed watchdogs of the mutual fund industry to Chihuahuas.

FIDELITY'S JOHNSON ARGUES AGAINST PROPOSED BOARD REFORM

New emphasis on corporate accountability has led to renewed urgency on the part of board members. Some boards started hiring full-time investigators and others started holding more frequent meetings that are independent of management in efforts to increase the objectivity of their oversight responsibilities. Some reformers call for requirements that the chairperson of a fund's board of trustees be independent and separate from the chairman of the fund management company.

There are those that oppose having two different people fill the roles of chairman of the fund company and board of trustees. Among them is Fidelity Investments Chairman Edward Johnson, who also serves as chairman of Fidelity funds' trustees. Johnson is an industry guru, and his firm was able to survive the fund-industry crackdown unscathed. Fidelity commissioned a study that suggests that insiders are better equipped to act in the interest of investors. The results of this study were communicated in a letter to the SEC. This letter stated that management-chaired funds outperformed 59 percent of peer funds, compared with only 48 percent of independently chaired funds. In addition, the study showed that Fidelity's funds outperformed more than 60 percent of comparable funds. The expense ratios of the two approaches are comparable. "The results of the study raise serious questions regarding the wisdom of forcing independent chairmen upon funds that have delivered superior performance to their shareholders," wrote Fidelity funds general counsel Eric Roiter to the SEC. Critics of the study point out that a relatively small number of large fund firms have independent directors and call coincidental any correlation in the study.[56]

In June 2004, the SEC decided to require that two separate individuals serve as chairman of the fund trustee boards and fund company chairman. This ended the controversy.

COMMISSION BUNDLING AND SOFT DOLLAR PAYMENTS

Fidelity suggested that the SEC consider an end to commission bundling by brokerage houses. The proposal suggested a breakdown clearly showing the value of the trade commission itself, as well as a quantified value of research and other services provided.[57]

Soft dollar payments have also come under fire by regulators. A soft dollar arrangement is created when the commission charged by a broker is higher than the actual "hard" cost of executing the trade. The "soft" remainder pays for research and other "value-added" services. Those that favor the elimination of soft dollar payments call them inefficient. The Investment Company Institute proposes a ban on soft dollar payments, except to large firms that also handle trading volume. Many fund managers criticize this proposal as potentially devastating for innovative research that often comes from smaller research houses to whom these soft dollar payments would be prohibited.[58] While some fund companies already avoid soft dollars, in March 2004 MFS may have become the first major fund company to forgo them.[59]

These issues are significant when one considers the impact of commissions on the cost of owning mutual fund shares. A study of

2,000 funds by Lipper on behalf of the *Wall Street Journal,* shows that brokerage commissions can more than double the cost of owning fund shares.[60] Many fund companies admit that of the five cents paid on each trade, only two cents goes towards the actual trade execution, while the other three cents is attributed to research and other services.[61]

MALFEASANCE AT INSURANCE COMPANIES

Insurance companies offering variable annuities have drawn the eye of regulators in the market timing investigation. Variable annuity plans have much of the same properties as traditional mutual funds, but are structured in a manner that should provide more protection against market timers. These products generally cannot be sold without significant penalties, and brokers realize commissions of as much as 10 percent each time a new plan is created or an existing policyholder transfers into another plan. These restrictions should encourage the participation of long-term investors only. However, regulators are investigating the possibility that some insurance companies may have allowed select investors to frequently trade in and out of variable annuity plans without incurring such costs. Other investors, who normally face these high penalties for selling, would pay the costs of these frequent trades. To date, there has been no formal action taken against this type of insurance provider.[62]

CASH WITHDRAWALS AND THE EFFECT ON FUNDS SIZE

The Investment Company Institute reported that investors withdrew $40 billion from mutual funds involved in the market-timing scandal of 2003. In the months prior to the scandal, these firms reported net redemptions averaging a $1 billion a month. However, in the last four-months of 2003, the average monthly withdrawals ballooned to $10.7 billion. Though some firms experienced sharp reductions in cash, the mutual fund industry as a whole did not experience this problem. On the contrary, firms not cited by regulators had new money flow that averaged $28.9 billion a month from September through December of 2003. Mutual funds attracted a total of $216 billion in new investor money during 2003, which is an 80 percent increase from the previous year. A great portion of this money undoubtedly came from investor withdrawals from money-market accounts as the stock markets rebounded in 2003.[63] This influx of "new" money into some mutual funds was also partially due to investors withdrawing cash from scandal-clad funds and transferring to those who stayed "clean" through the ordeal.

SEC Reform

In an attempt to crack down on the core abuses of the fund-trading scandal, the SEC is considering new measures:
- to discourage or prevent market-timing and late trading
- to require disclosure of fund managers' compensation and personal investments
- to promote and empower independent fund directors and enhance overall directors' accountability
- to disclose fund fees
- to crack down on long-criticized directed brokerage and 12b-1 fees.

Table 6-1 illustrates the initiatives as of June 2004.[64]

Final Thoughts

In the saga of the mutual fund scandals, the SEC's poor performance is clearly evident. Since the inception of the Investment Company Act of 1940, the SEC has had sole authority to regulate this now $7 trillion industry. However, it was Spitzer and not the SEC who actually exposed most of the scandal. It was primarily his office, though the SEC cooperated, that pursued serious resolutions and settlements with specific mutual fund companies. The SEC had allowed this industry to regulate

Table 6-1: SEC Reform Initiatives

Issue	Proposal	Description	Status in 2004
Market Timing and Late Trading	4 p.m. ET trading close	To receive today's price, a fund trade must be received by 4 p.m. ET.	Public comment period closed Feb. 6. No meeting date set.
	Formalize compliance	Mandate that funds have clear compliance procedures, review them annually and hire a chief compliance officer who reports to fund board, not the fund company.	Adopted Dec. 3, 2003, compliance deadline Oct. 5, 2004.
	Market-Timing and Fair-Value disclosures	Funds must disclose policies regarding market-timers and fair-value pricing in fund prospectuses, in addition to disclosing if they have market-timing arrangements.	Adopted April 13, compliance deadline Dec. 5.
	Portfolio Holdings disclosures	Funds must disclose in their prospectuses if they selectively disclose holdings between standard quarterly reports to the SEC.	Adopted April 13, compliance deadline Dec. 5.
	Mandatory redemption fee	A requirement that most funds charge a 2 percent redemption fee on shares sold within five days of purchase, with the money going to the fund.	Public comment period closes May 10. No meeting date set.
Fund-Manager Disclosures	Code of ethics and insider fund-trade monitoring	Investment advisers would be required to have clear codes of ethics and fund managers would be required to report fund trades in their personal accounts.	Public comment period closed March 15. No meeting date set.
	Identifying managers	Funds would be required to in their prospectus list the names of a team-managed fund's portfolio managers	Public comment period closed May 21.
	Conflicts with other funds	Funds would be required to list the other mutual funds, hedge funds, or separate accounts its manager(s) run and any potential conflicts of interest in their SAI.	Public comment period closed May 21.
	Pay	The structure of a fund's manager(s) pay would be listed in a fund's SAI.	Public comment period closed May 21.
	Fund ownership	Funds would have to disclose ownership of the fund and others the firm managers by its portfolio managers in the SAI.	Public comment period closed May 21.

Source: "Cleaning Up the Fund Industry". Damato, Karen and Burns, Judith. *Wall Street Journal.* 5 Apr 2004.

Table 6-1: SEC Reform Initiatives (continued)

Issue	Proposal	Description	Status in 2004
Fund Governance	Independent board chairman	Require each fund to have an independent chairman.	Public comment period closed March 10. No meeting date set.
	More independent directors	Raise the percentage of independent fund-board directors from a majority to at least 75 percent.	Public comment period closed March 10. No meeting date set.
	Support staff for independent directors	Require funds to give trustees authority to hire their own staffs so that they don't have to rely on fund-company employees.	Public comment period closed March 10. No meeting date set.
	Mandate board self-evaluation	Require boards to evaluate their performance on shareholders' behalf annually, with independent board members meeting separately from insider board members at least quarterly.	Public comment period closed March 10. No meeting date set.
	Management contract recordkeeping	Require funds to retain for SEC examiner review all documentation related to management contract negotiations.	Public comment period closed March 10. No meeting date set.
	Disclose why fund fees are reasonable	Mandate that fund directors explain why they deem a fund's fees reasonable in annual reports to shareholders.	Public comment period closed March 10. No meeting date set.
Fee Disclosure	Improve breakpoint disclosure	Clearer disclosure of "breakpoints" or discounts in fund prospectuses.	Public comment period ended Feb 13.
	Disclose fees in dollars	Require annual reports to state fees paid over the past year based on a $10,000 investment, in addition to quarterly holdings disclosure	Adopted Feb. 27, compliance deadline May 10.
	Measure transaction costs	A "concept release" asking for suggestions on how fund transaction costs can be fairly and fully disclosed to investors.	Public comments due Feb. 23. No meeting date set.
	Conflict of interest disclosure	Advisers would have to tell clients of any revenue-sharing agreements or other incentives they have to sell a given fund. The information would be provided both at the point of sale and in a trade confirmation.	Comment period closed April 12.

Issue	Proposal	Description	Status in 2004
Directed Brokerage and 12b-1 Marketing Fees	Brokerage for fund sales	Funds will not be allowed to use trading commissions to compensate certain brokerages for selling fund shares.	Public comment period closes May 10.
	Rethinking 12b-1 rules	Regulators have asked for comment whether 12b-1 fees should be eliminated or charged differently to avoid conflicts of interest.	Public comment period closes May 10.

Source: "Cleaning Up the Fund Industry". Damato, Karen and Burns, Judith. *Wall Street Journal.* 5 Apr 2004.

itself. Not only did the industry not do so, but also the industry participants actually seemed to violate the moral, if not legal, basis of business. The investigations found late trading, illegal timing, illegal sales practices, and illegal dispersal of fund information to be pervasive.

Equally questionable is the industry's governance structure wherein often the chairman of the fund management company serves as chairman of its Board of Trustees, yet this individual has a fiduciary duty to look out for the interests of fund shareholders. On its face, this dual role appears to be inherently conflicted. Further, it was found that the other trustees were either internal company personnel or friends of the company who obviously did not take their fiduciary obligations seriously. The reform movement to install different people as chairmen of the fund company and of the Board of Trustees, select independent trustees, and review/prosecute trustees for fiduciary compliance holds great promise.

Additional reform aimed at tightening the internal controls and enforcement of the policies of the various fund groups are also long overdue. The establishment of compliance officers with independence and authority should assure these reforms are effective.

The subject of fees charged by various mutual funds is one of the more interesting and certainly controversial pursuits by Spitzer. The SEC objected to fees being part of settlement agreements whereas

Spitzer went ahead and included several hundred million dollars of fee reductions for investors in his various settlements. The SEC's philosophical view in this matter is credible in that free enterprise systems work best when governments do not involve themselves in setting prices. The SEC is instituting strict and broad fee disclosure requirements in hopes of encouraging investors to do more comparison shopping. A key point: The industry took pricing advantage of its investors and generally neglected important fiduciary responsibilities.

Since the mutual fund industry now knows how time consuming and expensive misconduct can be, future violations will perhaps be minimized. In any event, the SEC now has the industry's major issues in sight—trading, timing, fees, sales practices, and governance.

CHAPTER SIX QUESTIONS:
MUTUAL FUNDS SCANDALS

1. What kinds of illegal activities occured in the mutual fund industry?
2. Why are late trading and market timing illegal?
3. Who is Ed Stern? What did he do wrong?
4. Evaluate the SEC's reform program for mutual funds.
5. Who is Richard Strong? Why is he noteworthy?
6. What was the SEC's view regarding negotiating fee reductions as part of settlements with specific mutual funds?
7. What are "soft dollars"?

7

EXECUTIVE PERVERSION OF FINANCIAL MANAGEMENT

In Chapters three to six we discussed the systematic evolution of corporate malfeasance and corruption both on and off Wall Street, noting the laxity of the SEC and of various self-regulated professions and stock exchanges. Understandably, the drama of all this corruption and scandal captured virtually all of the headlines at the time. It is curious, therefore, that a very large subplot was ignored, one involving the financial management of America's corporations.

A major shift in the historical role of dividend policy occurred as corporate profits were increasingly used for share repurchase strategies as opposed to dividend payments. The widespread use of share buybacks in the 1990s not only reduced the market capitalization of various firms, but also left the door open to a $1.679 trillion "heist" by corporate management in the aggregate. This theft was feasible because, in short, the massive corporate share buybacks covered up an explosive issuance of executive stock options.

Record high wealth creation occurred during the economic boom of the 1990s as a result of the stock market's appreciation. Corporate stockholders failed to recognize management's capture of a significant portion of overall stock market wealth because they were contented with the gains in their own stock portfolios.

In this chapter, we will look first at a theory of agency costs that describes what is referred to as "the agency problem." This problem became so large in the 1980s that it led to widespread leveraged buyouts (LBOs) that significantly changed the ownership structure of America's corporations. The chapter next explores the era when LBOs and junk bonds reigned, then examines executive stock options, a by-product of the LBO movement. Their increased use represented an attempt to minimize the effects of the agency problem. After that, the economic boom of the 1990s is discussed in relation to corporate financial decision-making during the period. In this section we evaluate the violation of dividend conventions and the inappropriate use of share repurchase strategies or buybacks as substitutes for dividends. Finally, we address the huge amount of wealth accumulated via stock options by management in those years. Although no conspiracy or illegality occurred, it is the fact that management made off with approximately $1.697 trillion that leads us to see the maneuvers as something akin to a "heist."

AGENCY THEORY

The modern corporation can be analyzed from several perspectives. For example, a stakeholder model says that the corporation is beholden to the various stakeholders of the company, i.e., its investors, customers, employees, etc. From another perspective the corporation is created to fulfill some societal need, e.g., food production and distribution. The dominant model of the corporation continues to be the neoclassical theory of the firm derived from Adam Smith's idea of the relationship between producers/owners and consumers. The model assumes that the only duties the firm has to outsiders are financial, and that these duties are owed to the owners, which in the case of modern corporations are stockholders. This perspective is referred to as agency (contractual) theory, which emphasizes efficiency over other values.

The U.S. legal system supports agency theory and views a corporation as a nexus of contracts among the various corporate constituencies. The most important constituent is the stockholder (shareholder). A principal-to-agent relationship exists between stockholders and corporate executives. Principals are the owners or stockholders, agents are the top-level managers of the firm. By this model and theory, managers act *on behalf of* stockholders and their interests. In this regard the managers are to behave much as travel agents or real estate agents might act on behalf of their clients. Senior managers of publicly owned U.S. corporations are routinely advised to adhere to the following principle: carry out only those policies that maximize the value of the firm.[1] The underlying assumption is that stockholders create firms (or invest in them) only to increase their wealth; managers of firms, as shareholders' agents, will act solely to enhance the firm's stock price to increase wealth relative to that provided by other available investment opportunities.

In the 1930s, Berle and Means addressed the divergence of the interests of the owners of the corporation from the professional managers who are hired to run it. They warned that widely dispersed ownership "released management from the overriding requirement that it serve stockholders."[2] That is, when ownership disperses no one shareholder owns enough shares to warrant the effort or cost to monitor problematic agent behavior. In this regard, it has been noted that the essence of agency theory rests on the assumptions that: (1) the desires or goals of the principal and agent conflict; and (2) that it is difficult or expensive for the principal to verify what the agent is doing.[3]

The U.S. legal system has addressed these concepts. In 1916, the Michigan Supreme Court ruled (in a case that two minority shareholders, the Dodge brothers, had brought against Henry Ford) that, "a business corporation is organized and carried on primarily for the profit of the stockholders."[4] Berle and Means[5] addressing the issue of dispersed ownership, argued that passivity of millions of shareholders had solidified "absolute power in the corporate managements."

To invest to acquire wealth implies that investors/owners expect those who run the firms will work to achieve that end. The principal-agent model of the firm rests on the normative principle that managers should maximize stockholder value. The model, however, does not necessarily describe the actual principles most managers of various firms follow.

THE AGENCY PROBLEM IN FULL BLOOM

One of the most interesting, if not most important, advances in the field of finance during the decade of the 1970s involved the theory of agency costs or "the agency problem." Professors Michael C. Jensen and William H. Meckling describe the agency problem in "Theory of the Firm: Managerial Behavior, Agency Costs and Ownership Structure."[6] Managerial behavior can often be at odds with the goal of shareholders. In fact, whenever the management and ownership of a firm is separate, one should expect such a problem.

Jensen and Meckling point out that although manager's (the agent's) behavior was often wasteful and involved the enjoyment of various perquisites ("perks"), it was nonetheless economically rational. That is, the agents of shareholding principals would rationally prefer maximizing their own profits and benefits to maximizing stock value for the benefit of shareholders. The resulting differences between the potential, maximized values and actual stock values are termed "agency costs."

In the 1980s U.S. corporations had a massive "agency problem." Stated differently, the corporate economic system sustained huge agency costs. Large publicly traded corporations spent wastefully and inefficiently. Theory suggested that investors were cognizant of the problem and consequently penalized stock prices. That, in turn, made equity capital costs much higher. It should be noted that managers at the time were also observed to use relatively less debt capital (financial leverage) than was thought to be optimal. It was believed that management purposely stayed under-leveraged to keep its' own personal risk low. That is, if a company's risk profile gained attention or resulted in financial difficulty, managers and executives could lose their jobs. So why take any risk? As a result, the aggregate average cost of capital (both debt and equity) of America's corporate entities was materially higher than their competitor's costs in Japan and Germany. This managerial waste and inefficiency coupled with the high costs of capital gave rise to the major economic policy problem of the day: Would the U.S. permanently lose its manufacturing base to Japan and Germany?

LEVERAGED BUYOUTS AND JUNK BONDS

The magnitude of the corporate agency problem during 1980s caught the attention of numerous leverage buyout (LBO) funds, especially Kravis, Kohlberg and Roberts (KKR), Fortsman Little, and Tom Lee. Junk bond guru Michael Milken and his investment firm, Drexel Lambert, provided the intellectual and financial capital to underwrite an unprecedented number of increasingly large deals. The drama was probably best captured in a book and movie entitled *Barbarians At the Gate*,[7] based upon a mega-deal wherein KKR bought RJR Nabisco for approximately $25 billion. In doing so, KKR trumped a competing bid by Ross Johnson, who led a management buyout effort. The entire LBO saga ended in the late 1980s with the bankruptcy of Drexel Lambert and the conviction of Michael Milken for violation of federal securities law. Milken served prison time and was permanently barred from working in the securities industry.

OPTIONS: THE MAJOR BY-PRODUCT OF THE LBO MOVEMENT

Agency costs also affect debt, whether bonds or bank loans. Companies have a strong incentive to borrow funds for very risky projects because if these investments are successful, then the large resultant profits go directly to equity holders. On the other hand, if these risky investments fail, then the creditors would have to take the loss of their capital. In other words, "heads" the stockholders win, and "tails" the creditors lose. To address this double-bind, Jensen and Mecking suggest that creditors receive convertible bonds or bonds and/or loans with stock warrants. They state "…warrants represent a claim on the upper tail of the distribution of outcomes…"[8] That is, only with equity conversion rights or warrants could creditors enjoy any of the potentially large cash flows.

In this context, Jensen and Mecking argue that participation in equity profits better aligns the interests of creditors or managers with those of shareholders. This notion became widely applied by LBO investors, such as KKR, who installed stock options into their compensation programs to provide incentives for their management operators. In doing so, they indicated that this was to better align management interests with shareholders and, thus, to narrow the inherent divergence between their interests.

In this way both the theoretical and practical bases of stock options were put in place. Concurrently, U.S. media interests began a persistent campaign against corporate executive salary levels. Headlines and content featured the theme: "CEOs now make a record 350 times what custodians earn. This is outrageous." CEO's were beginning, in fact, to earn $2–$4 million in annual salary. Corporate CEOs and their Boards of Directors cleverly responded to this criticism by immediately rolling back their base salaries to under $1 million. However, they simultaneously instituted several salary supplements such as profit sharing, performance bonus awards, and stock options. The latter concept had already received some degree of acceptance from its application within LBO programs. In essence, the media is partially responsible for changing executive pay from being salary-centered to being driven by supplements such as options.

THE ECONOMIC BOOM OF THE 1990s

The decade of the 1990s began with an economic slowdown. The severity of the 1991-1992 recession and the resistance of the economy to a recovery probably cost President George H. Bush a second term. The recovery did accelerate under President Bill Clinton in the spring of 1993. This economic pick-up gained further momentum as a result of a Clinton tax hike aimed at reducing federal budget deficits. Both the stock and the bond markets reacted positively to this initiative. The economy and the capital markets began what was to become one of the strongest performances in U.S. economic history during the ensuing seven years. As noted in chapter three, the United States created over twenty million jobs, and the Dow Jones Industrial Averages, as well as other stock indexes, hit new record high marks. The wealth created was unparalleled in history.

This economic boom ended in a barrage of scandals. Our concern here is to evaluate the way executives at U.S. corporations made financial management decisions during this boom period.

DIVIDEND CONVENTIONS VIOLATED

Investors have long viewed U.S. dividend taxation negatively. Unlike other countries, the United States effectively "double taxes" dividends. First, the corporation pays taxes on dividends in that they were paid out of after-tax profits. Second, after dividends are distributed to shareholders, they were taxed again at an individual's ordinary tax rate. President George W. Bush finally addressed this issue in his 2003 tax reform package. This law limits qualified dividends to a fifteen percent individual ordinary rate tax ceiling.

This is background to the fact that during the 1990s, two time-honored dividend relationships were routinely ignored. First, as Figure 7-1 indicates the dividend yield for the Standard and Poor's (S&P) 500 has ranged between three percent and nine percent between 1871 and

Figure 7-1: S&P 500 Dividend Yield since 1871

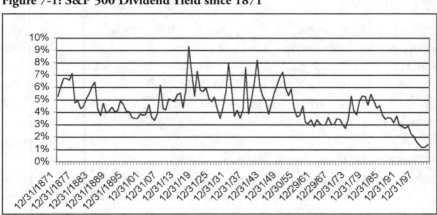

Sourece: Lehman Brothers

169

1991. In every case throughout history, when stock market prices rose to bring the dividend yield (dividend per share divided by price per share) down to 3 percent, stock prices were viewed as overvalued and would not increase any further. In 1992, stock prices ignored this long-standing relationship and continued to rise until record stock price highs were reached in the year 2000. At this point, dividend yields approached 1 percent! At this level, dividends constituted perhaps only ten percent of the total return on equity investments. (Total return is defined as the dividend yield plus appreciation of a stock's price, that is its' capital-gain yield). This ten percent relationship was greatly different than the dividend yield's historical role of thirty-five percent to forty percent of a stock's total return.

Corporations had long been sensitive to investors' dislike of dividends—versus an alternative use of cash—company share repurchase or buyback programs. Accordingly, instead of increasing dividend payments with rising cash flows, companies increasingly chose to buy back their own stock in the open market. This activity was believed to "support" a stock's market price, and thus was viewed as friendly to shareholders.

THE FUNDAMENTALS OF SHARE REPURCHASE STRATEGIES

Virtually every sector of the U.S. economy embarked upon major share-buyback initiatives in the 1990s. In fact, most major corporations announced multiple buyback plans. These programs often involved hundreds of millions, if not multiple billions, of dollars per firm. Before exploring this important financial management tactic, it is important to review the fundamentals of a share repurchase strategy (SRS).

Financial theory suggests that corporations should pursue a SRS when two conditions are present. First, the firm must have accumulated excess cash. That is, a firm should never send cash out to shareholders that might be needed for internal working capital and/or capital expenditures either presently or prospectively. Second, the firm must believe its stock price is seriously undervalued. In considering its earnings and growth record, the firm must conclude that the market's valuation of at least one of two factors is simply too low:

- multiple of earnings: price divided by earnings per share or ("P/E" ratio)
- multiple of book value: price divided by book value per share ("P/BV")

In these circumstances the best investment for the firm is to buy back its own shares. The internal rate of return on this action would far exceed any rate of return that the company could earn on the various capital projects in which it normally invests. A typical example could involve a company with a consistent record of double-digit earnings selling in the stock market at a low P/E (perhaps only a fraction of the average stock market P/E) and at a price that was a low multiple of the firm's book value, or in some cases below book value.

If a particular buyback plan is successful, then the SRS reduces the number of shares outstanding. The reduction, in turn, should increase earnings per share (EPS) in future reporting periods. These higher EPS should give rise to higher stock prices.[9] Higher EPS and stock prices imply a high rate of return achieved on the cash invested or committed to buybacks.

BUYBACKS SUBSTITUTED FOR DIVIDENDS

As the 1994-2000 economic boom and bull stock market roared, companies flush with cash flows and highly valued stock prices (record P/E and P/BV ratios) increasingly chose to de-emphasize dividend payouts while emphasizing SRSs. Figure 7-2 highlights the relevant data. In 1994, cash flows expressed as a percentage of the rising sales for the aggregate of the S&P 500 jump from about a 3.5 percent level to over 7 percent in 1999 and 2000. Figure 7-2 also indicates that share repurchases expressed as a ratio to the dividends per share paid by the entire S&P 500 index rose dramatically and synchronize with cash flows during these same years.

Figure 7-2: Share Repurchases compared to Dividends

Corporate Policy Cycle: Repurchases Soon to Outpace Dividends

Source: Thomson Financial; S&P/Barra; Federal Reserve.

The data show that dividend yields which were traditionally "sticky" or stable at the three percent level fall to nearly one percent. The dividend portion of a stock's total return consequently became minute.

Companies' "violation" of historical dividend policy norms are probably not that objectionable from a financial-theory perspective. Companies appeared to respect investors' disdain for the "double taxation" of dividends. Also, the stock market explicitly approved the reduced role of dividends by allowing stock prices to continue to escalate, thus allowing price appreciation (capital gains) to become a larger part of an investor's total return. Interestingly, when the market later corrected itself and a "bear market" became a destabilizing force in the broad economy, the administration of George W. Bush was finally able to enact a law that significantly lessened taxation of dividends. In addition, the stock market encouraged companies to bring dividend payouts back up to their historical levels.

THE INAPPROPRIATE USE OF SHARE BUYBACKS

Although one can defend the reduced role of dividends during the 1990s, it is more difficult to rationalize the vast amount of share buybacks that occurred. Although companies were facing the first condition that may signal SRSs indicated above—the existence of excess cash—they routinely ignored the second required condition, which is that the firm's stock price must be significantly undervalued.

Recall that during the 1994-2000 "bull market," corporations enjoyed record stock market valuation. That is, most firms sold at very high P/E and P/BV ratios. As a result, the internal rates of return on the cash used for a SRS, were miniscule and, in most cases, lower than the firm's cost of capital. Accordingly, a large amount of stock value was destroyed through the stock buyback process. Companies were allowed to proceed anyway because SRSs were perceived as shareholder friendly and it appeared that investors simply did not want dividends. Since companies could not assure that the rate of return of a buyback exceeded its cost of capital, companies adopted less rigorous standards. The standard most frequently employed involved dilution of EPS. As long as the price paid, even though a high or record price, did not dilute EPS, it was acceptable.

A few examples may illustrate the inappropriateness of the buy-back activity in the 1990s. Historically in the banking industry, firms would buy back stock when P/Es were single digit and below one-half the stock market average. In these cases, banks sold at or below their book value. Buybacks would significantly enhance EPS and book values while earning rates of return exceeding 25 percent. In the 1990s, industry participants routinely paid record, double-digit P/Es and as much as three times book value. The returns implicit in these applications were always single-digit and below the bank's cost of capital.

In the industrial sector, when a blue chip firm such as General Electric would adopt a SRS, it would pay a P/E as high as 35 times and a P/BV of about six times. Their stock's price was not undervalued; the basic tenets of share buybacks were cast aside.

ANYTHING BUT CHUMP CHANGE

So far we have documented there was a major shift in the historical role of dividend policy vis-à-vis investor rates of return and overall stock market price and yield relationships. Additionally, corporations broadly substituted share buyback programs for the payment of dividends when flush with the huge corporate cash flows emanating from the boom economy of the 1990s.

Figure 7-3 indicates the value of share buybacks from 1991-2003 for the S&P 500. These amounts are netted against the value of equity issued by the S&P 500 to derive net equity value issued for each year. The data clearly indicate how share buybacks escalated during the 1990s. Note that share buyback totals ranged from $18.7 billion to $29.9 billion during 1991-1993. However, buybacks exceeded $140 billion during 1998-2000. Net equity issuance (equity issued less share buybacks) was positive in 1991 and 1992. However, given the huge magnitude of the buybacks that took place for the remainder of the decade, net equity issuance became large and negative thereafter. For example, net equity issuance averaged a negative $85 billion for the years 1997-2000.

The effect of buybacks on net equity issued propped up stock share prices because it resulted in a lower supply of equity shares relative to the demand for shares.

Figure 7-3: S&P 500 Share Repurchases and Equity Issuance

Year	Share Buybacks ($ billions)	Equity Issuance ($ billions)	Net Equity Issuance ($ billions)
1991	$18.7	$26.9	$8.2
1992	23.8	34.6	10.8
1993	29.9	29.0	-0.9
1994	35.9	23.5	-12.4
1995	64.2	22.0	-42.2
1996	77.2	32.4	-44.8
1997	116.8	33.0	-83.8
1998	140.5	46.0	-94.5
1999	150.2	63.6	-86.6
2000	150.0	73.3	-76.7
2001	126.3	82.2	-44.1
2002	132.0	44.8	-87.2
2003	101.6	43.0	-58.6
Total	1,167.1	554.3	-612.8

Source: Lehman Brothers Fact Set, 2004, New York.

Note the total value of shares repurchased for the entire 1991-2003 period was $1.167 trillion. Recall that this figure accounts for only the five hundred corporations included in the S&P 500 index. Thousands of other firms were also buying back their shares.

WHAT HAPPENED AT THE END OF THE DAY?

Most of the share buybacks executed during the 1990s were ill-advised. That is, they occurred at times when individual stock prices were not undervalued, which accepted theory would suggest is inappropriate. Accordingly, most of these programs destroyed the market capitalization value at the various firms. It is not clear that shareholder disdain for dividends rationalizes all the value destruction resulting from the widespread misuse of buybacks. The question must be asked: Were there other motives?

Casual inspection of the shares-outstanding counts at numerous large corporations who bought back billions of dollars worth of their own shares indicates that, on balance, their number of shares outstanding were generally only slightly lower in each successive year examined. Yet given the huge dollar amounts of their buybacks, one would have expected very large reductions in an individual company's shares outstanding. And, if that were the case, very large EPS would have occurred as well as higher share (stock) prices, which are based upon EPS.

Unfortunately, there may have been another explanation or motivation for both the questionable use of buybacks and the actual management of shares outstanding. Recall that during this 1992-2000 period, the role of stock options in executive compensation grew dramatically. Option issuance became commonplace and pervasive throughout corporate America. Many executives enjoyed compensations exceeding $50 or $100 million per year due to option supplements. A colorful example of the potential impact of option compensation involved Disney CEO Michael Eisner. He reportedly earned over $300 million in a single year. Unfortunately for his reputation, a large number of his shareholders seriously questioned his management skills and performance.

Given the volume of options that corporations were using to supplement the compensation of their executives, and how lucrative these programs had become, it was imperative that something be done to cover up or hide what would otherwise be very large increases in shares outstanding. Indeed, there would have been explosions in the shares outstanding of individual firms as a result of options being exercised. Without comprehensive and continuous buyback strategies, the number of shares outstanding would have reached levels that would have significantly diluted EPS and brought down stock prices. Undoubtedly, shareholders would have complained and taken action to stop the root cause—that is, stock option programs for executives.

It is also important to note that the U.S. accounting authority, the Financial Accounting Standards Board (FASB), ruled that options were technically not compensation and, thus, need not be expensed. So corporations did not have to reflect huge option expenses that undoubtedly would have significantly "dragged" the EPS of most corporations down. The executives were giving significant slices of the company to themselves while the entire transaction was barely reflected in the firm's income statement. Serious shareholder objections were cleverly averted.

A TRILLION DOLLAR HEIST

On several occasions during the 1990s, the popular financial press such as *Fortune* and *Business Week* studied the relationship between executive pay and objective performance. In most cases, these studies showed little consistent correlation between pay levels and performance. Although the amounts involved were very large and the related performance levels were, at the very least, suspect, there have been few attempts to assess just how much money was misappropriated throughout the decade. To address this matter it is useful to review the Federal Reserve's Flow of Funds database (See Figure 7-4).

We are presently involved in a project to determine the extent of ill-gotten wealth collected by America's executive class. Though the final verdict is not yet in, one can still guess at the magnitude of the

Figure 7-4: Market Value of U.S. Corporate Equities and Foreign Depository Receipts Owned By U.S. Residents

Year	(trillions $)
1989*	$3.8
1990	3.5
1991	4.9
1992	5.4
1993	6.3
1994	6.3
1995	8.5
1996	10.3
1997	13.3
1998	15.5
1999	19.5
2000	17.6
2001	15.3
2002	11.9

*Data in each year are for December 31,
Source: Federal Reserve Flow of Funds, Federal Reserve Bulletin 1989—2003.

problem. Our compilations to date suggest that the entire management group of U.S. publicly traded firms owned between one and one-half percent to two percent of the public market value of U.S. equities at the beginning of the 1990s. In December 1989, Figure 7-4 indicates that this public market value was $3.8 trillion. Accordingly, two percent ownership would amount to $76 billion. Our work suggests that management's aggressive exploitation of option packages increased their equity ownership to the nine to ten percent level. The nine percent level, applied to the December 1999 equity public market value of $19.5 trillion suggests management's ownership value rose to $1.755 trillion ($19.5 trillion times nine percent). In short, management increased its wealth $1.679 trillion ($1.755 trillion minus $76 billion). That is a lot of money for a lot of managers judged to be mediocre performers by *Business Week, Fortune*, and others.

How could shareholders and their fiduciary representatives stand by and permit their corporations to be looted to the tune of $1.679 trillion? Obviously, they were very complacent and anything but vigilant.

Perhaps the record equity returns they experienced during the roaring bull stock market of the 1990s accounts for most of this complacency. Other seemingly honorable considerations also tended to disguise the problem. The corporate bias against dividend payments, the payment of options "to better align" managerial and shareholder interests, and the stock market's relative lack of interest in dividend conventions, as well as the view of share buybacks as inherently pro-investor, all appeared to be rational and legitimate. Nevertheless, shareholders were grossly abused by their managers. Corporate financial management theory regarding the practice of dividend policy, SRSs, and agency costs minimization was routinely misapplied, and the divergence between shareholders' and managers' interest were not narrowed, but widened to an extreme.

In short, it was a confluence of forces that gave rise to the "heist," but it did not rise to the level of a conspiracy. Management and their respective Boards of Directors were clever and in fact very greedy, but not conspiring robbers in any legal sense.

WHAT ABOUT AGENCY THEORY?

Agency theory was unequal to the task of the decade. Although the focus of the 1980s was on attacking waste and managerial behavior that ran contrary to shareholder interests, the end result was an even worse equilibrium. That is, agency costs accelerated and many of the natural "controls" supposed to contain the agency problem were ineffective. Specifically, assumptions of shareholder "monitoring" are central to agency theory, but we have noted that complacent shareholders and their representatives did not really do this to any meaningful degree. The watchdog role of public auditors and financial reporting simultaneously became corrupted. Similarly, the monitoring role of security analysts was entirely nullified by their lucrative subversion to their investment banker function. As we discussed in chapter five, this subversion was so perverse and unfair that the Wall Street settlements called for an absolute ban on contact between analysts and their investment bankers.

CONCLUDING THOUGHTS AND ANALYSIS

It is widely believed that shareholders' returns will be inherently inferior during the next few decades. Stock market guru Warren Buffet has admonished that six percent to seven percent total equity returns may be the most that can be expected for the foreseeable future. Accordingly, it seems likely that in the future shareholders will be less inclined to be silent about abuses such as outrageous pay packages, severance agreements, and empire-building acquisitions. Also, the Sarbanes-Oxley Act now assures that the Board Audit Committees, their public auditors, and senior management will take their certification of financial results seriously.

The FASB may soon require that corporations must expense options and their EPS effects. This added transparency should limit the more outrageous option programs. The prospective role of security analysts is unclear. Their ties to investment banking have been cut, and that will make it difficult to draw in and nurture new talent to the career. That is, given that retail commissions are virtually non-existent, who can pay for the analyst function? Already there are deep cuts in analysts' pay levels. This begs the question of what will be the quality of the talent attracted to the analyst profession. Historically, their high pay attracted some of the brightest and the best. That is bound to change.

CHAPTER SEVEN QUESTIONS:
EXECUTIVE PERVERSION OF FINANCIAL MANAGEMENT

1. What is an LBO and how did it change the ownership of America's corporations?

2. Discuss agency theory.

3. What is the difference between a principal and an agent? Describe the relationship between them.

4. What was considered the major by-product of the LBO movement?

5. What is the effect of a corporate share repurchase strategy (SRS) or stock buyback?

6. What exactly is the $1.679 trillion dollar heist and how did it happen?

7. If you were to give away one dollar bill per second, how much time, in days or years, would it take you to give away one million? One billion? One trillion??

MARKET SYSTEM AND SOCIAL INSTITUTIONS CALLED INTO QUESTION

After the burst of the high-tech bubble and subsequent corporate finance scandals, serious questions arose about the standards of corporate governance and the societal institutions that allowed such malfeasance to flourish. Since the appalling Enron scandal first hit the headlines, government investigations into corporate wrongdoing have reached unprecedented levels. The enormous public mistrust engendered by such wrongdoing has prompted government officials to re-examine corporate governance and financial regulation.

The SEC began implementing the Sarbanes-Oxley Act (SOA) in August 2002. The SOA represents the most radical and comprehensive redesign of U.S. regulation since the 1930s. Eliot Spitzer, the New York Attorney General, provided another line of attack by pursuing investment banks that had abused investors through conflicts of interest between their corporate finance and research activities. Spitzer also successfully pursued mutual fund companies that similarly manipulated the investing public.

Our society largely avoids public dialogue on the subject of the moral, cultural, and political ramifications of the market system. Yet, the profoundly unethical and even illegal nature of the management decisions leading to recent scandals calls into question the character of the market system itself. Nevertheless, some analysts assert that historic social institutions like family, religion, and politics are being invaded by the forces of commerce. Others argue that civic virtue is disappearing in part due to excessive consumption. Does work increasingly lose its' meaning while the populace is besieged by consumer goods that they desire but do not need? In short, the spread of market-oriented values like greed and consumption, combined with a general decline in the popular value of virtuous behavior, may erode important traditions and institutions upon which the market system depends.

This chapter begins by examining specific social institutions and the role they play in fostering cooperation and establishing the "rules of the game" by which the economy operates. The market economy is a fundamental institution that works in conjunction with other "nonmarket" institutions—such as the family, the state, and cultural associations—to help set generalized cultural expectations of moral behavior. The chapter closes by examining incentives and executive compensation. Markets set prices, rents, and wages. Executive compensation levels are established within the cultural constraints of what a society accepts in terms of differential pay levels, along with the economic forces of supply and demand.

INSTITUTIONS ESTABLISH THE RULES OF THE GAME

The choices individuals make are shaped by the past, which is intimately connected to the institutions of society. All societies depend on human cooperation which permits the economy to grow and prosper. In the economic realm, institutions like private property and the judicial system foster the type of cooperation that permits an economy to flourish.

Although human nature seems to dictate that people tend to first look after themselves and those significant to them, we also know that cooperation among human beings does occur and that, in fact, our civilization is based upon it. Yet, in situations where an individual has a distinct incentive to be selfish, how can cooperation for mutual benefit develop? One answer to this question was provided by Thomas Hobbes, the noted British philosopher of the seventeenth century. Unfortunately, his answer was rather pessimistic. Hobbes argued that before governments existed, societies were hindered by the problem of selfish individuals who competed on such ruthless terms that life was "solitary, poor, nasty, brutish, and short."[1] In his view, cooperation could not be maintained without a central authority, making a strong government a necessity. Since then, arguments about the proper role and scope of government have often focused on whether one can, or cannot, expect cooperation to emerge in a particular domain in the absence of an authority to police the situation. According to political scientist Robert Axelrod, who examined the evolution of cooperation in societies, the most effective way for an authority to encourage cooperation among members of an organization is to structure relationships so as to provide frequent and durable interactions among individuals.[2]

Institutions are humanly devised constraints that shape and reduce the uncertainties involved in human interaction, enabling individuals to behave in a more cooperative manner. Institutional constraints prohibit and permit certain activities and conditions. Institutions structure incentives that motivate human exchange, whether political, legal, social, or economic. They provide the "rules of the game" in a society analogous to the rules of the game in a competitive team sport.[3] Such rules include both formal written rules as well as unwritten codes of conduct that underlie and supplement the formal rules. Using the sports analogy, both formal and informal rules exist to prohibit the deliberate injury of a player on an opposing team, for example. Taken together, these formal and informal rules, as well as the type and effectiveness of enforcement, influence the character of the game.

Jack Knight, a noted institutional analyst, identifies two important aspects of institutions. First, an institution is a set of rules that structure social interactions in particular ways. Second, for a set of rules to constitute an institution, knowledge of these rules must be shared by the members of the relevant community or society.[4] Thus, idiosyncratic "rules of thumb" that guide the behavior of individual actors are not considered institutional rules. At the same time, informal conventions form the base on which a vast range of formal institutions organize and influence economic and political life. Political decision-making, for example, is framed by formal and informal institutional rules and procedures. Most countries are regulated by a constitution, the most all-encompassing form of institution found at the national level. Many economic and political institutions are fortified by a legal system and the force of law, itself a pervasive institution that in many ways is the mere formalization of informal conventions and norms.

THE ROLE OF ORGANIZATIONS

Douglas North[5] makes a useful distinction between organizations and institutions. Organizations are "the players," while institutions serve as "the rules" that define the way "the game" is played. Organizations include political bodies (political parties, a city council, a regulatory agency), economic bodies (firms, trade unions, family farms, cooperatives), social bodies (churches, clubs, athletic associations), and educational bodies (schools, universities, vocational training centers). Organizations are groups of individuals bound by a common purpose to achieve objectives. How organizations come into existence and how they evolve are fundamentally influenced by the institutional framework of a society. Organizations, in turn, influence how institutions evolve and, in the course of attempts to accomplish their objectives, can be major agents of institutional change.

Institutions affect the performance of the economy through their impact on the costs of exchange and production. For example, the number of levels of bureaucracy in government can raise the cost of doing business and the ease with which laws are written and understood can foster or impede business activity. Together with technology, institutions determine the transaction and transformation (production) costs that make up the total costs of goods and services. In regard to the economy then, the major role of institutions is to reduce uncertainty by establishing a stable structure for human interaction and limiting the degree of social change. So, institutions provide predictability and stability which encourages production and economic exchange.

THE MARKET ECONOMY AS AN INSTITUTION

Economic markets are influenced by institutions that operate within systems that support private property rights and define economic exchanges. Before the rise of government institutions to regulate and safeguard commerce, an informal system of judges was used to enforce commercial law. Known as the "Law Merchants," this European institution of the early middle ages promoted honest exchange and, by extension, promoted trust between those exchanging goods and services.[6] "Law Merchants" evolved from the efforts of merchants to enact their own private code of laws, a code that could be upheld by a judge who might actually be a local official or a private merchant. Such a system exemplifies the way in which the market itself has long served as an important social institution connecting people within a community.

According to Scottish economist Adam Smith, in a market economy based upon exchange, every person "becomes in some measure a merchant."[7] The pursuit of self-interest in the market, with its division of labor and resulting dependence on others, leads every individual to adapt his behavior to the expectations of others. Thus, the market is a key institution of society, both for developing a sense of individual self-worth in its citizens and for encouraging people to have regard for others. Smith saw the market as a disciplining institution. The work of being a merchant requires discipline in the development of virtues like persistence, frugality, and trustworthiness. Smith believed, "The real and effectual discipline which is exercised over a worker, is not that of his corporation (guild)," [but] "that of his customers.... It is the fear of losing his employment which restrains his frauds and corrects his negligence."[8] Thus, in order for an individual to become successful in his economic exchanges with others, he or she must develop an acceptable standard of moral behavior that Smith calls "propriety" (as discussed in chapter nine). The characteristics of the individual that the market promotes, then, include prudence, the disciplined pursuit of self-interest, and the ability to defer short-term gratification for long-term benefits."[9] In Smith's formulation, the market is a social institution that encourages people to act in a more pro-social manner. Because an individual's material needs are met through the production for others, individuals are forced to orient themselves to other people and take an interest in what they think and do.

The power of the market to stimulate new knowledge and creativity is evident throughout history in the efforts of entrepreneurs to discover new uses for things previously considered to be of negligible worth. Whatever its benefits as an institution, however, the market system has sometimes been considered irreconcilable with human well-being. Critical analysis of the market system have focused on three major concerns: 1) a market economy gives rise to a constant lack of satisfaction among individuals by increasing their wants faster than the means necessary to satisfy them; 2) a market economy leads to a decline in virtue, defined as the willingness to sacrifice one's own needs on behalf of one's community or society; and 3) a market economy fosters an ever-increasing division of labor, leading to specialization and the development of one-sided, "atrophied personalities."

PUBLIC EDUCATION IS NECESSARY TO AVOID "ATROPHIED PERSONALITIES"

Adam Smith's observation that the intellect of most men was formed largely by their work is related to this last concern about market systems. Writing at a time when public education did not exist and the long workday hours of manufacturing left little leisure time, Smith provided a harrowing portrait of the development of the great mass of the populace:

> The man whose whole life is spent in performing a few simple operations...has no occasion to exert his understanding.... He naturally loses, therefore, the habit of such exertion, and generally becomes as stupid and ignorant as it is possible for a human creature to become. The torpor of his mind renders him, not only incapable of relishing

or bearing a part in any conversation, but of conceiving any generous, noble, or tender sentiment, and consequently of forming any just judgment concerning many even of the ordinary duties of private life. Of the great and extensive interests of his country he is altogether incapable of judging; and unless very particular pains have been taken to render him otherwise, he is equally incapable of defending his country in war. The uniformity of his stationary life naturally corrupts the courage of his mind…. It corrupts even the activity of his body, and renders him incapable of exerting his strength with vigor and perseverance, in any other employment than that to which he has been bred. His dexterity at his own particular trade seems, in this manner, to be acquired at the expense of his intellectual, social, and martial virtues. But in every improved and civilized society this is the state into which the laboring poor, that is, the great body of the people, must necessarily fall, *unless government takes some pains to prevent it* (emphasis added).[10]

Had Smith believed that this portrait of the working man was the inevitable effect of the market system on the majority of the population, he would simply have concluded that the losses brought about by such a system outweighed its gains. The key to Smith's purpose in this dark portrait, however, lies in the last phrase: "unless government takes some pains to prevent it." His intention became very clear when he advocated some very extensive and expensive recommendations for new public expenditures, including those for education, in his book *The Wealth of Nations.*

As a remedy for the mental degradation brought about by the mind-numbing work engendered by the division of labor, Smith recommended the establishment of universal public schooling (largely at government expense) so that even those in the lower ranks of society could acquire the essential skills of reading, writing, and arithmetic. The benefits of education were not only important to the individual, Smith maintained, they were also a prime political consideration for the state. Smith believed that an educated populace would behave in a more decent and orderly fashion. Since the market system, did not promote the use of the mind, the visible hand of the state might be required to rectify the potentially character-draining, invisible hand of the market.

In summary, criticisms of the market system boil down to an apprehension about the development of a population that has as its overriding goal the pursuit of money or material gain. The solution to these concerns, according to both Smith and Hegel, involves non-market institutions.

TRANSACTION COSTS AND PROPERTY RIGHTS CREATE INSTITUTIONS

People in all societies develop institutions to lessen uncertainty and give structure to their commercial relations with one another. In relationships of economic exchange, such structures reduce the costs associated with ensuring the integrity of transactions. The cost of obtaining information that provides more assurance of the veracity and reliability of a transaction is the key to understanding the concept of transaction cost. The costs of measuring the valuable attributes of what is being exchanged (such as, quality, price competitiveness, availability, etc.), the costs of protecting rights associated with the transaction, and the costs associated with policing as well as enforcing the agreement need to be determined. These measurement and enforcement costs provide the impetus for the creation of social, political, and economic institutions in a society with a market economy. In other words, various institutions come into existence due to transaction costs.

These costs of economic exchange distinguish the transaction costs approach from the traditional theory of economics inherited from Adam Smith. For the last 200 years, the gains from trade made possible by the increasing specialization and division of labor have been the cornerstone of markets. As the world's economy grew, in part as a result of this ever more specialized division of labor, the number of exchanges involved in the operation of economies expanded. At the same time, economic theory developed without regard for the costs associated with this ever-increasing process of specialized exchange.

An exchange process involving transaction costs suggests significant modifications in economic theory and very different implications for economic performance.

Wallis and North[11] measured the size of transaction costs that pass through the market in the U.S. economy. That is, they measured the costs associated with banking, insurance, finance, wholesale trade, retail trade, and professional services such as lawyers and accountants. They found that more than 45 percent of national income was devoted to transacting. Moreover, this percentage had increased from approximately 25 percent a century earlier.

Property rights are the rights of individuals to own their own labor and the goods and services they possess.[12] This right of ownership is a function of legal rules, organizational forms, enforcement, and norms of behavior—in other words, the rules of the game or institutional framework. With any property rights structure, transaction costs are positive and rights are never perfectly specified and enforced. The costs of transacting have changed greatly throughout history and vary greatly between different economies. For example, in countries where education systems are better and people more literate, transaction costs will tend to go down. Also, the mix between the formal protection of rights and individual attempts to capture rights or devote resources to protection of their rights varies widely.

Institutions guide how exchange of goods and services take place, and, together with the technology employed, determine the costs of producing and transacting. How well institutions solve the problems of coordination and production is determined by three variables: (1) the motivation of the players, (2) the complexity of the environment, and (3) the ability of the players to understand and order the environment (measurement and enforcement).[13]

The institutions necessary to accomplish economic exchange vary in their complexity, from those that solve simple exchange situations to others that extend across space and time and large numbers of individuals. The degree of difficulty in economic exchange is a function of the complexity of the contracts necessary to undertake exchange in economies of varying degrees of specialization. As a general rule, the greater the degree of specialization in an economy and the greater the number and variability of valuable attributes (such as quality, price competitiveness, availability, etc.), the greater the need for reliable institutions that allow individuals to engage in complex contracting with a minimum of uncertainty about whether the terms of the contract can be realized.

NON-MARKET INSTITUTIONS THAT COUNTER THE NEGATIVE EFFECTS OF THE MARKET

The notion that social order relies on virtues that are not necessarily cultivated by a society's dominant institutions is at least as old as Aristotle. In keeping with this tradition, those who are favorably disposed toward a market economy have always emphasized the importance of institutions that could serve to counteract the negative effects of the market. Time and again, social philosophers have asserted or implied that the dispositions, virtues, character traits, and experiences promoted by the market were insufficient for human flourishing. Market relationships are almost by definition contractual relationships, motivated by self-interest and capable of dissolution when contracts are not effective. Of course, there is more to life than contractual relations. Relationships of friendship and love, with their accompanying altruism, make individual interest subordinate to the needs of others. The family is the best example of such relations as stressed by both Smith and Hegel.

THE FAMILY AS AN INSTITUTION

The family is probably the most ancient of social institutions and, in all likelihood, the oldest economic organization. The family is usually the most important social institution that transforms self-interest into something larger. German philosopher G.F.W. Hegel argued that earning a living in the marketplace is one of the most important ways in which love and the deep obligation of family life is expressed. As Catholic University history professor Jerry Muller notes, "The power of perpetuating our property on our families is one of the most valuable and interesting circumstances belonging to it, and that which tends the most to the perpetuation of society itself."[14] Similarly, economist Joseph Schumpeter saw the drive to build a trans-generational family fortune as an important spur to entrepreneurial activity.[15] The desire to provide opportunities for one's children is central to many life decisions in a capitalist society.

For Hegel, the family is a realm of relationships based upon emotional altruism. In this unit humans learn to become ethical beings through the experience of an immediate, emotional form, the relationship of love between two adults, and the relationships of love and obedience between parents and children.[16] Hegel was critical of those who conceived of marriage merely as a civil contract. Marriage, he thought, begins as a contract, but then supersedes that arrangement,[17] reverting to its original contractual form only when it dissolves.[18] Hegel saw marriage as an ethical institution based upon "love, trust, and the sharing of the whole of individual existence" such that we ultimately put the interests of other family members above our own.[19] In marriage, natural drives become part of an ethical order. That is, love itself is only one element of marriage, other essential elements being the sharing of wealth, sharing of worries, and raising children.[20]

THE STATE AS AN INDISPENSABLE INSTITUTION

Another counter-institution to the forces of the market is the State. To be sure, many political economists have emphasized that self-seeking behavior occurs in the political realm as well as in the market, and that such self-seeking can become a major barrier to the market's effective functioning. But because thinkers like Smith and Hegel saw the State as both indispensable for societal cooperation and the existence of the market, and yet threatened by organized interests, they believed it necessary for the State to cultivate a real commitment to the public good among at least part of the population. Smith's *Theory of Moral Sentiments,* for example, reserves its highest praise for "legislators and generals," rather than for prudent men of business. Hegel championed the role of a publicly minded civil service, and one hundred years later, economist J.M. Keynes became an embodiment of that ideal. In our time, the difficulty for legislators and civil servants is to remain pubic-minded while resisting the pressures to expand government endlessly. A natural inclination exists among civil servants to expand the scope of their power and control, a temptation that is built into the reward and survival structure of a representative democracy. Great minds like Smith have sought institutional limits on governmental power and published works intended to cultivate the desire among potential legislators and civil servants to be public-minded while limiting government power.

Hegel argued that the State should be characterized by relationships beyond those of individual self-interest, just as in the family. He disagreed with liberal thought on the role of the State, which regarded family only as an agency for the self-interested protection of individual rights and property. For Hegel, the State was the institutional embodiment of the collective identity of its population. The limits of the liberal conception of the State were most evident in the phenomena of taxes and of war.[21] The State required taxes, the payment of which does not necessarily accrue to the self-interest of individual taxpayers.[22] Similarly, in times of war, the State required that its citizens be willing to risk their lives—a request that is impossible to justify on grounds of self-interest. A State whose citizens are not disposed to pay taxes cannot prosper in peacetime, and without the additional willingness of citizens to fight on its behalf in time of war, the state would ultimately disappear. War reminds individuals in civil society of what they ordinarily forget: that without the State, their person and property have no security.[23] Thus, the State takes a broader, more collective view of society than market forces, which, driven by individual interests, do not consider.

THE NATION AND CULTURAL INSTITUTIONS

Patriotism can be viewed as another counterweight to the market in that such regard for the nation represents allegiance and duties beyond self-interest. For Hegel, national identity served as mediator between the individual identity and our identity as humans in general. German sociologist Max Weber defended participation in the world capitalist market as a prerequisite for national power.[24] Both Hegel and Weber viewed national identity as a complement to the market, and as a further basis of identification with the indispensable institution of the State.

A variety of cultural institutions also allow for the development of sensibilities, tastes, and traits not fostered by the market. Churches, religious institutions, and universities play such a role. These institutions act as a source of cultural ideals and values different from those readily provided and even promoted by the market.

PROFESSIONAL ASSOCIATIONS LET US DOWN

Hegel asserted that individuals can gain a greater sense of their place in society through their participation in legally constituted organizations that regulate entry into urban trades and educate members to the demands of their profession. Such entry must be voluntary, of course, and based on individual choice and talents. Hegel's hope was that such organizations could form an essential intermediary source of commitment between the individual and the State, providing a forum for mutual assistance and drawing the individual into a concern with interests wider than his own. Hegel also saw political representation occurring through these professional associations. The individual would identify with the welfare of his profession and, in turn, acquire a sense of worth and identity through the honor that accrued to him as a member of the profession. According to Hegel, recognition from one's professional peers could save an individual from the temptation to seek recognition through the display of wealth, and from the "bad infinity" of unlimited wants.[25]

Hegel's notions about professional organizations suggest that meaning and direction in the lives of individuals could be provided by memberships in associations such as unions and professional societies. The solution to the problem of unbounded wants lies in part in the fulfillment of needs and desires through the family, the State, and professional associations, all of which are essential elements of civil society.

It is in professional associations that individuals gain a sense of what level of wants is appropriate or consistent with the profession and the way of life they have chosen. In terms of being a socializing force on the market, professional associations of accountants, lawyers, financial analysts, and investment bankers were found to be grossly ineffective in the role they were to play in the corporate scandals of the past few years. Lack of enforcement of ethical standards by professional organizations was a systemic failure that contributed to the scandals surveyed in this text.

Professional organizations have influence over individuals and, as such, hold power in a society. Self-interested individuals working through professional organizations can manipulate their association as well as other societal institutions. There is a need to guard against these conflicts of interests.

CHOICES DEVOID OF MEANING

The importance of institutions that counterbalance the antisocial, self-interested forces of the market is connected to a persistent worry: that the market, sometimes in tandem with other forces in modern society, like science and technology, can lead individuals to live a life filled with choices but devoid of meaning. There are several ongoing sources of concern in this regard. Hegel revived the Aristotelian theme of *pleonexia,* the danger that arises from the open-ended desire for acquisition without limit or reflective purpose. For Aristotle, *pleonexia* was a psychological disposition most often associated with merchants. In a market economy, where, as Smith wrote, "every man becomes in some measure a merchant," the hazards posed by unbounded acquisitiveness might be institutionally limited, but never extinguished. Without a firm mooring in institutions like the family or professional associations, or in cultural frameworks that provide an independent notion of appropriate wants, the individual might be attracted to one commodity after another, in an endless round of joyless consumption. Like many others, Aristotle and Smith were aware of the danger of a triumph of means over ends. That is, individuals could become so caught up in their quest for means that they lose a sense of what those means are for.

Many have regarded the growth of new wants as itself harmful, although Smith welcomed new wants that arose from the refinement of tastes. What is of great concern is that the growth of new commodities, new wants, new means, and new choices is unsatisfying if it does not fit into some larger scheme, reflectively chosen by individuals and linked to their institutional attachments. Further, although non-market institutions are indispensable for human well-being in a market driven society, they are constantly transformed by the market.

The very dynamism of U.S. capitalism might appear to constantly threaten and undermine various formal and informal institutions. However, old institutions are often reshaped by the market rather than destroyed by it. This constant evolution is exemplified by changes in the structure of the family or in the move away from guilds to labor unions and professional associations. The current configuration of institutions in the U.S., in combination with the market, form the parameters of our society. We now turn to the issue of how the market affect the incentives of managers in our corporations.

SPILL-OVER EFFECTS OF THE MARKET

A purely economic view of business primarily measures success in financial terms (revenues, profits, returns on investment, etc.) and tends to de-emphasize the responsibilities and potential non-financial contributions of business to society. Money and material goods dominate the sense of satisfaction of individuals in one important respect: people tend to seek status, and therefore tend to judge their success in terms of money and/or material goods. Because these measures of success constantly rise in a market economy, the resulting struggle to "keep up" becomes a never-ending process.

Currently, many of the values and orientations that emanate from a market system have spilled over into non-market institutions. One area is the institution of marriage. In recent years industrialized nations have noted a decrease in family size throughout the last century. Basically, smaller families or different organizations of families have resulted, as prospective parents calculate relevant benefits and decide that children are difficult to justify. As such, the modes of thought and action derivative of a market system seem to have permeated human relations, at least in the United States. The result is the disabling of an important institution on which a vibrant society depends.

To advance the idea that the family, the State, universities, and other "non-market" institutions are separate from the world of commerce is not realistic. The market depends on each of these institutions. The proliferation of print, radio, television, and the Internet have all extended the reach of the market into the home. If family decisions are sufficiently influenced by values associated with the market, its members lose the sense of subordinating their individual interests to the larger interests of the family. Higher education, too, is sought with at least one eye on its ultimate payoff in the marketplace. Also, the State is intertwined with the market because virtually every group seeks to make use of its political power for its own economic self-interest. In the United States, the common occurrence of business contributions to political campaign finance has emerged as a major problem. In this regard, it is interesting to note that the Arthur Andersen accounting firm was one of the largest donors in the contested presidential election between George W. Bush and Al Gore.

Non-market institutions that have failed to hold up against the onslaught of the market system include professional associations and cultural institutions, both of which have been impacted greatly by the market emphasis on the bottom line over all other values. Although both types of institutions still function, they have in response continued to develop ever new codes of ethics. Professional associations often abandon any sense of pubic responsibility while cultural institutions are often dominated by the market, as evident by the exorbitant salaries of pop stars and professional athletes.

Although under the throes of change, the family, as a non-market institution, is still embedded in local communities and can act as a factor to bring about change through political institutions. As citizens become increasingly outraged by the vested interest, unethical behavior, and extravagance of business, the State is called upon to respond with legislation. Unfortunately, the increasing disappointment of citizens with political leadership and the resulting lack of voter participation has muted the potential power of the people.

Institutional change is a complicated process because changes tend to be small and can be a consequence of alterations in rules (through lobbying), informal constraints, and the effectiveness of enforcement. Moreover, institutions typically change incrementally and in a discontinuous fashion. As such, reform of our current market system will be slow in coming.

ORGANIZATION THEORY: INCENTIVES VERSUS LEADERSHIP

As discussed earlier, organizations are groups of individuals bound by a common purpose to achieve objectives. They are the actors within an institutional framework. Organizational control can be viewed as the mechanistic problem of designing incentive systems and sanctions so that either self-interested or intrinsically unmotivated employees find it in their interest to work to support the organization's goals. In other words, management shapes subordinate behavior through a system of rewards and punishments. This view is associated with Fredrick Taylor, the father of scientific management, who was a devout advocate of incentive wage systems as a way of motivating workers. The more recent "principal-agency theory" in the field of management and economics falls almost entirely within this mechanistic approach.

A contrasting view of organization theory contends that "leadership" is used to motivate employees to pursue organizational goals. This view is less mechanistic since the manager's goal is essentially the human engineering of the organizational machine. Thus, managerial leadership is thought to motivate desirable behavior through charisma, vision, and identity rather than the traditional "carrot and stick." A manager's primary job is to lead—that is, inspire a willingness to cooperate, take risks, innovate, and go beyond the level of effort that a narrow, self-interested analysis of the incentives would summon. As

North[26] notes,

> Human motivation is simply more complicated than simple wealth maximization. Human beings do trade off wealth or income for other values. And, because the price one pays for one's convictions are frequently lowered by institutions, institutions are important to choices.

EXECUTIVE COMPENSATION

An informal examination of executive compensation indicates that CEOs significantly control the process of appointment to a company's board of directors and may well control the composition of the compensation committee that sets managers' salaries. Thus, the disciplining forces of the market are prevented from having any direct impact on CEO compensation as salaries and other managerial perquisites are a controllable aspect of firm policy. Perquisites (known as perks) are goods or services that may be given to, used by, or provided at reduced cost to managers—essentially additional compensation above and beyond the manager's regular pay or that reduce their normal personal expenses.

PAYING FOR PERFORMANCE AS A JOKE

In many large corporations greater emphasis is placed on pay-for-performance contracts, linking executive bonuses to stock price or short-term earnings levels. However, the linkage is not nearly as strong as economic theory suggests. If the managers themselves own a great deal of the company's stock, then they might have sufficient incentive to act in the interest of the shareholders. The evidence however, suggests that managers who own little stock have no stronger incentive than mangers who own much stock. Jensen and Murphy conclude, "whatever the metric, CEO compensation is independent of business performance."[27]

Popular business magazines, such as *Business Week* and *Fortune*, often document the lack of correlation between CEO compensation and performance. Empirical evidence documents that the variation in executive compensation is more closely associated with firm size than with performance. A firm that is ten percent larger than another will pay its executives, on average, three percent more.[28] Managers have a strong incentive to engage in behavior that does not maximize shareholders' benefits. Once efficient levels of inputs are selected and purchased, managers have no reason to hand the resulting residual profits over to the shareholders in the form of dividends: According to Jensen, "Conflicts of interest between shareholders and managers over payout policies are especially severe when the organization generates substantial free cash flow. The problem is how to motivate managers to disgorge the cash rather than investing it at below the cost of capital or wasting it on organizational inefficiencies."[29] Managers find it unattractive to pay out dividends to shareholders for several reasons:

> Payouts to shareholders reduce the resources under managers' control, thereby reducing mangers' power, and making it more likely they will incur the monitoring of capital markets which occurs when the firm must obtain new capital.... Managers have incentives to cause their firms to grow beyond the optimal size. Growth increases the managers' power by increasing the resources under their control. It is also associated with the increases in managers' compensation, because changes in compensation are positively related to the growth in sales.[30]

According to this analysis, self-interested managers may make managerial decisions that increase the size of the firm beyond the efficient level and divert resources to managerial perquisites and salaries. As discussed in great detail in chapter seven, executive management actually developed an option-based scheme that, in the name of addressing ongoing concerns about agency costs and double taxation of dividends allowed them to enhance their wealth to the tune of $1.697 trillion. We characterized this scheme as "the great heist."

Shareholders, of course, have the power to remove managers who are using the firm's resources for excessive managerial salaries, company planes, or inefficient growth. However, exercising this power requires resolving a huge collective action problem, and for this reason, infrequently happens. Shareholders also may choose to sue managers in court for larger dividends, as the Dodge brothers sued Henry Ford early in his career. Ford was especially open about his disinterest in shareholder profits, and the Dodge brothers were successful. Normally, however, the courts are closed off to unhappy shareholders because of the "business judgment rule." This rule is a long-held principle of the U.S. court system that declares that the judgment of managers or a board of directors may not be challenged in court. Thus, managers typically are liable only for gross violations of their fiduciary responsibilities.

The legal ability of shareholders to control managers is further limited by the fact that many large firms have received their corporate charters from the state of Delaware, which successfully competes for the legal location of many large firms by offering a legal system that is very friendly to the rights of management. With or without the Delaware charter, any board of directors is charged with the responsibility of monitoring management in the interests of shareholders. However, the board of directors is normally selected by a nominating committee of directors, which is itself controlled, at least informally, by the CEO or management. The board is often thought of, then, more as an arm of management than as a legal representative of the mass of shareholders.

CEO Compensation Excesses: How Much is Enough?

As the story of corporate scandal has unfolded during the last few years, the issue of excessive CEO compensation surfaced often. In the 1970s, the average U.S. chief executive's total remuneration was just over twenty-five times that of the average worker. By 1980 it had jumped to a multiple of forty-two and by the year 2000, it was 600 times as much.[31] Today, even after falling share prices have slashed the value of their options, chief executives still earn 360 times as much as the average worker. The reality is that top executives often get rich despite their performance or level of income in proportion to those lower in the organization.

As discussed in chapter five, Richard Grasso, former director of the New York Stock Exchange (NYSE), had a pay package worth $187.5 million, an amount that angered many people, including traders on the NYSE floor. Giant pension funds, such as that of California's public employees and teachers, demanded his resignation in outrage. However, in contrast to other individuals surveyed in this book, Grasso may not have stolen anything. The NYSE board had offered him a huge sum of money and he accepted. Although one might think that the acceptance of such a remuneration package evidenced a certain amount of greed, one may not be able to conclude that benefiting from the terms of one's contract is unethical. In a May 2004 legal challenge of Grasso's pay package, Eliot Spitzer indicated that there may have been illegal acts by both Grasso and the NYSE Board in the salary process. Spitzer claimed that Grasso's nearly $200 million of compensation was not only "inappropriate" but illegal.

Regulations and stock exchange rules can influence systems of corporate governance but they will not, on their own, solve the problem of excessive executive pay. This is largely because even independent directors have an interest in ensuring that rewards remain high for all those at the top. Government legislators could conceivably outlaw the guaranteed bonus or limit severance payments, but it is difficult to see how they could regulate the overall level of pay. How could legislators enact a cap for the salaries of chief executives? Even if elected officials could come up with such a law, how long would it be before remuneration consultants found ingenious ways around it?

TRANSPARENCY AS A PANACEA

One possible solution might involve prompt disclosure of pay packages by corporate boards. Boards additionally could be required to explain how these packages are related to overall corporate performance. In market-based systems, shareholders are entitled to transparency in regard to the compensation of chief executives. The more information provided, the better. Most people in our capitalistic system accept that the rewards of chief executives should be substantially higher than those of the average employee, but they still have difficulty rationalizing the levels that have been reached. When these levels are associated with mediocre performance and/or CEO dismissals, both shareholders and the broader public are understandably angered.

Yet attempts at disclosure have had an unforeseen drawback. When remuneration becomes public, the pay of chief executives actually begins to rise. The competitive managerial labor market for chief executive officers dictates that they should not earn less than the average of their fellow CEOs or the company risks being seen as "below-average." Then, the company would have to come up with an even better pay package or find a new leader, one with above average ability and a remuneration package to match.

In addition, new chief executives make other kinds of demands on their respective corporate boards, such as long notice periods of up to three years before they can be terminated. A board may regard this as excessive, but published data of comparisons with other CEOs would support it. Then, when a company languishes with poor performance, the chief executive often gets to depart with a massive pay-off in lieu of that three years notice. U.S. chief executives who have left their companies over the past two years have received average termination payments of $16.5 million in cash.[32] Some received multiples of this average. These hefty sums do not include shares of stock, free offices, secretarial assistance, personal chauffeurs, use of the corporate jet, and Super Bowl tickets—all, non-pecuniary remuneration that often is included in various exit packages.

Increasingly, remuneration practices have been characterized as "obscene." Employees observing such "payment for failure," as it is commonly called, at an amount several times their expected lifetimes earnings, are understandably upset. Many employees tend to see chief executives as a "gang of bandits," especially when their poor performance puts employees' pension security at risk.

The primary problem with top management remuneration, and the source of popular anger, is that chief executives are the only people in the capitalist system who run little financial risk. If they succeed, they are richly rewarded. If they fail, their payoffs are usually great enough that they need never work again. Contrast the CEO's position with that of their employees, who fear not only for their jobs, but for their pensions (with Enron as a case in point). The tremendous unfairness of this dichotomy only can be described as a form of market failure and may point to the need for government regulation.

FINAL THOUGHTS AND ANALYSIS

In light of the numerous scandals and executive excesses discussed throughout this book, the market system as an institution can be called into question. Radical solutions to the problems of society are probably ill-advised in a period characterized by growth and wealth creation. However, complacency leads to denial that serious problems exist and/or helpful solutions are possible. The key is to retain the strength of our economic model while remedying its flaws. To this effect, the Sarbanes-Oxley Act (reviewed in chapter four) was enacted to address corporate conflicts of interests and grant greater enforcement capability to the SEC. Corporate governance will now be taken far more seriously by all concerned and the existence of an effective accounting oversight board will mean that audit responsibilities are clearly defined and penalties spelled out. These measures by themselves will not guarantee that all problems will subside, but they will do for the time being, since enacting additional regulations and laws could have resulted in an over correction and a concomitant loss of productivity and economic efficiency. The greatest missing element in the mix is a strong ethical business culture.

The fundamental question of the purpose of corporations cannot be avoided. As indicated in chapter seven, the modern corporation can be analyzed from several perspectives. From the stakeholder perspective, the corporation is beholden to the various stakeholders of the company, i.e., its investors, customers, and employees. The agency cost model assumes that the only duties the firm has to others are financial—these duties are owed to stockholders, thus emphasizing stock value and efficiency over other possible values.

A perspective that may be helpful in this regard is one that asserts that society should determine the goals that business pursues. In Japan, for example, managers are more concerned with market share than profit. European societies are much more concerned with employees than is the United States. So the question for the United States is: does our society want corporations generally to put profit above all other concerns? Perhaps in the process of answering this question, American confidence in the wealth-creating strength of the market system and in its central vehicle, the corporation, can be restored. New requirements of the Sarbanes-Oxley Act that make chief executives and chief financial officers responsible for attesting to the truth of their companies' financial statements will assist in this regard.

The heart of professionalism is the subordination of the individual to the "best standard" of performance of a given profession. Professionalism and formally stated personal standards that generate trust and predictable conduct in business situations are critical. Greater integrity and ethical behavior in business can be driven by the numerous professional associations implicated throughout this book, all of which were found wanting in the financial scandals of the late twentieth and early twenty-first centuries. These professional associations include those of accountants, lawyers, commercial bankers, investment bankers and security analysts. Awareness of social issues and the interrelationship between the market system and other social institutions is a necessary component of professionalism that should be incorporated into certification processes.

This chapter examined social institutions and factors that influence human cooperation and behavior. Organizations were cast as "players" in our economic system while institutions—political, social and professional—as entities that establish the rules that govern the players and guide all human interactions. The chapter pointed to the inclination of corporate managers to seek personal financial gain without regard to corporate ethical standards, personal professional standards, other societal values, and sometimes even the law. Organizational incentives and executive remuneration as discussed in this chapter shed light on the contradictions that exist in the current standards for management compensation. The next chapter examines individual integrity and the notion of virtue. The potential role of these positive traits in restoring public confidence and trust in corporations and social institutions is considered.

CHAPTER 8 QUESTIONS:
MARKET SYSTEM AND SOCIAL INSTITUTIONS CALLED INTO QUESTION

1. What are transaction costs?
2. Why does society have institutions and what purposes do they serve?
3. What is Adam Smith's concept of "propriety?"
4. How have some of society's major institutions contributed to the stability of the market economy?
5. Contrast organizations with institutions.
6. What is Thomas Hobbes' view of cooperation between individuals?
7. What is the difference between a market and a non-market institution?
8. What are some of the criticisms that Adam Smith leveled against market systems?
9. Why is a family unit considered one of the most important social institutions?
10. How might a system of corporate governance control the excessiveness of executive pay?

9

VIRTUE: MEDICINE FOR BUSINESS ETHICS

Thus far, this text has examined a wide variety of corporate scandals and malfeasance. These scandals involve securities fraud and corporate looting as well as gross negligence or outright fraud in public accounting. The scandals involve members of respected, indeed esteemed, professions such as public accountants, lawyers, commercial bankers, investment bankers, and security analysts. A widespread general laxity and, often, an embarrassing level of incompetence was found among relevant regulators and boards of directors. Our focus in this chapter is to view all of the corporate, professional, and regulatory misdeeds and shortcomings at the level of the individual. From that perspective, one saw an abundance of negative individual traits such as greed, dishonesty, immorality, unfairness, lack of integrity, and disrespect for the rights of others. Evidence of positive individual behavior such as generosity, fairness, integrity, and respect was regrettably scarce. Fortunately, there were a few whistleblowers who were willing to expose the various scandals. And also fortunately, state attorney general, Eliot Spitzer was able to use an esoteric New York law and a very small professional staff to effectuate billion dollar settlements with Wall Street's investment banking and mutual fund sectors.

Our economic system is widely assumed (as indeed it should) to reflect the values of U.S. society through the actions of its individual members. And clearly, in recent decades the character and judgment of a wide spectrum of finance professionals as well as that of a large number of management teams has been called into serious question. Given the dominance of negative individual tendencies such as greed, dishonesty, arrogance, and the pervasive immorality in our economic system, we might be well served by a serious study of virtue.

This chapter will examine the development and the theory of virtue, in an attempt to explain how virtuousness or its opposite can result from different social influences. Our purpose is not to advocate a particular philosophical view, but rather to stimulate the reader to reflect upon a wide variety of notions that potentially explain the development of character and of individual traits. We hope this discussion will lead to a better understanding of all the personal shortcomings that appear to be at the root of the era of *Corporate Scandals: the Many Faces of Greed.*

We begin this chapter with a review of trait theory in social psychology and a discussion of the experience of virtue. A historical review of early philosophers of virtue, such as Greek thinkers Plato and Aristotle is presented. Next, we move to the eighteenth century philosophies of Adam Smith and Georg Hegel. Smith, who wrote as the influence of classical moral theory was beginning to wane, focused on market economies and the "invisible hand" in an attempt to relate morality and virtuous behavior to economic activity. A third section will explore early writings from Asia on the topic of virtue, in particular, the works of Chinese philosopher Confucius. Next, we address the nexus between individual character and the development of virtuous behavior. The following section discusses the notion that our culture encourages placing greed at the front and center of most social activity. It considers the question of whether we have elevated greed to the status of a pseudo-virtue. The final section considers the role of education in conveying business ethics.

REFLECTIONS ON THE VIRTUOUS LIFE: EARLY PHILOSOPHIES

At the end of the twentieth century, researchers attempted to classify what were believed to be the most important character traits that contributed to the goodness of mankind. Using traits that could be assessed and measured, researchers in virtue ethics have established trait theory as a field of social psychology. Since classical times thinkers have asked, "What is the good of a person?" and answered by enumerating moral virtues readily interpretable as traits: general styles of behavior evident in thought, feelings and action that develop over time."[1] The categories of these traits can be represented by the head (thought), the heart (feelings), and the hand (doing), and together can represent the total person, how one thinks, feels, and does. These styles of behavior, or traits, are known in the fields of organizational behavior and social psychology as the major components of attitudes that have been identified through the concepts of cognition, affect, and behavior. The "cognitive factor" indicates what an individual knows, and is determined by their beliefs, opinions, and general knowledge. The "affective factor" is the emotional or feeling component. It can greatly influence the third area—behavior. The "behavior factor" refers to an intention or propensity to act in a certain way toward a person, place or thing.[2]

The meaning of the word "virtue," like "love" and "beauty," can only be truly understood and appreciated through experience. To live a virtuous life is to know its true quality. To know the pleasure of moral excellence, to have the feeling of intrinsic righteousness that comes from being just and doing good, is necessary to clearly understand the word "virtue." Engaging in virtuous behavior therefore produces a much deeper understanding of virtue than what might be learned merely from the surface of the concept. For example, you might come across a person who is perceived by others to be very kind and considerate, but then discover that their behavior is contingent on their momentary personal feelings. That is, when this person feels good on a particular day and all is going well in his life, he is full of kindness and consideration; but on other days when his mood is dark, he thinks only of himself. Suppose you then see another person who is also regarded as kind and considerate, but you happen to know that this person is experiencing difficulties in life and that all is not going well. Now, who would you say is the more virtuous? We also see plenty of instances of someone who supposedly exemplifies honesty, but who is honest only as long as they are not exposed to temptation. Of what value is such honesty? One gauge of a person's resilience in virtue is the ancient test which asks what a person would do if he had the ability to make himself invisible. Then, how honest would he be? If his virtuous behavior is contingent on the circumstances in which he finds himself, can he be a genuinely virtuous person?

Before the Sarbanes–Oxley Act (SOA) of 2002, the measure of honesty of CEOs' and CFOs' was never challenged and they were like the invisible people in the old test. Although these executives were technically responsible for the financial statements reported to the SEC, they did not bear much actual personal responsibility. Under the SOA, they now must do so. Recent evidence that shows a pivotal and significant increase in the number of restatements of financial reports, 250 in 2002, raises suspicion about the degree of honesty and truthfulness of such statements before SOA was enacted. Top executives are now much more cautious about the information that their companies submit, because there is a potential $1,000,000 fine and/or up to 10 years of prison time if those same CEOs and CFOs "knowingly" submit falsified information. Already, because of the SOA, several top executives from HealthSouth are facing the consequences of faking some $2.5 billion in earnings.

THE STUDY OF VIRTUE IN HISTORY

Historically, virtue theory is the oldest normative tradition in Western philosophy, having its roots in ancient Greek civilization [specifically with Plato and Aristotle]. Greek epic poets and playwrights, such as Homer and Sophocles, paint the morality of their heroes and antiheroes in terms of their respective virtues and vices. Plato believed that an integral part of one's quest for truth was understanding the ideal nature of virtues such as justice, piety, and courage.[3]

Many philosophers contend that morality consists of following precisely defined rules of conduct, such as "don't kill," or "don't steal." It was up to the individual to learn these rules of moral behavior, and then develop the behaviors that were necessary to follow these rules. Societies throughout the world have always presented these rules of correct behavior. Some codes are detailed in the manner of Ten Commandments, brought down from Mount Sinai by Moses, but a surprising number of the moral rules given throughout the history of mankind take the form of "The Golden Rule." Table 9-1 lists several examples.

Virtue theorists tend to approach the standards of moral behavior from a less prescriptive angle. They place less emphasis on learning predetermined rules established by someone else. Instead they stress the importance of developing what would be considered good habits of character, such as prudence or benevolence. When an individual practices these virtues over an extended period of time, he or she will then habitually act in a prudent and benevolent manner. This approach stresses an affective and behavioral process to personal character development.

In his writings Plato emphasized four preeminent virtues. Wisdom, courage, temperance and justice came to be known as cardinal virtues.[4] Plato also dealt with other important virtues, such as fortitude, generosity, self-respect, good temper, and sincerity. Yet he thought that the cardinal virtues were superior to all others. In addition to advocating good habits of character, classical virtue theorists held that individuals should make a special effort to avoid acquiring bad character traits (called vices), such as cowardice, insensibility, injustice, and vanity. Many emphasized the importance of developing strong moral character through a moral education, since virtuous character traits were assumed to develop during the early years of life. As a result of this philosophy, ancient Greeks felt that the shaping and molding of their children was a paramount responsibility of adult citizens, mainly parents

Table 9-1: Universal Symmetry: The Golden Rule Across Cultures

Culture	Teaching
Judaism	"Do not seek revenge or bear a grudge against one of your people; but love your neighbor as yourself." Bible, *Leviticus* 19:18 When he went to Hillel, he said to him,"What is hateful to you, do not do to your neighbor: that is the whole Torah; all the rest of it is commentary; go and learn." *Talmud*, Shabbat 31a
Zoroastrianism	"That nature only is good when it shall not do unto another whatever is not good for its own self." *Dadistan*-I-Dink 94:5 "What is disagreeable to yourself do not do unto others." Shayast-na-Shayast 13:29
Buddhism	"Hurt not others in ways that you yourself would find hurtful." Udana-Varga 5:18
Confucianism	Tsetung asked, "Is there one word that can serve as a principle of conduct for life?" Confucius replied, "It is the word shu—reciprocity: Do not do to others what you do not want them to do to you." *Analects* 15.23 "Try your best to treat others as you would wish to be treated yourself and you will find that is the shortest way to benevolence." *Mencius* VII.A4
Jainism	"A man should wander about treating all creatures as he himself would be treated." *Sutrakritanga* 1.11.33 "Therefore, neither does he [a sage] cause violence to others nor does he make others do so." *Acarangasutra* 5. 101-2
Socrates	"Do not do to others what would anger you if done to you by others."
Hinduism	"One should not behave towards others in a way which is disagreeable to oneself. This is the essence of morality. All other activities are due to selfish desire." *Mahabharata*, Anusasana Parva 113.8
Hinduism and Brahmanism	"This is the sum of duty: Do naught unto others which would cause you pain if done to you." *Mahabharata* 5:15-17
Christianity	"Whatever you wish that men would do to you, do so to them." Bible, *Matthew* 7:12 "Do to others as you would have them do to you." Bible, Luke 6:31
Epictetus	"What you would avoid suffering yourself, seek not to impose on others."
Islam	"Not one of you is a believer until he loves for his brother what he loves for himself." Forty Hadith of an-Nawawi 13
Baha'i	"And if thine eyes be turned towards justice, choose thou for thy neighbour that which thou choosest for thyself." *Epistle to the Son of the Wolf,* 30 "He should not wish for others what he does not wish for himself." Baha'u'llah

and teachers. Indeed, it was seen as key to the very future of the Greek civilization. This institutionalized approach worked to build excellence in character by way of virtuous behaviors: first, by implanting in the minds and hearts of the youth an appreciation for virtuous behavior through knowledge and understanding and, second, by helping the younger generation develop certain character traits through patterns of habit formation.

Aristotle gave the first systematic expression to virtue theory in his *Nichomachean Ethics.* He believed that virtues were a type of moral excellence and that through practice good virtuous habits would be instilled and this would help build a strong moral base in one's character development. After being internalized, this would also help control one's emotions.

For Aristotle, character had to do with an individual's enduring traits of behavior. That is, one's attitudes, sensibilities, and beliefs affect how one acts and, ultimately, how one actually lives. The character of an individual has a permanence about it that can explain not only why someone acts in a certain way, but also why he will act that way in the future. From a behavioral sense, a person's character gives a type of predictability to future propensities of behavior. For example, in response to the natural feelings of fear, an individual could develop the virtue of courage, one of Plato's cardinal virtues. This virtue allows an individual to be firm in the face of danger. As Aristotle analyzed specific virtues, he argued that most virtues fall at a mean between more extreme character traits. Again, using courage as an example, if a person did not have enough courage, he would develop the disposition towards cowardice, which is a vice. Conversely, if one had too much courage, he would develop the disposition towards rashness, which the Greeks also considered a vice. Aristotle argued that it was not an easy task to find the perfect "mean" between extreme character traits. In fact, he believed that one actually needed assistance from one's sense of reason to find or acquire the character trait that represented the mean.

After Aristotle, medieval theologians supplemented the Greek's cardinal virtues with the additional Christian theological virtues of faith, hope, and charity. Interest in virtue theory continued beyond the Greeks, on through the middle ages with the help of the Holy Roman Empire and the popularity of knighthood. Virtuous attitudes and behaviors were of paramount importance among the young men who joined together in the Crusades of that era. It was not until the 17th century that virtue theory started to decline, as a result of the rise of alternative moral theories expounded during the latter period of the Renaissance and further developed during the Scientific Revolution and Enlightenment periods.[5]

ADAM SMITH RELATES MORALITY TO THE INVISIBLE HAND

Even as the old ideas of virtue theory were losing influence, Adam Smith wrote a commercially successful book on ethics and human nature in 1759 entitled *The Theory of Moral Sentiments*. Smith argued that the same 'invisible hand' that brought balance to the market, also created beneficial social patterns out of our economic actions. He believed that our morality was the product of our nature not our reason. Smith argued in a completely new direction, holding that people were born with a moral sense, just as they had inborn ideas about beauty or harmony. Our conscience tells us what is right and wrong, he said, and that is something innate, not something given to us by lawmakers or developed from rational analysis.[6] Adam Smith recognized the influence that virtues have in a market economy, and he understood the advantage of analyzing a society and its institutions from a virtues perspective.

The great strength of a market economy, according to Adam Smith, is its tendency to promote the "inferior virtue" of prudence that is typically associated with striving for rank and fortune with the "prudent" pursuit of self-interest. The virtues of these "prudent" men "who are content to walk in the humble paths of private and peaceable life," as he said, are "temperance, decency, modesty, and moderation…industry and frugality."[7]

At the root of the attempt to "better our condition," wrote Smith, lies the desire "to be observed, to be attended to, to be taken notice of with sympathy…and approbation." The better off men appear, the more likely they are to get the attention and approval and praise of others.[8]

This fascination with wealth fuels the avarice of many of our industry captains. For example, Tyco's CEO Dennis Kozlowski's desire to appear better off led, through greed, to outrageous spending of his company's funds. He regularly reached into Tyco's treasury to finance his extravagant lifestyle and enhance his personal image (see chapter three). All in all, Kozlowski used more than $135 million in Tyco's funds. Another CEO, Richard Scrushy, formerly at HealthSouth, allegedly bought diamond jewelry, a plane, a yacht, expensive automobiles, works of art by famous artists, land, and even an armor-plated sport-utility vehicle. Maintaining this type of lifestyle resulted in his indictment on 85 criminal counts.

The dominant motive for economic activity—once the basic bodily necessities are obtained—is the desire for social status. Smith observed that "moralists in all ages" had complained of the undeniable fact that "the great mob of mankind are the admirers and worshippers…of wealth and greatness." This human failing, as Smith understood, did not begin with a market economy but unfortunately remains a problem within it. Smith believed that the moral advantage of the market economy lay in the fact that those "in the middling and inferior stations of life" who were neither rich and powerful nor wise nor of superior virtue—that is, the majority of people—were compelled by social institutions to channel their desires for wealth and distinction into decent forms of behavior. For them, "the road to virtue, and that to fortune…are, happily in most cases, very nearly the same." For their success depended on "real and solid professional abilities, joined to prudent, just, firm, and temperate conduct," and on "the favor and good opinion of their neighbors and equals," who demanded such conduct of them.[9]

The greatest achievement of the "invisible hand of social institutions" in a market economy was to convert the potentially base desire for status and approval into relatively virtuous forms of conduct, at least among most of the population. Twenty-first century media continuously remind us of these desires. Print and television advertising, along with entertainment and television programming, influences our everyday culture to create and reinforce a "virtue" of acquisitiveness in the minds of the unsuspecting populace.

Yet, Adam Smith also believed that if society was to flourish, some people have to possess virtues not readily promoted by any market. Thus another role for the academic professional, as Smith understood it, was to encourage character traits beyond prudence: the superior virtues of wisdom, benevolence, self-sacrifice, and public-spiritedness. "The wise and the virtuous," Smith believed, were actually a "small party."[10] Smith insisted that the survival and prosperity of society depended on the cultivation of these superior virtues, at least in some men—namely legislators and statesmen, those individuals who are guiding our leading institutions and therefore society at large. From a modern psychological perspective, they should be authentic leaders who develop, high levels of confidence, hopefulness, optimism, resilience, and strong ethical and moral character.[11]

The German philosopher G.W. F. Hegel wrote during the early part of the nineteenth century that to be virtuous in an ethical society is to live up to one's institutionally imposed duties. "In an ethical community, it is easy to say 'what' someone must do and 'what' duties he has to fulfill in order to be virtuous. He must simply do what is prescribed, expressly stated, and known to him within his situation."[12]

For Hegel, the question of what our social and political institutions ought to be is linked to the philosophical issue of what a person ought to wish to become. In part, the answer depends on how much potential for human development has been created, or allowed, by historical institutions. That is why, for Hegel, ethical theory is both a social and a political theory, and all three are tightly linked to historical developments.

Hegel had to defend his idea that a developing market economy was compatible with virtuous behavior and the well being of human kind. His critics thought that a market economy would lead to a decline in virtue and that individuals would eventually not be willing to sacrifice for the betterment of the community or society.

To prove that prediction wrong, modern man must understand

that it is the institutions of his society that make possible his sense of individual self.[13] For Hegel, the market is a key institution both for the development of a sense of individual self-worth and for habituating us to respect others as individuals.

While some philosophers think that virtues must be weakened by the operation of the market, others believe that institutions and society can maintain a balance and constantly add to its stock of virtues.[14] To do this and have a successful market economy, society must be capable of carving out sanctuaries like family, school, church, and community. There the virtues necessary to the proper functioning of an individualistic, contractual economy can be nurtured. Virtues such as truth, trust, tolerance, and restraint create obligations that make social cooperation possible. A market economy based on such virtues then creates a setting where individuals in the economic system have powerful inducements to conform to prevailing standards of behavior.

For Hegel, the significant fact about man is that he is capable of being free, but that does not mean that he is born free. To the extent that men act spontaneously upon their natural instincts and drives, Hegel thinks they are the opposite of free. In that condition they are slaves to their passions. They are liberated from this enslavement of natural drives by social and cultural institutions, which transform the individual so that he acts in ways that are good for him. Ethical life, for Hegel, involves the reorientation of natural drives by a higher self that is the product of culture and institutions. It is the replacement of nature by this "second nature," that helps develop an ethical life. It is his emphasis on the fact that ethical behavior must be instilled by habit that sets him apart from Kant and many other thinkers. Hegel clearly associated his line of thinking with the writings of Aristotle.

The market, Hegel points out, is a social institution that makes men more social. Because an individual's needs can only be met through the production of others, that individual must orient himself to other people and take an interest in what they think.[15] He must acquiesce to the requirements of others.

If a market economy is to be successful, then there are some fundamental virtues that are necessary to support the effectiveness of successful business transactions. Table 9-2 indicates five virtues that Ian Maitland identifies as necessary in an individualistic, contractual economy that rests on a foundation of credit, handshakes, mutual confidence, and implicit commitments.

Table 9-2: Virtues that Support Business Transactions

Virtue	Business Impact
Trust	The predisposition to place confidence in the behavior of others while taking the risk that the expected behavior will not be performed. Trust prevents activities that monitor compliance with agreements, contracts, and reciprocal agreements and saves costs associated with them. There is the expectation that a promise or agreement can be relied on.
Self-Control	The disposition to pass up an immediate advantage or gratification. It indicates the ability to avoid exploiting a known opportunity for self-interest. The tradeoff is between short-term self-interest and long-term benefits.
Empathy	The ability to share the feelings or emotions of others. It promotes civility because success in the market depends on the courteous treatment of people who have the option of recourse to other competitors. The ability to anticipate needs and satisfy both customers and employees contributes to a firm's economic success.
Fairness	The disposition to deal with perceived injustices to others. Fairness often entails doing the right thing with respect to small matters in order to cultivate a long-term business relationship.
Truthfulness	The disposition to provide the facts or correct information as known to the individual. Telling the truth involves avoiding deception and contributes to trust in business relationships.

Source: Ian Maitland, "Virtuous Markets: The Market as School of the Virtues," *Business Ethics Quarterly*, January 1997, 97.

In any system of ethics there needs to be a sensitive appreciation of human character and a familiarity with human psychology. Virtuous behavior is not innate, not something that you have at birth. It can only be developed from a variety of individual lifetime experiences. Experience is a precondition for acquiring prudence, one of the key virtues for living a correct moral life. Prudence gives the ability to deliberate rationally and arrive at the "right" decisions; it can only come from making decisions and observing their results. It was Aristotle's view that only persons with moral virtues would possess prudence and only persons with prudence would possess fully developed moral virtues. In the words of Robert Louden, "A truly good person will have both."[16]

CONFUCIUS

In reviewing the field of virtue theory, one finds that discussion of the classical writings of Asia, specifically from the countries of China and India, is unfortunately a bit scanty in contemporary works by the West's prominent historical virtue theorists. A brief survey of early Asian work may be helpful.

K'ung Fu-Tse was born in the year 551 B.C. He was a conservator of ancient Chinese truth and ceremonial propriety. He did not address theology or metaphysics, but his teachings and exemplary personal conduct led to a moral and cultural renaissance among the people of China. Despite the many foreign influences and internal political conflicts, his influence on Chinese civilization has been more or less permanent.[17] Confucius (the Latinized name that westerners use), a great figure of Asian philosophy, was a contemporary of Pythagoras. He taught his students through conversational lessons about propriety in moral and political conduct. He promulgated an ideal conduct of life, the basis of which was learning, wisdom, moral perfection, and decency in behavior.[18] Thomas Cleary offers a concise and articulate exposition of the philosophy of Confucius.

> Confucius worked for the revitalization of culture in its role as a means of cultivating human feelings and maintaining the integrity and well-being of a people. [Confucius] envisioned a social order guided by reasonable, humane, and just sensibilities, not by the passions of individuals arbitrarily empowered by hereditary status, and warned of the social consequences if men in positions of power considered personal profit and advantage over public humanity and justice. Confucius believed in the regeneration of public and private conscience through education and the influence of unifying cultural ideals.[19]

The Confucian philosophy was promulgated through four great books, written by Confucius and his disciples. *The Analects* (Lun Yu) was an "affirmation of humanist ethics and the universal brotherhood of man; it inspired all the nations of Eastern Asia and become the spiritual cornerstone of the most populous and oldest living civilization on earth."[20] The second book, *The Great Learning* (the Ta Hsueh) was written by several of Confucius' disciples, about two generations after he died. It presents the idea that "a state can only be healthy to the extent that the leader maintains a high personal standard of virtue."[21] The third book attributed to Confucius was *The Doctrine of the (Golden) Mean* (the Chung Yung). It was written by Confucius' grandson, and is summarized "as the Chinese adage puts it: 'Anything which is carried to the extreme will inevitably bring about just the opposite effect.' Thus, if the goal is to attain prolongation and propagation of life, one must neither be excessive nor be insufficient, but always try to hold the Golden Mean as the best policy."[22] The thoughts from this particular book are very similar to the philosophy of Aristotle, who argued that the virtuous man had to find the perfect "mean" between extreme character traits. Through reason, he said, one would find the character trait that represented the (Golden) Mean. The fourth and final great book was *Mencius* (the Meng-tzu), named after its author and written 150 years after the death of Confucius. Mencius was a student of one of the disciples of Confucius' grandson. His book indicates that, "Confucianism represents the sensible medium between total self-love and total indiscriminate 'altruism.' …[Mencius'] central task is to prove in the face of a doubting world that the achievement of a good society depends wholly on the inherent moral intentionality of good men."[23]

During Confucius' time, China was in a state of turmoil with corrupt government officials.

> Confucius advocated the restoration of just government and the revivification of society through the cultivation of what he called the ideal cultured person, the exemplary individual. The word Confucius used to express this ideal was a class term that formerly meant scion of the ruling class, but he subtly transformed it into an abstract moral ideal, a quality of character. Because [Confucius] thought that the rule of personal example was the most effective, Confucius

believed the virtues of the exemplary individual should especially be cultivated by the ruling class.[24]

In the long history of mankind, corruption was never considered extraordinary and neither were the proposals for dealing with it. For example, the Indian political analyst, Arthashastra Kautilya, in the fourth century B.C., artfully distinguished among forty different ways in which a public servant can be tempted or financially corrupted and described how a system of spot checks followed by penalties and rewards could prevent these activities.[25] He believed that a clear system of rules and penalties, along with rigorous enforcement, could make a difference in behavior patterns.

Confucius believed the same result could be achieved by clearly outlining the hierarchy of society, designating the subordinate-superior axis in most relationships, and requiring strict adherence to traditions of respect and obedience for all. As Park and Peterson explain,

> Confucius identified six relationships as crucial, those between: ruler and subjects, parents and children, husband and wife, older brother and younger brother, teacher and student, and friend and friend. These relationships each have a "superior" and "subordinate" member, except for friend and friend, although even here, if one individual is older than the other, it may become an older-younger brother relationship. In each relationship, the "subordinate" individual has the responsibility of obedience to the "superior," but only when the superior in turn displays benevolence and care.[26]

A synopsis of the Confucian philosophy is presented by a pair of authors, Boardman and Kato, whose writings traced the historical connection between Confucian philosophical principles and the Japanese concept of kyosei. Although the philosophy of kyosei was initially developed during the sixteenth century in Japan, it was not until the twentieth century that the concepts were used to describe the business environment from an ethical viewpoint. The two Japanese characters of kyo (working together) and sei (life) suggest that corporations respect the interests of their stakeholders, including customers, staff, shareholders, suppliers, and competitors.... It is noteworthy that kyosei explicitly endorses a macro view of business ethics and corporate responsibility that encompasses the local and regional communities, the nation, the broader global community, in addition to the corporate community itself.[27]

The Caux Round Table Report, which is presented as an Appendix at the end of this book, was created by a group of Japanese, European, and U.S. business, education, and community leaders, and has as its foundation the ethical ideals of kyosei.

These principles are rooted in two basic ethical ideals: kyosei and human dignity. The Japanese concept of kyosei means living and working together for the common good enabling cooperation and mutual prosperity to coexist with healthy and fair competition. Human dignity refers to the sacredness or value of each person as an end, not simply as a means to the fulfillment of others' purposes or even majority prescription.[28]

The philosophical background of kyosei, lies squarely in "the way" of Confucius. The following is a sampling of what Confucius says.

- Reciprocity should be practiced throughout one's life. In short, one should treat others the way you would like to be treated.[29]
- Virtue, not profit, should be the goal of the superior man.[30]
- Life should be a balance between self-interest and altruism.[31]
- One does not exist in isolation; we are a part of a larger and more complex family (literally and figuratively) where harmony can be achieved by acting appropriately with one another.[32]
- Risk should be avoided by operating near the average, or the "golden mean," of possibilities.[33]
- With respect to relationships, filial obedience to and respect for one's parents is paramount.[34]
- One should love learning, live the simple life, practice what has

been learned, and seek good teachers from whom one could continue learning throughout one's life.[35]

The strength of Confucian philosophy contributed much to the concept of kyosei, and helped it to become a significant descriptor of corporate behavior in Japan and the rest of the world by the end of the twentieth century.[36]

The dispersal and development of this cultural ideal, within all levels of society, helped to establish a virtuous process that became a cultural standard. The training of the young through family relationships most definitely helped to enshrine the Asian concept of filial piety that is still very prominent in Asian society today.

Many societies rely on voluntary compliance with codes of behavior rather than on financial incentives to avoid corruption. A variety of behavioral norms, however, prevail in different societies. Plato suggested in *The Laws* that a strong sense of duty would help to prevent corruption, but he also noted that instilling this would be "no easy task." What is required is not just the general sense of dutifulness, but a particular attitude of compliance with rules, of strict conformity, which has a direct bearing on corruption. All of this comes under the general heading of what Adam Smith called "propriety." Rules of honest and upright behavior are not necessarily given priority in all codes of duty, but they certainly can provide a bulwark against corruption.

How people behave often depends on how they see—and perceive—others behaving. Much depends on the reading of prevailing behavioral norms. A sense of "relative propriety," a norm established by following the actions of a comparison group (in particular, others similarly placed) can be an important influence on behavior. Indeed, the argument that "others are doing the same" is one of the more commonly cited "reasons" for unethical behavior. The importance of imitation, and of following established "conventions," has been emphasized by commentators who felt moved to study the bearing of "moral sentiments" on social, political and economic life. Adam Smith noted:

> Many men behave very decently, and through the whole of their lives avoid any considerable degree of blame, who yet, perhaps, never felt

the sentiment upon the propriety of which we found our approbation of their conduct, but *acted merely from a regard of what they saw were the established rules of behavior*" (emphasis added).[37]

In establishing "rules of behavior," importance may be particularly attached to the conduct of people in positions of power and authority. This makes the behavior of senior corporate officers especially important in setting norms of conduct. Indeed, writing in China in 122 B.C., the authors of Hui-nan Tzu stated the problem:

> If the measuring line is true, then the wood will be straight, not because one makes a special effort, but because that which it is *ruled* by makes it so. In the same way if the ruler is sincere and upright, then honest officials will serve in his government and scoundrels will go into hiding, but if the ruler is not upright, then evil men will have their way and loyal men will retire to seclusion.[38]

Corrupt behavior in "high places" can have effects far beyond the direct consequences of that behavior, and the insistence on starting moral regulation at the top does have sound reasoning behind it. For example, the case of Adelphia, is perhaps the most egregious instance of corporate self-dealing and financial chicanery in U.S corporate history. The infamous Rigas family, the founders of Adelphia, hid $2.3 billion in debts and treated the company as their personal "piggy bank," resulting in tens of billions of dollars in losses to investors. When the officers of a corporate body behave so, it is pointless to preach to the less powerful.

DEVELOPING CHARACTER THROUGH VIRTUOUS BEHAVIOR

"Character is simply habit long continued."   —Plutarch

"Virtue ethics assumes that what is moral in a given situation is not only what conventional morality requires, but also what the mature person with a 'good' moral character would deem appropriate."[39] Good character can be defined as a composite of qualities, typically of moral excellence and firmness blended with resolution, self-discipline, high principles, and sound judgment.[40] Our character existed yesterday and will be with us tomorrow; character establishes both our day-to-day demeanor and our destiny.[41] Can these virtues be instilled through education? If so, can they build character? Virtue is given as "a moral practice or action; conformity to a standard of right (divine law); moral excellence; integrity of character: uprightness of conduct."[42]

Popular newspaper columnist Leonard Pitts writes that "reputation is about who you are when people are watching; character is about who you are when there is nobody in the room but you. Both matter, but of the two, character is far and away the most important. The former can induce others to think well of you, but only the latter allows you to think well of yourself."[43] The ImClone scandal involving Martha Stewart is an example of how reputation and character are interrelated. Martha Stewart built an empire atop beautiful living. Yet, her involvement with ImClone and her conviction for making false statements to federal agents, cast suspicion on her character and tainted her reputation. The evidence of her unethical behavior and dubious character dragged down the reputation of her business.

Stephen R. Covey, the author of the best seller *The 7 Habits of Highly Effective People*, contends that:

> Character is made up of those principles and values that give your life direction, meaning and depth. These constitute your inner sense of what's right and wrong based not on laws or rules of conduct but on *who you are*. They include such traits as integrity, honesty, courage, fairness and generosity—which arise from the hard choices we have to make in life.... Many have come to believe that the only things we need for success are talent, energy and personality. But history has taught us that over the long haul, who we are is more important than who we appear to be.[44]

Character can be developed through the practice of virtuous behavior. According to Aristotle, although we are endowed by nature with the capacity to acquire virtue, one is not naturally virtuous. One becomes virtuous by performing virtuous acts repeatedly until such acts become "second nature."[45] At this point virtue is internalized, no longer a virtue of deed, but of character.

The Aristotelian assumption that virtuous behaviors (if practiced habitually) will help people develop into better human beings, would also support the assertion that good people can be good students, good business persons, good politicians and vice versa. The integration of virtue into the multiple roles that people play in their lives, at home and at work, will determine their ethical behaviors, and ultimately will define their character. Table 9-3 identifies six core virtues and example behaviors that emerge consistently in philosophical and religious discussions of human goodness: wisdom and knowledge, courage, love, justice, temperance, and transcendence.[46] These are the main strengths and virtues of individuals of good character. These virtues could certainly serve to further a harmonious environment within an educational or organizational setting. Would they not also create harmonious life experiences in the society at large?

BLINDSIDED BY GREED

"Greed is all right.... Greed is healthy. You can be greedy and still feel good about yourself."
—Ivan Boesky, Commencement address at the School of Business Administration, University of California, Berkeley, 18 May 1986

During the early nineteen thirties, J.M. Keynes recognized that our modern economic practice was based on a moral inversion. He had written "of the pseudo-moral principles which have ridden us for two hundred years, by which we have exalted some of the most distasteful of human qualities into the position of highest virtue."[47] Bald, disrespectful and single minded aggressiveness that is understood to be destructive in other circumstances has become celebrated in corporate trenches as "competitiveness." Angry, egocentric lust for power that would qualify as tyranny in politics has been elevated to "strategic

Table 9-3: Six Core Virtues

Core Virtues	Examples
Wisdom and Knowledge	Creativity, Curiosity, Good Judgment
Courage	Bravery, Industry, Integrity
Love	Kindness, Altruism, Niceness
Justice	Loyalty, Fairness, Equity
Temperance	Mercy, Modesty, Prudence

mastery" and "leadership" in business. And runaway greed has been sanctioned as "wealth creation," making heroes out of billionaire work-aholics. The end seems to make the means irrelevant, so what is bad taste, bad judgment, or bad character in life has been made admirable and to be emulated in business.[48]

Jane Eisner, a senior fellow at the University of Pennsylvania, explains how most Americans fail to acknowledge the degree to which greed has seeped into our national psyche and how it is skillfully justified by continued prosperity. Greed has become a sin masquerading as a reward and we seem to be absorbed by a false notion that wealth is a virtue. We have become "blinded by reality," or blinded to reality, and have come to believe that the wealthy must be virtuous. We no longer really recognize greed for what it is except in its most exaggerated displays.[49]

USA Today reported in a major cover story how the former CEO of Tyco purchased a $15,000 umbrella stand and a $6,000 shower curtain.[50] These are not virtuous acts. They are vicious ones, shameful products of the capital sin of avarice. Avarice (or greed) is "an insatiable desire to possess or acquire wealth or property far beyond what one needs or deserves; wanting or taking all one can get with no thought of the needs of others."[51] Most of us can probably name a majority of the seven capital (or deadly) sins, but can you name the seven virtues? If you need a hint, see Table 9-4.[52]

Table 9-4: The Seven Capital Sins and The Seven Capital Virtues

SEVEN CAPITAL SINS	SEVEN CAPITAL VIRTUES
Gluttony	Temperance
Lust	Chastity
Avarice (Greed)	Liberality
Sloth	Diligence
Envy	Love
Pride	Humility
Wrath	Meekness

Eisner also argues that "built deep into the foundations of the advertising process [a major force behind our market driven economy] is the belief that we, as consumers, never have enough. Enough of what can vary with every 60-second commercial, but it's the sense of dissatisfaction, of yearning for some thing we didn't know we wanted that has turned citizens into consumers and 7-year-olds into the new target demographic." She adds, "who doesn't want more in a culture founded on manifest destiny, in an economy fueled by desire for the next new thing?"[53]

So as a culture of consumers, what have we become? What is the result of this conditioning process that has caused us to believe in the pseudo-virtuous way of life? How has this way of living affected our relationships in our families, work groups, neighbors, and communities? Has this attitude of egotistic self-fulfillment affected our perceptions of right and wrong? If it has, is there hope of repairing this torn fabric in our society? Eisner sees the irony in the American psychological makeup that allows us to have strong religious beliefs while ignoring the fact that "every great religion in the world treats greed as the Mother of All Sins. Jesus, Muhammad, Buddha, the Tao Te Ching—all preached against the wanton desire of more than one requires or deserves."[55] What are we to do?

EDUCATION AND BUSINESS ETHICS

> Education is not merely a means for earning a living or an instrument for the acquisition of wealth. It is an initiation into life of spirit, a training of the human soul in the pursuit of truth and the practice of virtue.
>
> —Vijaya Lakshmi Pandit

An alternative approach to educating future business leaders involves supplementing the traditional methods of teaching Business Ethics. Ethics are mainly taught on a purely cognitive level, with reading assignments, class lectures, group discussions of ethical dilemmas, and "case studies." This approach has been used for several decades in many business programs. Some of the content includes:

- studying business ethics issues, definitions, theories, and frameworks
- identifying and recognizing ethical issues
- understanding the interrelationship of ethics and social responsibility
- relating an ethical controversy in business to moral philosophy
- understanding the impact of significant others, of group influences, and of the corporate culture on an individual's decision making process
- choosing and defending a theory or principle that is used in resolving an ethical dispute or business decision
- examining the consequences of unethical and ethical business decisions[56]

An alternative approach would include behavioral activities that attempt to help the individual student internalize the ethical information presented. Giving students the opportunity to practice good behaviors through various campus, community, industry, or volunteer service settings is one way that virtuous behavior could be internalized and reinforced, helping to cultivate character. Modules to address emotional change should also be considered. This might be accomplished through required "role playing" and/or transactional analysis. The goal would be to achieve both an affective and behavioral transformation in attitude patterns towards ethical behavior.

This suggested alternative for creating change involves an educational process that more comprehensively addresses the attitudes and moral character of graduates who will lead us in the future. As an alternative pedagogy, we would have a holistic approach to teaching business ethics. This holistic approach can be integrated into the Business Ethics course by teaching not only to the mind (cognitively), but also to the body (behavioral), as well as to the heart (affective).

Business programs have clearly proven the positive influence that their pedagogy can have on students. They, in general, graduate a very highly skilled group of individuals who join corporate America as leaders. The very power of their teaching suggests, however, that there is much more that can be done. The following suggestions surfaced at the 2003 meeting of the Academy of Management:

1. Too many business schools do not take ethics training seriously as part of their business curricula. Ethics courses are not perceived as serious or "core" courses, such as finance, accounting, and economics. As a result, the teaching of ethics, corporate social responsibility, and other business-and-society courses have been marginalized.

2. External organizations that do business school rankings, both nationally and regionally, could be of more assistance. Ethics courses and training should be a measured criteria that helps to determine these rankings. Currently, they are largely ignored and have no influence on the rankings.

3. The economic perspective dominates business school curricula. For all the good that economic perspectives do, they nonetheless emphasize a view of the world in dollars, profits, returns on investment, etc. which de-emphasizes other ways in which we might conceptualize the responsibilities and contributions of businesses to society.

In summary, the authors agree with these suggestions to effectively bring change to the business programs throughout the nation to assure the study of business ethics is taken as seriously as other academic core courses. It might be necessary to change the criteria of standards adopted by the accreditation agencies, i.e., the American Assembly of Collegiate Schools of Business, (AACSB) and include Business Ethics courses in the core of various curricula. In addition, the study of ethics should become part of the criteria used in the annual rankings of educational programs, which influences many individual decisions on where to study.

Overall, the importance of business ethics to any organization should be self-evident. It is just good business to have a reputation of ethical integrity among employees as well as customers and the general public. Instilling a greater sense of trust and honesty into our business culture will help to shape and support a corporate culture that will benefit all stakeholders: customers, employees, suppliers, and investors.

Sadly enough, as we have come to find out, when CEOs are bent on self-destruction, no amount of incentives to be good and no threatened punishments will stop their dysfunctional and/or illegal behavior. The cable operating company, Adelphia, is a case in point. The founding family that stood to gain the most from a successful and prosperous company, instead, chose to steal resources from the company coffers and consistently lied about it to their stockholders and board of directors. For change to be lasting, the laws of the land and the supervision by regulators must be buttressed by a healthy and ethical corporate culture. The culture must be buoyed by a set of values that are systematically established and constantly nurtured by corporate leaders, as well as by the society at large.

FINAL THOUGHTS AND ANALYSIS

Despite the contributions of critical thinkers through the ages, most cultures and their associated institutions have had only limited success in achieving truly virtuous societies in which the behavior of individuals conformed with the culture's highest ideals. Various cultural codes have produced significant positive traits, but negative traits, sins, and other undesirable characteristics often appear. Given this time-tested reality, one must consider how a society such as the United States can promote virtuous behavior and simultaneously limit the presence of unavoidable negative traits such as greed, arrogance, dishonesty, and immorality.

Although the role of social institutions such as schools, religious groups, and family are relevant, our economic system puts a particular faith in the power of U.S. business schools to inculcate the "right" values and traits into its graduates, the individuals who will lead our economy in the future. Business schools' main course for addressing this important chore is Business Ethics. Unfortunately, this course has been found, for the most part, to be ineffective. For this reason we suggest several modifications and innovations to increase the efficacy of these courses.

In the larger context, it is ironic if not ridiculous that the general emphasis on ethics and much of the initial push for new ethics courses came from corporate executives in their role as advisors to business schools. As we discovered in our earlier chapters, large numbers of these same individuals were often found to be arrogant, greedy and insensitive to the broader community, if not actually engaged in some form of implicit and/or explicit corruption.

It would appear that business school professors could do a lot more, not only in their teaching but also in their consulting, public speaking, research and writing to speak out against these negative behaviors. Educators must clearly stand up against institutional failures such as those we have seen: the laxity of regulators at the SEC and various self-regulating organizations such as the New York Stock Exchange and public accounting and auditing firms; the laxity and incompetence of responsible Boards of Directors or Boards of Trustees; and outrageous compensation packages for CEOs who performed poorly or were discharged.

When more difficult cases must be appraised or boundaries of acceptable behavior need to be established, academics can provide balanced perspective. Former General Electric CEO Jack Welch's retirement pay package appears deserving of this type of attention. Because he was undoubtedly one of the most effective and valuable corporate CEO's in U.S. history and played the lead role in enhancing GE's market value by tens of billions of dollars, few would question his receiving very large compensation. Nevertheless, when his divorce case resulted in the public disclosure of his huge retirement payments and seemingly endless perquisites, most Americans were aghast. Although Welch agreed to modify his package and lower his total compensation prospectively to quell criticism, it once again highlighted how complacently arrogant and greedy the U.S. management sector had become and that corporate directors remained complicit.

As a society, we must accept the fact that even if our cultural institutions, including business schools, work reasonably well, there will always be individual character defects and "fashionable," or broadly shared, negative traits that threaten to subvert the ethical code. For this reason, great attention must be given to the legal, regulatory, professional, and governance apparatus that oversees our free enterprise economic system to assure that our system continues to produce great wealth and concomitant standards of living.

CHAPTER NINE QUESTIONS:
VIRTUE: MEDICINE FOR BUSINESS ETHICS

1. Discuss the relationship between character and reputation.

2. How did the ancient Greeks define a virtue?

3. List and explain the seven virtues and the seven vices.

4. What can American businesses learn from the sayings of Confucius?

5. Is advertising fundamentally deceptive?

6. Does a market economy promote virtuous behavior?

7. Is greed a basic and necessary condition in a market economy?

10

REFLECTIONS ON CORPORATE SCANDALS

The plethora of problems that surfaced during the corporate scandals of 2000–2003 leads to reflection about causes. Clearly, some systemic breakdowns in our financial system occurred, particularly in relation to: 1) accounting, 2) an array of activities on Wall Street and in the financial marketplace, and 3) regulation. With the benefit of hindsight, it is apropos to consider how well the various responses of government to corporate malfeasance and misdeeds will serve us in the future. Have such responses actually minimized the likelihood that history will one day repeat itself, so that U.S. investors and other stakeholders will not have to experience yet another wave of scandal, greed, and corruption?

A number of corollary questions appear relevant when analyzing the response to the recent financial scandals in the U.S. What role has the media played in the difficult problems we have experienced? Are there better ways to approach executive compensation? Are there any broad social implications of the "great heist" perpetrated by the managerial class of corporate America? In reflecting on all the problems and issues discussed in this book, the six questions examined below capture the most salient issues.

SIX KEY QUESTIONS

1. Why did our financial caretakers fail to use the lessons of history to guard against the bubble and its subsequent burst?

Several observations are relevant here. First, many safeguards existed at the time of the financial scandals of the 2000s. The first of these involved investors. Prior to the financial crises that occurred at this time, the United States had experienced a decade of rapid economic growth in which money flowed very freely and normal accountability and behavioral standards were overlooked. Few were concerned that management might be skimming off the top (ultimately estimated to be $1.679 trillion) or presenting misleading financial statements when the price of stocks were going up routinely—and everyone was making lots of money—even when some of the profits or underlying value that were being created were bogus, if not illegal.

Secondly, because government regulatory authorities were inept at meeting their responsibilities, self-regulation turned out to be an oxymoron. The various professional associations of public accountants, lawyers, bankers, and securities analysts did not have the professional courage or ethical standards to police their members. Indeed, they participated in implementing a variety of questionable schemes. The issue of corrupt financial statements has been addressed, to some extent, with the enactment of the Sarbanes-Oxley Act (SOA). Still, to this day, the problem of regulatory laxity may not be entirely remedied. In particular, the SEC's ultimate responsibility for supervising the various self-regulated stock exchanges and professions (such as public accounting) has yet to be proven.

A third type of safeguard in existence at the time of the recent financial crises concerns Federal Reserve policy. Driven and characterized by record stock market prices, the economic boom of the 1990s was christened the era of the "New Economy" and symbolized by the dot.coms and the development of the Internet and telecommunications powered by fiber optics. In short, the way America did business was revolutionized. As the stock market continued its speculative rise, a pivotal speech by Federal Reserve Chairman Alan Greenspan addressing the speculative bubble garnered much attention. In speaking to the American Enterprise Institute in December 1996, Greenspan uttered the now famous words "irrational exuberance," noting that a sudden plunge in real estate prices had triggered Japan's descent into a broad state of economic paralysis. Pundits knew it was the United States, rather than Japan, to which he was referring.

Greenspan acknowledged that it is hard to know when a speculative market might be due for a sudden contraction and when such a contraction might prove to be a disaster for the economy at large. Greenspan asked, "How do we know when irrational exuberance has unduly inflated asset values? The day after Greenspan's speech, the stock market fell by 2 percent as investors steeled themselves for a possible interest rate increase. However, nothing happened. The Fed did not raise interest rates and the stock market continued setting records with continuous regularity for the next four years. Not until January 2000, when the Dow Jones Industrial Averages reached over 11,600, did the bubble burst.

The minutes of a Federal Open Market Committee meeting around that time revealed that Greenspan had discussed his bubble-related concerns and his arguments for not taking action to address the overvaluation of the stock market.[1] Greenspan knew that bubbles are dangerous because they wreak havoc once they burst. The challenge for Greenspan was to figure how to let the air out of the bubble, that is, to bring stock prices down to the underlying value of their companies without causing a major economic downturn. Raising interest rates would not necessarily be an effective measure, since the effect of doing so would not be limited to the stock market.

In August 2002, in Congressional testimony after the bubble had burst, Greenspan recalled that he had carefully considered how to attack the bubble and rejected action for two reasons. First, he was not sure that the stock market's continuous climb was indeed a bubble, "as it is very difficult to definitively identify a bubble until after the fact, that is, when its bursting confirmed its existence."[2] Second, he did not feel certain that he possessed an effective remedy. Greenspan was probably correct in ruling out interest rate increases as they are not the appropriate instrument for fine-tuning the stock market. However, Greenspan could have raised margin requirements that govern how much stock people can buy with borrowed money. The present requirements, dating back to 1974, dictate that a minimum of fifty percent of any stock purchase must be made with cash, that is, only half can be financed with credit. In all likelihood, a move to create greater limits on margin buys would have dampened the bubble. Because this intervention goes beyond the usual money supply calibration, it would probably have been opposed by Congress, banks, and investors. Nevertheless, this instrument was available. Greenspan argued that changing the requirements on margin buying was not guaranteed to burst the bubble and there was no idea of what collateral damage could result from it. Political caution ruled the day, and no action was taken. In retrospect, it is interesting to note that the most extreme part of the stock market bubble was corrected without any government policy action. What finally caused the air to come out of the bubble of Internet/dot.com stocks was the October 2, 2000 *Barron's* magazine cover story entitled "Smoldering." The article exposed the fact that these companies were rapidly "burning through" their cash and predicted that each would go bankrupt according to a specified time table indicated in the article.[3]

2. To what extent is the free enterprise system broken? How well has it been fixed?

Slowly but surely, the financial crises of the past decade inflicted serious damage to one of our greatest assets: the credibility of our free enterprise system. When the equity markets collapsed in 2000, over $7 trillion of market value and the savings of millions of Americans were wiped out. The recession of 2001 occurred and the bankruptcies of Enron, WorldCom, Kmart, and others occurred in short order. The role of several key components of our economic system—the Federal Reserve, the SEC, the NYSE, and the Financial Accounting Standards Board (FASB)—were all called into question as a result. Public auditors, Boards of Directors, investment and commercial banks, lawyers, mutual funds, security analysts, and floor traders were all found derelict in their responsibilities to various degrees. Above all, the ethics of business reached a historically low level.

As illustrated in chapter two, the economic history of the world is replete with incidents of corporate scandal and malfeasance. In the light of this history, it is reasonable to ask whether present efforts to address systemic breakdown of the free market system will prove to be lasting. Or, will we again experience widespread accounting scandals, laxity in regulation, and greedy, if not immoral, schemes to enrich the managerial class?

One improvement has been a change in corporate governance such that corporate boards are more independent and transparent. Unfortunately, current reforms, by and large, have left the director class basically immune from serious punishment or prosecution for laxity or failure to meet their oversight responsibilities. In the wake of the entire scandal episode of the early 2000s, America's corporate directors ultimately avoided the consequences that should have resulted from their culpability. Making a few blameworthy directors face prosecution probably would have sent a healthy message to the rest of corporate America. Enron's board, for example, could have been held to account for their role in the company's misdeeds.

As stated earlier, the 2002 Sarbanes-Oxley Act sought to ensure that future accounting malfeasance is infrequent. The Public Company Accounting Oversight Board provides yet another important layer of review to assure accounting compliance.

Yet, the SEC remains a wild card. Will its widespread laxity reoccur? Will it continue to delegate its responsibilities to self-regulated stock exchanges, professional standards boards such as FASB, and industry groups such as the Investment Company Institute (ICI), a mutual fund organization, without the follow-through required to ensure that self-policing responsibilities are fulfilled?

At the present time, all of the parties mentioned above are on "good behavior" and are vigilantly watched by the media, Congress, and regulators. The important question is whether this "good behavior" and high vigilance will disappear over time? Much of what has gone wrong is obviously due to serious ethical lapses on the part of a variety of business leaders. One can easily imagine yet another wave of corporate scandals should the historic root causes of such financial misdeeds be allowed to reemerge. The belief of the authors is that "the jury is still out" on the question of the future effectiveness of regulation.

3. New York State Attorney Eliot Spitzer led the reform of Wall Street investment banking as well as mutual fund practices. How enduring will these reforms prove to be?

Upon reflection, the widespread evidence of conflicts of interest, corruption, greed, immorality, and outright illegal behavior on Wall Street is not only shocking but despicable. The wrong doing foisted misery upon investors, many of whom, were simply hard working, "average" Americans whose only mistake was to trust the companies and specific mutual or pension funds in which they were invested, as well as the regulators of our financial marketplace.

This book lauds Eliot Spitzer's work with respect to addressing a myriad of Wall Street's shortcomings. The requirements of the $1.6 billion investment banking settlement he spearheaded seems to guarantee that we will be rid, once and for all, of the outrageous conflicts of interest that existed between investment bankers and security analysts in the same firm. Under the terms of the settlement, analysts are better postured to provide objective research to investors. However, given the strict separation of analysts and investment banking dealmakers and the very low levels of stock trading commissions that now exist, the future salary levels of analysts will be much more modest than they have been in the past. The new, lower pay levels will, most likely, not attract the top talent that they have historically. Accordingly, to the extent analysts are critical to the process of establishing correct stock prices, the efficiency of our capital markets may be impaired.

On the mutual fund front, once again Spitzer led a reform agenda. It is noteworthy that the SEC has joined in most of the specific settlements of suits involving mutual funds. The estimated aggregate amount of the settlements with numerous mutual fund organizations is $2 billion. These settlements have been very comprehensive, addressing the specific wrong doings of various mutual fund groups, such as late trading, market timing, and illegal sales practices. Additionally, Spitzer has negotiated significant reductions in the fees that mutual funds charge investors in several of the agreements.

The reforms brought about by Spitzer have also included significant modifications of mutual fund governance. The complicit mutual fund groups not only fired and replaced all the executives and portfolio managers involved in the scandals, but also established strictly independent compliance officers to monitor potential violations in the future. These officers report directly to the funds' Board of Trustees. These trustees have also attracted Spitzer's attention. In investigating whether they met their fiduciary responsibilities in the various cases of wrongdoing, Spitzer indicated that in the future they can be expected to be reviewed and prosecuted if their duties are not fulfilled.

Looking ahead, it would appear that legal and regulatory responses to the mutual fund industry's widespread corruption have effectively resulted in better internal controls and compliance programs throughout the industry. Certainly mutual fund organizations now have a keen sense of how costly it can be to "stray." In addition, the discovery that the SEC had been lax, if not completely negligent, in its sole responsibility for overseeing the mutual fund industry has provided a "wake-up call" that will hopefully prove enduring.

4. How do media and other cultural influences feed greed?

The advertising industry has become a somewhat nefarious institution. Advertising strongly influences the perceptions and expectations of the general public, creating an unquenchable desire to possess or acquire wealth far beyond what one needs for a comfortable life. The unfortunate result of the relentless reinforcement of material values is that the emphasis on wanting or taking all that one can get de-emphasizes concern for the needs of others. The unethical, illegal and avaricious behaviors of John Rigas and his family members at Adelphia, Kenneth Lay and Andrew Fastow of Enron, and Dennis Kozlowski and Mark Swartz of Tyco, are but a small sample of such avarice gone unchecked.

The United States has developed a consumer-oriented culture wherein the strength of our market economy is based on the creation and promotion of material goods. The desire of human beings to always better their condition was recognized earlier by economist Adam Smith. The "reality show" phenomena that dominates the television airways of the early twenty-first century gives credence to Smith's observation in 1776 that, "the better off men appear, the more likely they are to get the attention, approval, and praise of others." Our society tends to feed the notion that richer is better, and print and visual media are more than happy to bolster our fantasy. Is it any surprise that the star quality of CEOs perpetuates this ideal as well? The success of the television program *The Apprentice,* in which Donald Trump, a billionaire, gives advice on how to become rich and successful exemplifies this point. In the United States, television and print media are replete with images of luxury and opulence. The idea that success equates with the possession of luxurious things is continuously fed into the minds of viewers, many of whom are young business students who will be starting their careers at salaries in the $60,000 to $150,000 range. Although these salaries are substantial, they certainly will not support the type of lifestyle promoted on "The Apprentice." Maybe after years of sacrifice and wise investments such material trappings might become a reality, but with the short-run orientation and attitudes so prevalent among our current generation, it is doubtful that they will always have the strength of character to defer the need for immediate gratification. Sadly, it is likely that the temptation to take short-cuts or engage in unethical actions to achieve their goals will often prevail.

5. Are the current high levels of CEO pay appropriate? How can our management compensation systems be improved?

Several arguments are made to justify excessive CEO compensation. Most are questionable. First, the receipt by CEOs of enormous share options and share grants was supposed to align the interests of chief executives with those of their shareholders and address the agency problem (see chapter seven for a full discussion of this concept). In fact, however, our calculations indicate that management used options to capture about $1.697 trillion of wealth for themselves during the 1990s. We labeled this "the great heist." In reality, stock options not only did not forge an alignment between CEOs and investors, but also actually worked to widen the divergence of the interests they were supposed to correct.

A second assertion used to justify the outrageous remuneration of CEOs is the misleading claim that the payment of chief executives is set by the market. In fact, it is set by remuneration committees usually made up of peer senior executives from other companies. The compensation these committees approve in effect set the standard for their own compensation. In fact, several chief executives entitled to large termination payments sit on the compensation committees of other companies with similar arrangements. This was the case with Richard Grasso of the NYSE. He hand picked his compensation committee from a group of top executives with similar pay packages, and who were, not surprisingly, friendly to the management compensation programs suggested by Grasso.

A third argument used to justify high management pay is that chief executives are a breed apart from the rest of us. Corporations argue that they often have to search for chief executives outside their company and offer large incentives to recruit them. However, research by Jim Collins, author of the best selling book, *From Good to Great*, found that the most successful chief executives were not outsiders enticed aboard by vast contracts. Rather, they were internal appointments, managers who rose through the ranks.

Certainly, chief executives should be paid substantially more than the average employee. They typically work longer hours, bring very high skill sets, and have greater responsibilities. These factors suggest that CEOs should receive substantial salaries irregardless of the multiple of the salary to that of the average worker. Further, to the extent that actual management performance is objectively rated high, performance bonuses and profit sharing should reflect such accomplishment. In this regard, as many workers as possible should participate in bonus pools. The magnitude of salary supplements should be correlated to the actual performance level reached by a management team as a means of correcting the lack of correlation that has so often prevailed in the past—to the rightful dismay of shareholders and other interested observers. Finally, the use of options for executive compensation should be greatly curtailed since they were found to only exacerbate the divergence between the interests of the shareholders and the managers. Options as a compensation tool have contributed to some of the more outrageous pay levels documented in this book.

The establishment of a fair system of remuneration has several advantages over the alternatives described above. First, such a system would make clear that success is a team endeavor. Second, if everyone is to share the benefits of short- and long-term incentives, they must truly be tied to performance; otherwise the company will not be able to afford them. Finally, when chief executives benefit financially, they can say that everyone else has too. If the company suffers, so do they.

In the end, it is unrealistic to expect chief executives to remedy the problem of unwarranted compensation themselves. Nor can any one Board of Directors act alone. If it does, its top executives will be vulnerable to poaching by competitors. In the absence of legislation, chief executives will have to be tamed by investors or some combination of their institutional representatives, the media, and public opinion.

6. Does the shift of wealth to a managerial elite signify a larger social problem?

Our findings in regard to the redistribution of wealth from general stockholders to the management elite are consistent with recent wealth distribution economic data and analysis. Since 1974, the share of pretax income in the United States that goes to families in the top twenty percent of the income distribution has risen steadily while the share going to those in the bottom twenty percent has fallen. Not only has the share of income going to the top twenty percent risen, but also that of the top five percent has increased even more as well. Economists estimate that since the mid-1970s, roughly seven-eights of the aggregate increase in the nation's wealth goes to families in the top five percent of income.[4]

This recent trend stands in contrast to the broader trend evident throughout most of the twentieth century, when incomes in America grew more equal over time as strong gains for those at the top of the income scale came alongside even stronger gains for those in the middle and at the bottom. The widening inequality that had marked much of the nineteenth century was increasingly seen as a historical artifact, attributable to the nation's initial transformation into an industrial economy.

The recent widening of wealth distribution in the U.S. should be cause for great concern. Too much economic inequality can pose serious problems for a democratic society, particularly if the privileged use their economic strength to gain unfair advantage in the political and/or economic arena. Because money buys access, the general negative consequence of the more highly skewed distribution of income that resulted from the "great heist" (documented in chapter seven) exacerbates this unfairness. Our nation's commitment to fair play and democratic processes are imperiled by great inequalities of income. The polarization of society that may result if these trends continue may be ominous.

A CENTRAL VILLAIN?

This book explores what are, perhaps, the largest financial scandals ever experienced by any country, a saga that produced both a hero and many villains. Chapter five hails Eliot Spitzer. Rhetorically, we ask where the U.S. economic system would be if Spitzer had not been "on the beat." The New York State Attorney single-handedly faced and exposed a plethora of corrupt Wall Street practices. After closing a comprehensive financial settlement that included wide-ranging reforms of Wall Street firms, he resurfaced to address a broad set of illegal practices that had become pervasive throughout the U.S. mutual fund industry. Again, he led several settlements with numerous mutual fund organizations which included broad reforms that should serve American investors well in the future.

Although not heroes in the strict sense of the word, the whistle-blowers who significantly assisted in the prosecution of both the corporate and mutual fund scandals deserve honorable mention. These individuals include Sherron Watkins of Enron, Cynthia Cooper of WorldCom, and Noreen Harrington of Canary Capital.

Given the many villains in this story, it is difficult to identify a "central" villain. One can place serious blame in a number of places. Numerous corporate CEOs, for example, qualify as "villains." Ken Lay and Jeff Skilling of Enron, Bernard Ebbers of WorldCom, Dennis Kozlowski of Tyco, and Richard Scrushy of HealthSouth are a few names that immediately come to mind. Wall Street investment banker, Frank Quattrone and security analysts Jack Grubman and Henry Blodgett probably deserve to be on this ignominious list as well. On the mutual fund side, Richard Strong of the Strong Funds must surely be included.

The accounting arena provides another fertile area for identifying villains. The chief accounting officers and chief financial officers at Enron, WorldCom, Tyco, and HealthSouth have all been involved in financial misdeeds. Interestingly, in the case of HealthSouth, all five CFOs since the company's initial public offering admitted to "cooking the books." Despite all these individual candidates for villain status, the largest villain in the accounting arena is undoubtedly a firm—Arthur Andersen LLP. The worldwide accounting company participated in so many individual company scandals and was so corrupt that the government closed Andersen's doors.

The SEC, the NYSE, the NASD, and the ICI each were lax and/or incompetent in meeting their responsibilities as self regulated organizations (SROs). Many individuals working at these entities can be criticized. Probably Richard Grasso, former Chairman and CEO of the NYSE, would be the media's choice for "Villain #1." However, we choose the the SEC. No other entity bears more responsibility for regulation and oversight of our economic and financial system. The SEC is the sole and ultimate authority for the public accounting/auditing sector. All U.S. public reporting is ultimately under SEC purview. Authority over various SROs (NYSE, NASD, and ICI) rests with this regulatory body. Additionally, the SEC has sole responsibility for regulating the mutual fund industry.

A major feature of our system of financial regulation is the delegation of responsibility for appropriate policy setting, conduct, and enforcement to relevant professions (e.g., public accounting) and associations (e.g., NYSE and NASD). In delegating this responsibility, the SEC relies upon these various professions and/or organizations to "police" themselves. In doing so, the SEC as the ultimate authority must ensure that all the responsibilities of the SROs are met. Clearly, the SEC lost sight of this vital duty with respect to the nation's public accounting/auditing profession and stock exchanges.

The tremendous laxity of the SEC in regulating the mutual fund industry is, perhaps, the most appalling evidence of its negligence in meeting its responsibilities. The SEC repeatedly argues that its budget is not remotely adequate to address the huge job it must do as a watchdog for virtually the entire financial/economic marketplace. This justification rings somewhat hollow when one considers that Spitzer did most of the clean-up work with a very small staff and budget. So as we close our story, we proclaim the SEC as the ultimate villain among many in this very painful era of corporate scandal.

CHAPTER 10 QUESTIONS:
REFLECTIONS ON CORPORATE SCANDALS

1. How do you assess Federal Reserve Chairman Alan Greenspan's handling of the handle the stock market bubble?

2. In your view, has the "broken system" been fixed adequately?

3. Does the media bear any responsibility for the breakdown in our free enterprise system?

4. What changes have been made to rectify the various aspects of the mutual fund scandal? Are these sufficient?

5. Are CEOs compensated appropriately? How might their compensation plans be modified?

6. Select three "villains" in the saga of corporate scandals. Provide your reasoning for each villain.

APPENDIX 1

CAUX ROUND TABLE
PRINCIPLES FOR BUSINESS

In a world which is experiencing profound transformations, the Caux Round Table of business leaders from Europe, Japan and the United States is committed to energizing the role of business and industry as a vital force for innovative global change.

The Round Table was founded in 1986 by Frederik Philips, former President of Philips Electronics, and Olivier Giscard d'Estaing, Vice-Chairman of INSEAD, as a means of reducing escalating trade tensions. It is concerned with developing constructive economic and social relationships between the participants' countries, and with charting their urgent, joint responsibilities toward the rest of the world.

At the urging of Ryuzaburo Kaku, Chairman of Canon Inc., the Round Table has focused attention on the importance of global corporate responsibility in reducing social and economic threats to world peace and stability. The Round Table recognizes that shared leadership is indispensable to a revitalized and more harmonious world. It emphasizes the development of continuing friendship, understanding and cooperation, based on a common respect for the highest moral values and on responsible action by individuals in their own spheres of influence.

INTRODUCTION

The Caux Round Table believes that the world business community should play an important role in improving economic and social conditions. As a statement of aspirations, this document aims to express a world standard against which business behavior can be measured. We seek to begin a process that identifies shared values, reconciles differing values, and thereby develops a shared perspective on business behavior acceptable to and honored by all.

These principles are rooted in two basic ethical ideals: kyosei and human dignity. The Japanese concept of kyosei means living and working together for the common good enabling cooperation and mutual prosperity to coexist with healthy and fair competition. "Human dignity" refers to the sacredness or value of each person as an end, not simply as a mean to the fulfillment of others' purposes or even majority prescription.

The General Principles in Section 2 seek to clarify the spirit of kyosei and "human dignity," while the specific Stakeholder Principles in Section 3 are concerned with their practical application.

In its language and form, the document owes a substantial debt to The Minnesota Principles, a statement of business behavior developed by the Minnesota Center for Corporate Responsibility. The Center hosted and chaired the drafting committee, which included Japanese, European, and United States representatives.

Business behavior can affect relationships among nations and the prosperity and well-being of us all. Business is often the first contact between nations and, by the way in which it causes social and economic changes, has a significant impact on the level of fear or confidence felt by people worldwide. Members of the Caux Round Table place their first emphasis on putting one's own house in order and on seeking to establish what is right rather than who is right.

SECTION 1. PREAMBLE

The mobility of employment, capital, products, and technology is making business increasingly global in its transactions and its effects.

Law and market forces are necessary but insufficient guides for conduct.

Responsibility for the policies and actions of business and respect for the dignity and interests of its stakeholders are fundamental.

Shared values, including a commitment to shared prosperity, are as important for a global community as for communities of smaller scale.

For these reasons, and because business can be a powerful agent of positive social change, we offer the following principles as a foundation for dialogue and action by business leaders in search of business responsibility. In so doing, we affirm the necessity for moral values in business decision making. Without them, stable business relationships and a sustainable world community are impossible.

SECTION 2. GENERAL PRINCIPLES

Principle 1.
The Responsibilities Of Businesses: Beyond Shareholders Toward Stakeholders

The value of a business to society is the wealth and employment it creates and the marketable products and services it provides to consumers at a reasonable price commensurate with quality. To create such value, a business must maintain its own economic health and viability, but survival is not a sufficient goal.

Businesses have a role to play in improving the lives of all their customers, employees, and shareholders by sharing with them the wealth they have created. Suppliers and competitors as well should expect businesses to honor their obligations in a spirit of honesty and fairness. As responsible citizens of the local, national, regional and global communities in which they operate, businesses share a part in shaping the future of those communities.

Principle 2.
The Economic and Social Impact of Business: Toward Innovation, Justice, and World Community

Businesses established in foreign countries to develop, produce or sell should also contribute to the social advancement of those countries by creating productive employment and helping to raise the purchasing power of their citizens. Businesses also should contribute to human rights, education, welfare, and vitalization of the countries in which they operate.

Businesses should contribute to economic and social development not only in the countries in which they operate, but also in the world community at large, through effective and prudent use of resources, free and fair competition, and emphasis upon innovation in technology, production methods, marketing, and communications.

Principle 3.
Business Behavior: Beyond the Letter of Law Toward a Spirit of Trust
While accepting the legitimacy of trade secrets, businesses should recognize that sincerity, candor, truthfulness, the keeping of promises, and transparency contribute not only to their own credibility and stability but also to the smoothness and efficiency of business transactions, particularly on the international level.

Principle 4.
Respect for Rules
To avoid trade frictions and to promote freer trade, equal conditions for competition, and fair and equitable treatment for all participants, businesses should respect international and domestic rules. In addition, they should recognize that some behavior, although legal, may still have adverse consequences.

Principle 5.
Support for Multilateral Trade
Businesses should support the multilateral trade systems of the General Agreement on Tariffs and Trade/World Trade Organization and similar international agreements. They should cooperate in efforts to promote the progressive and judicious liberalization of trade and to relax those domestic measures that unreasonably hinder global commerce, while giving due respect to national policy objectives.

Principle 6.
Respect for the Environment
A business should protect and, where possible, improve the environ-

ment, promote sustainable development, and prevent the wasteful use of natural resources.

Principle 7.
Avoidance of Illicit Operations
A business should not participate in or condone bribery, money laundering, or other corrupt practices: indeed, it should seek cooperation with others to eliminate them. It should not trade in arms or other materials used for terrorist activities, drug traffic or other organized crime.

SECTION 3. STAKEHOLDER PRINCIPLES

Customers
We believe in treating all customers with dignity, irrespective of whether they purchase our products and services directly from us or otherwise acquire them in the market. We therefore have a responsibility to:

- provide our customers with the highest quality products and services consistent with their requirements;
- treat our customers fairly in all aspects of our business transactions, including a high level of service and remedies for their dissatisfaction;
- make every effort to ensure that the health and safety of our customers, as well as the quality of their environment, will be sustained or enhanced by our products and services;
- assure respect for human dignity in products offered, marketing, and advertising; and
- respect the integrity of the culture of our customers.

Employees
We believe in the dignity of every employee and in taking employee interests seriously. We therefore have a responsibility to:

- provide jobs and compensation that improve workers' living conditions;

- provide working conditions that respect each employee's health and dignity;
- be honest in communications with employees and open in sharing information, limited only by legal and competitive constraints;
- listen to and, where possible, act on employee suggestions, ideas, requests and complaints;
- engage in good faith negotiations when conflict arises;
- avoid discriminatory practices and guarantee equal treatment and opportunity in areas such as gender, age, race, and religion;
- promote in the business itself the employment of differently abled people in places of work where they can be genuinely useful;
- protect employees from avoidable injury and illness in the workplace;
- encourage and assist employees in developing relevant and transferable skills and knowledge; and
- be sensitive to the serious unemployment problems frequently associated with business decisions, and work with governments, employee groups, other agencies, and each other in addressing these dislocations.

Owners / Investors

We believe in honoring the trust our investors place in us. We therefore have a responsibility to:

- apply professional and diligent management in order to secure a fair and competitive return on our owners' investment;
- disclose relevant information to owners/investors subject to legal requirements and competitive constraints;
- conserve, protect, and increase the owners/investors' assets; and
- respect owners/investors' requests, suggestions, complaints, and formal resolutions.

Suppliers

Our relationship with suppliers and subcontractors must be based on mutual respect. We therefore have a responsibility to:

- seek fairness and truthfulness in all our activities, including pricing, licensing, and rights to sell;
- ensure that our business activities are free from coercion and unnecessary litigation;
- foster long-term stability in the supplier relationship in return for value, quality, competitiveness and reliability;
- share information with suppliers and integrate them into our planning processes;
- pay suppliers on time and in accordance with agreed terms of trade; and
- seek, encourage and prefer suppliers and subcontractors whose employment practices respect human dignity.

Competitors

We believe that fair economic competition is one of the basic requirements for increasing the wealth of nations and ultimately for making possible the just distribution of goods and services. We therefore have a responsibility to:

- foster open markets for trade and investment;
- promote competitive behavior that is socially and environmentally beneficial and demonstrates mutual respect among competitors;
- refrain from either seeking or participating in questionable payments or favors to secure competitive advantages;
- respect both tangible and intellectual property rights; and
- refuse to acquire commercial information by dishonest or unethical means, such as industrial espionage.

Communities

We believe that as global corporate citizens we can contribute to such forces of reform and human rights as are at work in the communities in which we operate. We therefore have a responsibility in those communities to:

- respect human rights and democratic institutions, and promote them wherever practicable;
- recognize government's legitimate obligation to the society at large and support public policies and practices that promote human development through harmonious relations between business and other segments of society;
- collaborate with those forces in the community dedicated to raising standards of health, education, workplace safety and economic well-being;
- promote and stimulate sustainable development and play a leading role in preserving and enhancing the physical environment and conserving the earth's resources;
- support peace, security, diversity, and social integration;
- respect the integrity of local cultures; and
- be a good corporate citizen through charitable donations, educational and cultural contributions, and employee participation in community and civic affairs.

LISTING OF VIRTUES

Accountability: The state of being accountable; being responsible to someone or for some activity.

Altruism: The quality of unselfish concern for the welfare of others.

Benevolence: The disposition to do good and promote a sense of happiness.

Bravery: A quality of spirit that enables one to face danger of pain without showing fear.

Candor: The ability to make judgments free from discrimination or dishonesty.

Caring: Having or displaying warmth or affection towards another.

Charity: To have a kindly and lenient attitude towards the less fortunate and to freely contribute to their welfare.

Chastity: Refraining from unlawful sexual intercourse.

Compassion: Having a deep awareness of and sympathy for another's suffering.

Consideration: Showing concern for the rights and feelings of others.

Courage: That quality of mind which enables one to encounter danger and difficulties with firmness, without fear, or fainting of heart.

Courtesy: An act of civility or respect that is given out of kindness or favor and is performed with politeness; expressed concern for the well-being of others.

Curiosity: A state of wanting to learn more.

Decency: The quality of conforming to standards of propriety and morality.

Dependability: The trait of being reliable, of performing that which is undertaken.

Diligence: The quality of being devoted to a task and taking painstaking effort to accomplish what is undertaken.

Duty: The social force that binds you to your obligations and the courses of action demanded by that force.

Empathy: Having a sense of understanding another person, entering into another's feelings.

Equity: Giving, or desiring to give, to each person their due according to reason. To be fair and impartial in the determination of conflicting claims.

Excellence: The state of possessing good qualities in an eminent degree.

Fairness: Having the ability to make judgments free from prejudice or dishonesty.

Faith: The assent of the mind to the truth of what is declared by another, resting solely on their authority and veracity.

Filial piety: The act of loving one's parents, and showing it through courtesy and reverence.

Forgiveness: The compassionate feelings that support a willingness to forgive and excuse a mistake or offense.

Fortitude: That strength or firmness of mind which enables a person to bear pain or adversity with courage, without murmuring or despondency.

Frugality: The careful management of anything valuable which expends nothing unnecessarily, and applies what is used to a profitable purpose without being extravagant.

Generosity: The trait of being willing to give money or time for the welfare of others.

Good judgment: Having the capacity to assess situations or circumstances shrewdly and to draw sound conclusions.

Good Temper: The quality of resilience that maintains a cheerful and agreeable mood.

Goodness: The quality of moral excellence.

Gratitude: The state of being grateful, of having a warm feeling of thankfulness and appreciation.

Healthy: Fit, being physically and mentally sound.

Honesty: A disposition to be truthful and straight-forward in conduct, thought, speech, etc. The honest person is sincere, free from fraud, guile, and duplicity.

Hope: A desire for some future good, accompanied by an expectation of obtaining it, or a belief that it is obtainable.

Humility: The quality of being free from pride and arrogance; having a modest estimate of one's own worth.

Industry: Habitual diligence in any employment or pursuit, either bodily or mental.

Integrity: A high degree of moral soundness, honesty, and freedom from corrupting influence or motive. This virtue is used especially with reference to the fulfillment of contracts and the discharge of agencies, trusts, and the like.

Justice: Being fair, and conforming to the principles of righteousness and rectitude in all things.

Keeping promises: A declaration, written or verbal, made by one person to another, which binds the person who makes it to do, or to forbear to do, a specified act; a declaration which gives the person to whom it is made a right to expect or to claim the performance or forbearance of a specified act.

Kindness: Warm-heartednees, being considerate, humane, and sympathetic.

Liberality: The trait of being generous in behavior and temperament.

Love: A feeling of strong attachment induced by that which delights or commands admiration, a preeminent kindness towards another.

Loyalty: Feelings of allegiance of being bound intellectually or emotionally to another or to a course of action.

Meekness: A disposition to be patient or submissive; having a calm temper of mind.

Mercy: The inclination to exercise compassion or favor towards an offender or adversary.

Moderation: Taking a middle path, avoiding extremes.

Modesty: The quality of freedom from vanity or conceit; being unwilling to flaunt oneself before others.

Niceness: A courteous or unthreatening manner that respects accepted social usage.

Optimism: The feeling that all is going to turn out well.

Piety: The loving obedience to the will of God, and earnest devotion to spiritual service.

Playfulness: A festive, merry feeling. Having a disposition to find (or make) causes for amusement.

Prudence: The quality exercising due discretion in practical affairs, of showing a reasonable degree of caution.

Public-spiritedness: Having, or exercising, a disposition to advance the interest of the community or public.

Resilience: The ability to rebound from a setback; flexibility and toughness.

Resolution: Firmness in opinion, thought, or endeavor.

Respect: A courteous regard for people's feelings, acknowledgement of the significance of others.

Responsibility: The state of being accountable or answerable, as for a trust, debt, or obligation.

Restraint: The act of holding back any action, physical or mental.

Righteousness: The quality of adhering to upright moral principles.

Self-control: The act of denying yourself by controlling your impulses.

Self-respect: Esteeming oneself as worthy and respectable, and behaving so as to restrain that esteem.

Self-sacrifice: The act of sacrificing one's own interest for that of others.

Sincerity: Honesty of mind or intention; freedom from hypocrisy, disguise, or false pretense.

Temperance: Habitual moderation in regard to the indulgence of the natural appetites and passions.

Tolerance: The endurance of the presence or actions of objectionable persons, or of the expression of offensive opinions.

Transcendence: A state of being above and beyond the limits of material experience.

Trustworthiness: The trait of deserving the confidence of others.

Truthfulness: Consistent reporting of what one knows to be real.

Uprightness: Moral rectitude, a consequence of being honorable and honest.

Wisdom: The trait of being able to apply knowledge and experience with common sense and insight.

ENDNOTES

CHAPTER 1: CORPORATE SCANDALS

1. "Corporate America's Woes, continued," *The Economist*, 30 November 2002, 59-61.

2. Amartya Sen, *Development As Freedom* (New York: Anchor Books, 1999), 264.

3. *Merriam Webster's Collegiate Dictionary,* 10th Edition (Springfield, MA: Merriam-Webster, 1993).

4. Norman E. Bowie, "Companies are Discovering the Value of Ethics," *USA Today Magazine*, January 1998, 22-24.

5. John Plender, "What Price Virtue?" *Financial Times*, 2 December 2002, 21.

6. Max Bazerman, George Loewenstein, and Don Moore, "Why Good Accountants Do Bad Audits" *Harvard Business Review,* 80, No. 11 (November 2002), 102.

7. Ibid., 102.

8. T. A. Kochan, "Addressing the Crisis in Confidence in Corporations: Root Causes, Victims, & Strategies for Reform," Papers presented at the special presidential panel, *Academy of Management Meeting,* August 2002.

9. Michael Useem, *Investor Capitalism* (New York: Basic Books, 1996), 40.

10. Rakesh Khurana, *Searching for a Corporate Savior: The Irrational Quest for Charismatic CEOs* (Princeton: Princeton University Press, 2003), 45.

11. John Plender, op. cit., 13.

12. Joshua Ronen, "Post Enron Reform: Financial Statement Insurance and GAAP Revisited," *Stanford Journal of Law, Business, and Finance,* 39, 2002.

CHAPTER 2: A SHORT HISTORY OF BUSINESS SCANDALS

1. John Carswell, *The South Sea Bubble* (London: Cresset Publishers, 1960), 13.

2. Bray Hammond, *Banks and Politics in America from The Revolution to the Civil War* (Princeton: Princeton University Press, 1957), 268.

3. Charles Kindleberger, *Manias, Panics and Crashes: A History of Financial Crisis,* 4th ed. (New York: John J. Wiley and Sons, 2000), 16.

4. Edward Chancellor, *Devil Take the Hindmost: A History of Financial Specula-*

tion (London: Farrar, Straus & Giroux Publishers, 1999), 268.

5. Antoine E. Murphy, *John Law: Economic Theorist and Policy-Maker* (Oxford: Oxford University Press, 1997), 10.

6. John Micklethwait and Adrian Wooldridge, *The Company: A Simple History of a Revolutionary Idea* (New York: Random House, 2003), 28.

7. Niall Ferguson, *The Cash Nexus: Money and Power in the Modern World.* (New York: Basic Books, 2001), 313.

8. Early Hamilton, "The Political Economy of France at the Time of John Law," *History of Political Economy,* 1, no. 1 (Spring, 1969), 146.

9. Charles Franklin, *They Walked A Crooked Mile: An Account of the Greatest Scandals, Swindlers, and Outrages of All Time* (New York: Hart, 1969), 168.

10. John Baskin and Paul J. Miranti, *A History of Corporate Finance* (Cambridge: Cambridge University Press, 1997), 105.

11. Ibid., 176.

12. Larry Neal, *The Rise of Financial Capitalism: International Capital Markets in the Age of Reason* (Cambridge: Cambridge University Press, 1990), 98.

13. Ibid., 78.

14. Charles Kindleberger, op. cit., 134-35.

15. H. G. Lewin, *The Railway Mania and its Aftermath, 1845-1852* (New York: August M. Melley Publishers, 1968), 262, 357-64.

16. Brian Bailey, *George Hudson: The Rise and Fall of the Railway King* (Stroud, England: Alan Sutton, 1995), 139.

17. Edward Chancellor, op. cit., 184.

18. Charles Franklin, *They Walked A Crooked Mile: An Account of the Greatest Scandals, Swindlers, and Outrages of All Time* (NY: Hart, 1969), 25.

19. Ibid., 30.

20. John Baskin and Paul Miranti, *A History of Corporate Finance,* op. cit, 200.

21. Edward Chancellor, op. cit., 198.

22. *Time* magazine cover, 28 October 1929.

23. Forrest McDonald, *The Definitive Biography of Samuel Insull* (Chicago: University of Chicago Press, 1962), 12.

24. Ibid., 278.

25. Charles Kindleberger, op. cit., 85.

26. Maury Klein, *Rainbow's End: The Crash of 1929* (Oxford: Oxford University Press, 2001), 241.

27. Edward Chancellor, op. cit., 200.

28. Robert Sobel, *The Great Bull Market: Wall Street in the 1920s* (New York: W.W. Norton & Company, 1968), 134.

29. John Baskin and Paul Miranti, op. cit., 204.

30. Harold Ickes, *The Secret Diary of Harold Ickes: The First Thousand Days, 1933-1936* (New York: Simon and Schuster, 1954), 173.

31. Matthew Josephson, *Infidel in the Temple: A Memoir of the 1930s* (New York: Knopf, 1967), 307.

32. Timothy Curry and Lynn Shibut, "The Cost of the Savings and Loan Crisis: Truth and Consequences," (*FDIC Banking Review*, Vol. 13, No. 2, Dec. 2000).

33. John Micklethwait and Adrian Wooldridge, op. cit., 141.

34. Niall Ferguson, op. cit., 311-312.

35. Edward Chancellor, op. cit., 69.

36. Adam Smith, *An Inquiry into the Nature and Causes of the Wealth of Nations*, ed, Edwin Cannan (New York: Random House, 1994), Book I, Chapter XI, 287-288.

CHAPTER 3: CORPORATE MALFEASANCE: FRAUD, THEFT, AND REGULATORY LAXITY

1. "Former Enron Chief Financial Officer Andrew S. Fastow Charged With Fraud, Money Laundering, Conspiracy," *United States Department of Justice Press Release,* 2 October 2002.

2. Ibid.

3. "Enron Justice," *Review & Outlook, The Wall Street Journal,* 15 January 2004, A14.

4. Elizabeth MacDonald, "Tyco's Goodwill Games," Forbes.com [Article on-line]; available from http://www.forbes.com/2002/06/13/0613tycaccount.html; Internet; accessed 13 June 2002.

5. "Tyco to cut costs by $3 billion in next 3 years," *Reuters*, 29 December 2003.

6. "There's No Magic in Mergers," [Businessweek on-line]; available from http://www.businessweek.com/magazine/content/02_41/b3803160.htm; Internet; accessed 14 October 2002.

7. Elizabeth MacDonald, op. cit.

8. "Tyco Fraud," [Securities Fraud FYI on-line]; available from http://www.securitiesfraudfyi.com/tyco.html; Internet; accessed 14 October 2002.

9. Ibid.

10. Ibid.

11. "SEC Sues Former Tyco Director…," *SEC Government News 2002-177,* 17 December 2002.

12. "Healthsouth Timeline," [Article on-line]; available from http://www.nbc13.com/news/2101600/detail.html; Internet; accessed 17 April 2004.

13. "Global Crossing Accounts Probed," BBC News Co. United Kingdom [Article on-line]; available from http://news.bbc.co.uk/1/hi/business/1801871.stm; Internet; accessed 22 February 2004.

14. "Gary Winick Should Go To Jail," *The New York Observer*, 1 April 2002, 4.

15. "Watchdog probes Qwest Accounts," BBC News Co. United Kingdom [Article on-line]; available from http://news.bbc.co.uk/1/hi/business/1867238.stm; Internet; accessed 11 March 2003.

16. "Cable flop sues former Auditor," BBC News Co. United Kingdom [Article on-line]; available from http://news.bbc.co.uk/1/hi/business/2415145.stm; Internet; accessed 7 November 2003.

17. "Adelphia Execs Arrested for Fraud," BBC News Co. United Kingdom [Article on-line]; available from http://news.bbc.co.uk/1/hi/business/2149956.stm; Internet; accessed 24 July 2003.

18. "ImClone Founder Jailed," BBC News Co. United Kingdom [Article on-line]; available from http://news.bbc.co.uk/1/hi/business/2979672.stm; Internet accessed 10 June 2003.

19. Ibid.

20. "Martha Stewart Sued by Investor," BBC News Co. United Kingdom [Article on-line]; available from http://news.bbc.co.uk/1/hi/business/2210598.stm; Internet; accessed 22 August 2003.

21. "Stewart Resigns as Company head," BBC News Co. United Kingdom [Article on-line]; available from http://news.bbc.co.uk/1/hi/business/2964478.stm; Internet; accessed 5 June 2003.

22. "Unsure of Shell," *Financial Times*, 23 January 2004, 15.

23. "A Damning Verdict," *Economist Global Agenda*, 25 August 2004, 2.

24. *Financial Times*, "Ahold: The Fall-out," 25 February 2003, 16.

25. Peter S. Goodman, "7 More Executives Arrested in Parmalat Probe," *Washington Post Foreign Service*, 1 January 2004, E01.

26. Jack Grone "Financial Scandals Test Regulators European Authorities Are Under Pressure to Show They Are Up to the Tasks" *DOW Jones Newswires*, 20 January 2004.

27. Ibid.

28. "UK Strives to Avoid Enron-Style Scandals," BBC News Co. United Kingdom [Article on-line]; available from http://news.bbc.co.uk/1/hi/business/2096445.stm; Internet; accessed 5 July 2002.

29. Ibid.

30. Ibid.

CHAPTER 4: ADDRESSING CORPORATE SCANDALS: THE SARBANES-OXLEY ACT AS A PANACEA?

1. Public Company Accounting Oversight Board," [Homepage on-line]; available from http://www.pcaobus.org; Internet; accessed 21 January 2004.

2."Sarbanes-Oxley Act of 2002, "Perkins Coi Law Firm [Library on-line]; available from http://www.thecorporatelibrary.com/special/practices/; Internet; accessed 21 January 2004.

3. Ibid.

4. Ibid.

5. Ibid.

6. Ibid.

7. Joann S. Lublin. "Companies Seek To Recover Pay from Ex-CEOs," *Wall Street Journal,* 7 January 2004, B1.

8. "Healthsouth Timeline," [Article on-line]; available from http://www.nbc13.com/news/2101600/detail.html; Internet; accessed 17 April 2004.

9. Tom Bassing, "Five ex-HealthSouth executives sentenced," *Birmingham Business Journal,* 12 December 2003, 15.

10. John Goff, "So Who Was Arthur Andersen Anyway?" CFO.com [Article on-line]; available from http://www.cfo.com/article/1,5309,7639,00.html; Internet; accessed 13 March 2004.

11. Ibid.

12. Ibid.

13. David Brancaccio, *Marketplace* News: Wednesday 29 May 2002.

14. "Derivative Instrument," Risk Glossary.com [Glossary on-line]; Available from http://www.riskglossary.com/articles/derivative_instrument.htm; Internet; accessed 21 January 2004.

15. "Freddie Mac Scandal Deepens" *The Banker,* 3 November 2003, 12.

CHAPTER 5: SCANDAL SPREADS TO WALL STREET

1. "Pitt the Gamekeeper," *The Economist,* 14 February 2002, 69.

2. David Schepp, "Bush delivers too little too late," BBC News Co. United Kingdom [Article on-line]; available from http://news.bbc.co.uk/1/hi/business/2118700.stm; Internet; accessed 9 July 2002.

3. "US Financial Regulator Resigns," BBC News Co. United Kingdom [Article on-line] available from http://news.bbc.co.uk/1/hi/business/2408157.stm; Internet; accessed 6 November 2003.

4. David Schepp, op. cit.

5. Ibid.

6. Ibid.

7. Ibid.

8. SRI Media News Corporate Governance, Joint Press Release, SEC, NYSE, NASD and New York Attorney General, 28 April 2003.

9. "SEC, NYSE, NASD and Elliot Spitzer settle with U.S. Investment Banks," *SRI Media,* 28 April 2003.

10. Ibid.

11. Ibid.

12. "Blodget Pays Out $4m and Gets Life Ban," *Financial Times,* 29 April 2003, 21.

13. "Grubman The Poster Child for Conflict of Interest," *Financial Times,* 29 April 2003, 21.

14. "SEC Details "Quattrone's Influence," *Financial Times,* 29 April 2003, 21.

15. "The Grasso Resignation," *Financial Times,* 19 September 2003, 20.

16. "140M Payday For Big Board Chief," CBSNews.com [Article on-line]; available from http://news.codewind.com/go,10997; Internet; accessed 28 August 2003.

17. Ibid.

18. Ibid.

19. Ibid.

20. Ben White and Brooke Masters, "Exchange Looks for New Leader," *Washington Post,* 19 September 2003, E01.

21. Ben White, "Pension Fund Officials Seek NYSE Split: Group Wants Business Regulation Separated," *Washington Post,* 25 September 2003, E01.

22. Ibid.

23. Ibid.

24. Allan Sloan, "Grasso's Gone, but Plenty of Corporate and Political Excesses Remain," *Washington Post,* 23 September 2003, E03.

25. Ben White, "Grasso Backer to Quit NYSE's Board," *Washington Post,* 26 September 2003, E01.

26. Ben White, "New NYSE Head Plans Changes," *Washington Post,* 27 September 2003, E03.

27. Ben White, "NYSE's Interim Chief A Master of Analysis," *Washington Post,* 14 October 2003, E01 .

28. *The Economist,* "A Bleak Future," 28 February 2004, 71.

29. Ibid.

30. Ben White & Kathleen Day, "NYSE to Fine Five Floor-Trading Firms," *Washington Post,* 16 October 2003, E01.

Chapter 6: Mutual Funds scandals: More than a Few Bad Apples

1. Christine Dugas, "Spotlight Hits Whistle-Blower," USAToday.com [Article on-line]; available from http://www.usatoday.com/money/perfi/funds/2003-12-09-whistleblow_x.htm; Internet; accessed 10 December 2003.

2. Ibid.

3. Ibid.

4. Ibid.

5. Peter Elkind, "The Untold Tale of the Great Mutual Fund Rip-off," *Fortune,* 19 April 2004, 106.

6. Paul Nowell, "Bank of America confirms three executives fired," *The Atlanta Journal-Constitution,* 12 September 2003.

7. "Spitzer, S.E.C. Reach Largest Mutual Fund Settlement Ever," *Press Releases, Office of New York State Attorney General Eliot Spitzer*, 15 March 2004.

8. Christopher Oster and Carrick Mollenkamp, "Mutual-fund Indictment Against Broker Reveals Startling Phone Dialogue," *Wall Street Journal,* 6 April 2004, C1.

9. Jayne O'Donnell, "The guy who blew the whistle on Putnman," USAToday.com [Article on-line]; available from http://www.yourlawyer.com/practice/news.htm?story_id=7077&topic=Putnam%20Mutual%20Funds; Internet; accessed 20 November 2003.

10. John Hechinger, "Putnam to Pay $110 Million in Settlement," *Wall Street Journal,* 9 April 2004, C1.

11. Ian McDonald, "Putnam board chief targets the gaps that lead to timing," *Wall Street Journal,* 13 January 2004, C1.

12. "Putnam Settles with SEC," CNN Money [Article on-line]; available from http://money.cnn.com/2003/11/13/funds/fundsfire_putnam/index.htm; Internet; accessed 13 November 2003.

13. Robin Sidel and Tom Lauricella, "Funds Allure Survives," *Wall Street Journal,* 9 January 2004, C3. Also, Kathleen Gallagher, "Word on Strong may Come Next Month," *Milwaukee Journal Sentinel,* 21 January 2004,

14. Karen Damato, "Strong's Fund Sale Faces a Hurdle," *Wall Street Journal,* 28 January 2004, D11.

15. Jonathan R. Laing, "Mercurial Man," *Barron's,* 26 January 2004, 27.

16. Ibid.

17. Ibid.

18. Ibid.

19. Ian McDonald, "Janus Executive Quits Amid Probe: Investigators Say

Garland Approved Rapid Trading of Mutual-Fund Shares," *Wall Street Journal,* 18 November 2003, D9.

20. Ibid.

21. Ibid.

22. Christopher Oster, "Janus To Repay Fund Shareholders," *Wall Street Journal,* 22 December 2003, C13.

23. Ibid.

24. Ibid.

25. Ibid.

26. Ibid.

27. Ibid.

28. "MFS Settles Market-timing Issues." Office of New York State Attorney General, Press release, 5 February 2004.

29. Ibid.

30. Phil McCarty, "MFS Settlement Funds To Be Returned To Shareholders: CNBC," *Dow Jones Newswire,* 5 February 2004.

31. Judith Burns, "MFS Deal Cracks Down On Company, Two Top Executives," *Dow Jones Newswires,* 5 February 2004.

32. Phil McCarty, op. cit.

33. Judith Burns, op. cit.

34. Ibid.

35. Tom Lauricella and John Hechinger, "Alliance Settles Charges, MFS in Talks," *Wall Street Journal,* 19 December 2003, C1.

36. Gregory Zucherman and Randall Smith, "Bear Shakes Up Its Clearing House," *Wall Street Journal,* 1 April 2004, C1.

37. Matthew Goldstein, "Back-Office Figure Emerges in Bear Stearns Investigation," TheStreeet.com [Article on-line]; available from http://www.thestreet.com/_yahoo/markets/matthergoldstein/10158333.html; Internet; accessed 5 May 2004.

38. Matt Andrejczak, "Franklin Talks to Settle SEC Charges," CBSMarketwatch.com [Article on-line]; available from http://www.1800lawinfo.com/practice/news.htm?story_id=7578&topic=mutual1%20funds%20fraud; Internet; accessed 9 February 2004.

39. John Shipman, "Federated to Compensate Investors," *Wall Street Journal,* 4 February 2004, D9.

40. Matt Leitch, "Take A Perp Walk With Me: A Scandalous Score Card," Registered Rep., 1 January 2004.

41. John Shipman, "Schwab's Role in Mutual-Fund Probe Adds new Dimension," *Wall Street Journal,* 14 November 2003, C1.

42. Matthew Goldstein, "Three Merrill Brokers Fired in Hedge Fund Scandal," TheStreet.com [Article on-line]; available from http://www.thestreet.com/_yahoo/markets/matthewgoldstein/10117370.html; Internet; accessed 3 October 2003.

43. Matthew Goldstein, "A.G. Edwards Fired Brokers Over Fund Practices," TheStreet.com [Article on-line]; available from http://www.thestreet.com/_tscana/markets/marketfeatures/10132167.html; Internet; accessed 15 December 2003.

44. "Statement by State Attorney General Eliot Spitzer Regarding Mutual Fund Fee Reduction," Office of New York Attorney General Eliot Spitzer, Press Release, 18 December 2003.

45. "Spitzer Slams Putnam Settlement," Money.CNN.com [Article on-line]; available from http://money.cnn.com/2003/11/17/funds/spitzer_oped/; Internet; accessed 17 November 2003.

46. Ibid.

47. Ibid.

48. Marcy Gordon, "SEC Pushing for Dramatic Reforms for Mutual Funds," *Tallahassee Democrat,* 12 February 2004, E1.

49. Ruth Simon, "Why Your Broker Is Pushing That Fund," *The Wall Street Journal,* 14 January 2004, D1.

50. Laura Johannes and John Hechinger, *Wall Street Journal,* 31 March 2004, C1.

51. Ibid

52. Ibid.

53. Tom Lauricella and John Hechinger, "SEC's Agreement with MFS Puts Mutual Funds on Notice," *Wall Street Journal,* 1 April 2004, C1.

54. Ibid.

55. George Anders, "As Scandals Mount, Fund Boards Feel the Heat," *Wall Street Journal,* 17 March 2004, A1.

56. John Hechinger, "Fidelity's Johnson Seeks to Keep Both His Jobs, *Wall Street Journal,* 17 March 2004, C1.

57. Ann Davis, "Fidelity Wants Trading Costs Broken Down, *Wall Street Journal,* 15 March 2004, C1.

58. Ann David, "Soft Punch: Dreyfus Says A Mutual- Fund Reform Would Give Investors Less," *Wall Street Journal,* 26 January 2004, C1.

59. John Hechinger, "MFS Ends Soft Dollar Payments on Concerns Over Ethics," *Wall Street Journal,* 16 March 2004, C1.

60. Theo Francis, "How Variable Annuities Can Gnash Investors," *Wall Street Journal,* 5 February 2004, D1.

61. John Hechinger, "Deciphering Funds' Hidden Costs," *Wall Street Journal,* 17 March 2004, C1

62. Theo Francis, op.cit., D7.

63. Yuka Hayashi, "Tainted Funds Hurt by Withdrawals," *Wall Street Journal,* 1 April 2004, D7.

64. Ian MacDonald, "Mutual Fund Regulation Primer: The SEC's Flurry of New Rules," *Wall Street Journal,* 14 April 2004, C1.

CHAPTER 7: EXECUTIVE PERVERSION OF FINANCIAL MANAGEMENT

1. Peter Drucker. "The New Meaning of Corporate Social Responsibility," *California Management Review,* 26. (Winter, 1984): 53-63. Also, Michael Jensen, "Corporate Control and the Politics of Finance," *Journal of Applied Corporate Finance,* 4, no. 2 (1991): 13-33.

2. Adolf A. Berle and Gardiner C. Means, *The Modern Corporation and Private Property* (New York: Transaction Publishers, 1932, reprinted 1991), 45.

3. M. Eisenhardt. "Agency Theory: An Assessment and Review," *Academy of Management Review,* 14, no. 1 (1989), 57-74.

4. John Micklethait and A. Wooldridge, *The Company: A Short History of a Revolutionary Idea* (Modern Library, A Division of Random House Publishers, 2003), 113.

5. Adolf A. Berle and Gardiner C. Means, op. cit.

6. Michael C. Jensen and William H. Meckling, "Theory of the Firm: Managerial Behavior, Agency Costs, and Ownership Structure," *The Journal of Financial Economics,* 3, no. 4 (October 1976), 305-360.

7. Bryan Burrough and John Helyar, *Barbarians At The Gate* (Harper Business, New York, NY, 1990.)

8. Michael C. Jensen and William H. Meckling, "Theory of the Firm: Managerial Behavior, Agency Costs, and Ownership Structure," *The Journal of Financial Economics,* 3, no. 4 (October 1976), 352-353

9. The student of finance should quickly note that reduced shares outstanding and concomitant higher EPS resulting from stock buybacks do not automatically result in higher stock prices. Buybacks often weaken balance sheets by draining liquidity and increasing leverage. This tends to lower P/E's and, thus, stock prices.

CHAPTER 8: MARKET SYSTEM AND SOCIAL INSTITUTIONS CALLED INTO QUESTION

1. Thomas Hobbes, *Leviathan* (New York: Collier Books Edition, 1962 [1652]), 100.

2. Robert Axelrod, *The Evolution of Cooperation* (Basic Books, New York, 1984) 180.

3. Douglass C. North, *Institutions, Institutional Change and Economic Performance* (Cambridge University Press, Cambridge, 1990), 3.

4. Jack Knight. *Institutions and Social Conflict.* (Cambridge University Press, Cambridge, 1992), 2.

5. Ibid., 4.

6. Paul Milgrom, Douglas North and Barry Weingast. "The Role of Institutions in the Revival of Trade: The Law Merchant, Private Judges, and the Campagne Fairs," *Economics and Politics* Vol. 2, No. 1, March 1990, 1—23.

7. Adam Smith, *An Inquiry into the Nature and Causes of the Wealth of Nations*, ed, Edwin Cannan. (Random House Inc., 1994), Book I, Chapter IV, page 1. Cited hereafter as WN I.iv.i, 24.

8. Ibid., WN I.x.c., 146.

9. Adam Smith, *Theory of Moral Sentiments,* ed. A.L. Macfie and D.D. Raphael (The Glasgow Edition of the Works of Adam Smith, Oxford University Press, 1976; rep. Indianapolis, Ind., 1982) VI.iii.13, 212-7.

10. Adam Smith, op. cit., WN V.i., 840.

11. John Wallis and Douglass North, "Measuring the Transaction sector in the American Economy, 1870-1970." In S.L. Engerman and R.E. Gallman (eds.), *Long-Term Factors in American Economic Growth*, University of Chicago Press, Chicago, 1986).

12. Yoram Barzel, *Economic Analysis of Property Rights (*Cambridge University Press, Cambridge, 1989), 12.

13. Douglass C. North, op. cit., 33.

14. Jerry Muller. *The Mind and The Market* (Anchor Books, A Division of Random House, 2002), 162.

15. Joseph Schumpeter, *Capitalism, Socialism, and Democracy.* (Harper Perennial, New York, 1975 [1942]), 157.

16. Georg F. Hegel. *Elements of the Philosophy of Right.* Trans. H.B. Nesbit, ed. Allen Wood. (Cambridge University Press, 1991), 162.

17. Ibid., 163.

18. Ibid., 159.

19. Ibid., 163.

20. Ibid., 169-170.

21. Shlomo Avineri. *Hegel's Theory of the Modern State.* (Cambridge University Press, 1972), Chapters 9 and 10.

22. Georg F. Hegel. *Elements of the Philosophy of Right.* op. cit., 302.

23. Ibid., 258.

24. Max Weber, *The Theory of Social and Economic Organization*, ed. Talcott Parsons (The Free Press, 1947), 156.

25. Ibid., 617-27.

26. Douglass C. North, op. cit., 63.

27. Michael Jensen and Kevin Murphy, "CEO Incentives—Its Not How Much you Pay, But How," (*Harvard Business Review*, May-June, 1990), 143.

28. George Baker, Michael Jensen and Kevin Murphy, "Compensation and Incentives: Practice vs. Theory (*Journal of Finance*, 43, 1988), 609.

29. Michael Jensen, "Agency Cost of Free Cash Flow, Corporate Finance, and Takeovers" (*AEA Papers and Proceedings*, 76:323-9), 323.

30. Ibid., 323.

31. Michael Skapinker, "CEO: Greedy Liar with Personality Disorder," (*The Financial Times*, 2 July 2003), 8.

32. Paul Hodgson, "Golden Parachutes and Cushion Landings: Termination Payments and Policy in the S&P 500." (*The Corporate Library*, Portland, ME Feb. 2003), 3.

CHAPTER 9: VIRTUOUSNESS: MEDICINE FOR BUSINESS ETHICS

1. Nansook Park and Christopher M. Peterson, "Virtues and Organizations," in Kim S. Cameron, Jane E. Dutton, and Robert E. Quinn, eds., *Positive Organizational Scholarship: Foundations of a New Discipline* (San Francisco: Berrett-Koehler Publishers, Inc. 2003), 33

2. S. J. Breckler, "Empirical Validation of Affect, Behavior, and Cognition as Distinct Components of Attitude," *Journal of Personality and Social Psychology*, May 1984, 1191-1205.

3. The Internet Encyclopedia of Philosophy, "Virtue Theory," *http://www.utm.edu/research/iep/v/virtue,htm* (accessed 5 October 2003).

4. See appendix for a glossary of virtues with their definitions.

5. Ibid., The Internet Encyclopedia of Philosophy.

6. Eamon Butler, Director of the Adam Smith Institute (London), Preface to The Theory of the Moral Sentiments by Adam Smith, [book on-line]; available from http://www.adamsmith.org/smith/tms-intro.htm; Internet; accessed 25 January 2004.

7. Adam Smith, *The Theory of Moral Sentiments*, ed, A.L. Macfie and D.D. Raphael (The Glasgow Edition of the Works of Adam Smith, Oxford University Press, 1976; rep. Indianapolis, Ind., 1982). VI.iii.13, 242.

8. Ibid. 50.

9. Ibid. 63.

10. Ibid. 62.

11. Fred Luthans and Bruce Avolio, "Authentic Leadership Development," in Kim S. Cameron, Jane E. Dutton, and Robert E. Quinn, eds., *Positive Organizational Scholarship: Foundations of a New Discipline* (San Francisco: Berrett-Koehler Publishers, Inc., 2003), 243.

12. Georg F. Hegel. *Elements of the Philosophy of Right*, trans. H.B. Nesbit, ed. Allen Wood (Cambridge University Press, 1991), 150.

13. Ibid., 132.

14. Ian Maitland, "Virtuous Markets: The Market as School of the Virtues," *Business Ethics Quarterly*, January 1997, 97.

15. Ibid., 192.

16. *The Internet Encyclopedia of Philosophy*, op. cit., "Virtue Theory."

17. Dagobert Runes, ed. "Confucius," *Treasury of Philosophy* (New York: Philosophical Library, 1955), 272.

18. Ibid. 273.

19. Thomas Cleary, trans., *The Essential Confucius: The Heart of Confucius' Teachings in Authentic I Ching Order, A compendium of Ethical Wisdom* (Edison: Castle Books, 1998), 1.

20. Simon Leys (aka Pierre Ryckmans), translator of *The Analects of Confucius* (New York: W. W. Norton & Co., 1997), xvi-xvii.

21. T. R. Reid, *Confucius Lives Next Door* (New York: Random House, 1999), 99.

22. Li-Fu Chen, *Why Confucius Has Been Reverenced As The Model Teacher of All Ages* (New York: St. Johns University Press, 1976), 21

23. Benjamin I. Schwartz, *The World of Thought in Ancient China* (Boston: The Belknap Press of Harvard University Press, 1985), 259, 262.

24. Ibid., 2.

25. Arthashastra Kautilya, *The Arthashastre Kautilya*, trans. R. Kangle (Bombay: University of Bombay, 1972), 86-88.

26. Nansook Park and Christopher M. Peterson, op. cit., 40.

27. Calvin M. Boardman and Hideaki Kiyoshi Kato, "The Confucian Roots of Business Kyosei," *Journal of Business Ethics* 48 (2003) : 318.

28. Caux Round Table, "Principles for Business," [homepage on-line] ; available from http://www.cauxroundtable.org/principles.html, ; Internet ; accessed 3 April 2004.

29. Li-Fu Chen, op. cit., 21.

30. Fung Yu-Lan, *A History of Chinese Philosophy*, Vol. I (Princeton: Princeton University Press, 1952), 362.

31. Schwartz, op. cit., 259.

32. Tsai Chih Chung, *Confucius Speaks* (New York: Anchor Books, 1996), 15.

33. Huang Quanyu, Joseph Leonard, and Chen Tong, *Business Decision Making in China* (New York: International Business Press, 1997), 133.

34. Liu Wu-Chi, *Confucius, His Life and Time* (New York: Philosophical Library, 1955), 151.

35. Chen Jingpan, *Confucius as a Teacher* (Beijing: Foreign Languages Press, 1990), 183.

36. Calvin M. Boardman and Hideaki Kiyoshi Kato, op. cit., 318.

37. Adam Smith, *The Theory of Moral Sentiments*, op. cit., 162.

38. Hui-nan Tzu, *The Sociology of Corruption,* trans. Syed Hussein Alatas, Singapore: Times Books, 1980, 117.

39. O. C. Ferrell, John Fraedrich, and Linda Ferrell, *Business Ethics: Ethical Decision Making and Cases*, 5th edition (Boston: Houghton Mifflin Company, 2002), 57.

40. *Webster's Third International Dictionary of the English Language Unabridged,* s.v. "Character."

41. Gail Sheehy, *Character: America's search for Leadership* (New York: Bantam Books, 1990), 311.

42. *Webster's Third International Dictionary*, op. cit., s.v. "Virtue."

43. Leonard Pitts, "Your kid's going to pay for cheating—eventually," *Tallahassee Democrat*, 24 June 2002, 7A.

44. Stephen R. Covey, "Why Character Counts," *Reader's Digest*, January 1999, 133.

45. Christina Sommers and Fred Sommers, *Vice & Virtue in Everyday Life: Introductory Readings in Ethics,* Fourth Edition (Fort Worth: Harcourt Brace College Publishers, 1997), 577.

46. Nansook Park and Christopher M. Peterson, op. cit., Table 3.1: VIA Classification of Character Strengths, 35-36.

47. John Maynard Keynes, "Essays in Persuasion," in *The Great Thoughts,* ed. George Seldes (New York: Ballantine Books, 1985), 26

48. John Dalla Costa, *The Ethical Imperative: Why Moral Leadership Is Good Business* (Reading, PA: Perseus Publishing, 1998), 37.

49. Jane Eisner, "What's behind our high tolerance for the sin of greed?" *Tallahassee Democrat*, 31 July 2002, 9A.

50. Bruce Horovitz, "Scandals grow out of CEOs' warped mind-set," *USA*

TODAY, 11 October 2002, 2B.

51. Richard Paul and Linda Elder, *The Miniature Guide to Understanding the Foundations of Ethical Reasoning* (Dillon Beach, CA: Foundation for Critical Thinking, 2003), 36.

52. Second Exodus, "Catholic Definitions: Capital Virtue," [definitions online]; available from http://www.secondexodus.com/html/catholicdefinitions/capitalvirtue.html; Internet; accessed 22 December 2002.

53. Jane Eisner, op. cit.

54. Ibid.

55. O. C. Ferrell, John Fraedrich, and Linda Ferrell, *Business Ethics: Ethical Decision Making and Cases*, 4th edition, *Instructor's Resource Manual with Test Bank* (Boston: Houghton Mifflin), 2000, xiii.

CHAPTER 10: CORPORATE SCANDALS: REFLECTIONS

1. Federal Open Market Committee [minutes on-line], available from www.federalreserve.gov//FOMC/transcrips/1996/19960924meeting.pdf; Internet; accessed 10 May 2004.

2. The Federal Reserve, remarks by Chairman Alan Greenspan, 30 August 2002 [speech on-line] available from www.federalreserve.gov/BoardDocs/Speeches/2002/20020830/default.htm; Internet; accessed 10 May 2004.

3. Jack Willoughby, "Smoldering," *Barron's,* vol. 80, no. 40 (October 2, 2000), 38.

4. James Heckman and Alan Krueger, *Inequality in America: What Role for Human Capital Policies?* (Cambridge, MA: MIT Press, 2003), 10.

BIBLIOGRAPHY

Books

Avineri, Shlomo. *Hegel's Theory of the Modern State.* Cambridge: Cambridge University Press, 1972.

Axelrod, Robert. *The Evolution of Cooperation.* New York: Basic Books, 1984.

Bailey, Brian. *George Hudson: The Rise and Fall of the Railway King.* London: Stroud Publications, 1995.

Barzel, Yoram. *Economic Analysis of Property Rights.* Cambridge: Cambridge University Press, 1989.

Baskin, John and Paul Miranti. *A History of Corporate Finance.* Cambridge: Cambridge University Press, 1997.

Bell, Daniel. *The Cultural Contradictions of Capitalism.* New York: Basic Books, 1976.

Berle, A. A. and G.C. Means. *The Modern Corporation and Private Property.* New York: Transaction Publishers, 1932, reprinted 1991.

Buchanan, Allen. *Ethics, Efficiency, and the Market.* Totowa, NJ: Rowman and Littlefield Publishers, Inc., 1988.

Buchholz, Rogene A. and Sandra B. Rosenthal. *Business Ethics: The Pragmatic Path Beyond Principles to Process.* Upper Saddle River, NJ: Prentice-Hall, Inc., 1998.

Burrough, Bryan and John Helyar. *Barbarians At The Gate.* New York: Harper Business, 1990.

Cameron, Kim S., Jane E. Dutton, and Robert E. Quinn, ed. *Positive Organizational Scholarship: Foundations of a New Discipline.* San Francisco: Berrett-Koehler Publishers, Inc. 2003.

Carswell, John. *The South Sea Bubble.* London: Cresset Publishers, 1960.

Chancellor, Edward. *Devil Take the Hindmost: A History of Financial Speculation.* London: Farrar, Straus & Giroux Publishers, 1999.

Chen, Li-Fu. *Why Confucius Has Been Reverenced as The Model Teacher of all Ages.* New York: St. Johns Press, 1976.

Chen, Jingpan. *Confucius as a Teacher.* Beijing: Beijing Foreign Language Press, 1990.

Chew, Donald H. Jr. and Stuart L. Gillan. *Corporate Governance at the Crossroads: A Book of Readings.* New York: McGraw-Hill/Irwin, 2005.

Cleary, Thomas (trans.), *The Essential Confucius: The Heart of Confucius' Teachings in Authentic I Chang Order. A Compendium of Ethical Wisdom*. Edison: Castle Books, 1998.

Chung, Tsai Chih. *Confucius Speaks*. New York: Anchor Books, 1996.

Collins, Jim. *Good to Great*. New York: Harper Collins Publishers, 2001.

Costa, John. *The Ethical Imperative: Why Moral Leadership Is Good Business*. Reading: Perseus Publishing, 1998.

Csikszentmihalyi, Mihaly. *Good Business: Leadership, Flow, and the Making of Meaning*. New York: Viking, a Division of the Penguin Group, 2003.

DiPiazza Jr., Samuel A. and Robert G. Eccles. *Building Public Trust: The Future of Corporate Reporting*. New York: John Wiley and Sons, Inc., 2002.

Etzioni, Amitai. *The Moral Dimension: Toward a New Economics*. New York: The Free Press, 1988.

Ferguson, Niall. *The Cash Nexus: Money and Power in the Modern World*. New York: Basic Books, 2001.

Ferrell, O. C., John Fraedrich, and Linda Ferrell. *Business Ethics: Ethical Decision Making and Cases, 4th edition,* Boston: Houghton Mifflin Company, 1998.

_____. *Business Ethics: Ethical Decision Making and Cases, 4th edition. Instructor's Resource Manual with Test Bank*. Boston: Houghton Mifflin Company, 2000.

_____. *Business Ethics: Ethical Decision Making and Cases, 5th edition*. Boston: Houghton Mifflin Company, 2002.

Franklin, Charles. *They Walked A Crooked Mile: An Account of the Greatest Scandals. Swindlers, and Outrages of All Time*. New York: Hart Publishing Company, Inc., 1969.

Hammond, Bray. *Banks and Politics in America from The Revolution to the Civil War*. Princeton: Princeton University Press, 1957.

Heckman, Jack, and Alan Krueger. *Inequality in America: What Role for Human Capital Policies?* Cambridge, MA: MIT Press, 2003.

Hegel, G.F. *Elements of the Philosophy of Right*. Trans. H.B. Nesbit. ed. Allen Wood. Cambridge: Cambridge University Press, 1991.

Hobbes, Thomas. *Leviathan*. New York: Collier Books Edition, 1962 [1652].

Huffington, Arianna. *Pigs at the Trough: How Corporate Greed and Political Corruption Are Undermining America*. New York: Crown Publishers, 2003.

Ickes, Harold. *The Secret Diary of Harold Ickes: The First Thousand Days, 1933-1936*. New York: Simon and Schuster, 1954.

Josephson, Matthew. *Infidel in the Temple: A Memoir of the 1930s*. New York: Knopf, 1967.

Kautilya, Arthashastra. *The Arthashastre Kautilya*. Trans. R. Kangle. Bombay: University of Bombay, 1972.

Kelly, Marjorie. *The Divine Right of Capital: Dethroning the Corporate Aristocracy*. San Francisco: Berrett-Koehler Publishers, Inc., 2001.

Keynes, John Maynard. "Essays in Persuasion," in *The Great Thoughts*. Ed. George Seldes. New York: Ballantine Books, 1985.

Kindleberger, Charles. *Manias, Panics and Crashes: A History of Financial Crisis*, 4th edition. New York: John J. Wiley and Sons, 2000.

Klein, Maury. *Rainbow's End: The Crash of 1929*. New York: Oxford University Press, 2001.

Knight, Jack. *Institutions and Social Conflict*. Cambridge: Cambridge University Press, 1992.

Khurana, R. *Searching for a Corporate Savior: The Irrational Quest for Charismatic CEOs*. Princeton: Princeton University Press, 2003.

Levitt, Arthur and Paula Dwyer. *Take On the Street: How to Fight for Your Financial Future*. New York: Vintage Books, 2003.

Lewin, H. G. *The Railway Mania and its Aftermath, 1845-1852*. New York: August M. Melley Publishers, 1968.

Leys, Simon (aka Pierre Ryckmans) translator. *The Analects of Confucius*. New York: W.W. Norton & Co., 1997.

Luthans, Fred and Bruce Avolio. "Authentic Leadership Development." in *Positive Organizational Scholarship: Foundations of a New Discipline*. Ed. Kim S. Cameron, Jane E. Dutton, and Robert E. Quinn. San Francisco: Berrett-Koehler Publishers, Inc. 2003.

Mayer, Martin. *The Greatest-Ever Bank Robbery: The Collapse of the Savings and Loan Industry*. New York: Melley Publishers, 1992.

McDonald, Forrest. *The Definitive Biography of Samuel Insull*. Chicago: University of Chicago Press, 1962.

Micklethwait, John and Adrian Wooldridge. *The Company: A Simple History of a Revolutionary Idea*. New York: Random House Publishers, 2003.

Monks, Robert A. G. and Nell Minow. *Corporate Governance*, 3rd edition. Malden, MA: Blackwell Publishing Limited, 2004.

Muller, Jerry. *The Mind and The Market*. New York: Anchor Books, 2002.

Murphy, Antoine E. *John Law: Economic Theorist and Policy-Maker*. Oxford: Oxford University Press, 1997.

Neal, Larry. *The Rise of Financial Capitalism: International Capital Markets in the Age of Reason*. Cambridge: Cambridge University Press, 1990.

North, Douglass C. *Institutions, Institutional Change and Economic Performance*. Cambridge: Cambridge University Press, 1990.

Park, Nansook and Christopher M. Peterson. "Virtues and Organizations," in *Positive Organizational Scholarship: Foundations of a New Discipline*. Kim S. Cameron, Jane E. Dutton, and Robert E. Quinn, eds. San Francisco: Berrett-Koehler Publishers, Inc. 2003.

Partnoy, Frank. *Infectious Greed: How Deceit and Risk Corrupted the Financial Markets*.

New York: Henry Holt and Company, LLC, 2003.

Paul, Richard and Linda Elder. *The Miniature Guide to Understanding the Foundations of Ethical Reasoning.* Dillon Beach, CA: Foundation for Critical Thinking, 2003.

Quanyu, Huang, Joseph Leonard & Chen Tong. *Business Decision Making in China.* New York: International Business Press, 1997.

Reid, T.R. *Confucius Lives Next Door.* New York: Random House, 1999.

Runes, Dagobert, ed. *Treasury of Philosophy.* New York: Philosophical Library, 1955.

Schumpeter, Joseph. *Capitalism, Socialism, and Democracy.* New York: Harper Perennial, 1975 [1942].

Schwartz, Benjamin I. *The World of Thought in Ancient China.* Boston: The Belknap Press of Harvard University Press, 1985.

Sen, Amartya. *On Ethics and Economics.* Malden, MA: Blackwell Publishing Limited, 1987.

_____. *Development as Freedom.* New York: Anchor Books, 1999.

Sheehy, Gail. *Character: America's search for Leadership.* New York: Bantam Books, 1990.

Shleifer, Andrei. *Inefficient Markets: An Introduction to Behavioral Finance.* Oxford: Oxford University Press, 2000.

Smith, Adam. *An Inquiry into the Nature and Causes of the Wealth of Nations.* Edwin Cannan, ed. New York: Random House Inc., 1994.

_____. *Theory of Moral Sentiments.* A.L. Macfie and D.D. Raphael, eds. Indianapolis: Liberty Fund. The Glasgow Edition of the Works and Correspondence of Adam Smith, 1976. Reprinted 1982.

Sobel, Robert. *The Great Bull Market: Wall Street in the 1920's.* New York: W.W. Norton & Company, 1968.

Sommers, Christina and Fred Sommers. *Vice & Virtue in Everyday Life: Introductory Readings in Ethics,* Fourth Edition. Fort Worth: Harcourt Brace College Publishers, 1997.

Steidlmeier, Paul. *People and Profits: The Ethics of Capitalism.* Englewood Cliffs, NJ: Prentice Hall, Inc., 1992.

Stiglitz, Joseph E. *The Roaring Nineties.* New York: W. W. Norton and Company, Inc., 2003.

Tichy, Noel M. and Andrew R. McGill, ed. *The Ethical Challenge: How to Lead with Unyielding Integrity.* San Francisco: Jossey-Bass, a Division of John Wiley, Inc., 2003.

Tzu, Hui-nan. *The Sociology of Corruption.* Syed Hussein, trans. Alatas, Singapore: Times Books, 1980.

Useem, Michael. *Investor Capitalism.* New York: Basic Books, 1996.

Wallis, John and Douglass North. "Measuring the Transaction sector in the American

Economy, 1870-1970." In *Long-Term Factors in American Economic Growth.* S.L. Engerman and R.E. Gallman, eds. Chicago: University of Chicago Press, 1986.

Weber, Max. *The Theory of Social and Economic Organization.* Talcott Parsons, ed. New York: The Free Press, 1947.

Webster's Third International Dictionary of the English Language Unabridged. s.v. "Character."

Wu-Chi, Liu. *Confucius, His Life and Time.* New York: Philosophical Library, 1955.

Yu-Lan, Fung. *A History of Chinese Philosophy.* Vol. I, (Princeton: Princeton University Press, 1952.

ACADEMIC AND PROFESSIONAL JOURNALS

Baker, George B., Michael Jensen, and Kevin J. Murphy. "Compensation and Incentives: Practice vs. Theory." *Journal of Finance,* 43 (1988): 593-616.

Bazerman, Max H., George Loewenstein, and Don A. Moore. "Why Good Accountants Do Bad Audits." *Harvard Business Review,* 80, no. 11 (November 2002): 96-102.

Boardman, Calvin M. and Hideaki Kiyoshi Kato. "The Confucian Roots of Business Kyosei." *Journal of Business Ethics* 48, (2003): 317-333.

Breckler, Steven J. "Empirical Validation of Affect, Behavior, and Cognition as Distinct Components of Attitude." *Journal of Personality and Social Psychology,* 47 no. 6 (December 1984): 1191-1205.

Coase, R. "The Nature of the Firm," *Economica,* 4 (1937): 386-405.

Curry, Timothy and Lynn Shibut. "The Cost of the Savings and Loan Crisis: Truth and Consequences." *FDIC Banking Review,* 13, no. 2, (December 2000): 26-35.

Drucker, Peter. "The New Meaning of Corporate Social Responsibility." *California Management Review,* 26 (Winter 1984): 53-63.

Eisenhardt, M. "Agency Theory: An Assessment and Review," *Academy of Management Review,* 14, no. 1 (1989): 57-74.

Hamilton, Early. "The Political Economy of France at the Time of John Law." *History of Political Economy,* 1, no. 1 (Spring 1969): 123-149.

Jensen, Michael. "Corporate Control and the Politics of Finance." *Journal of Applied Corporate Finance,* 4, no. 2 (1991): 13-33.

Jensen, Michael and Kevin Murphy. "CEO Incentives – Its Not How Much you Pay, But How," *Harvard Business Review,* May-June 1990: 138-143.

Jensen, Micheal C. and William H. Meckling. "Theory of the Firm: Managerial Behavior, Agency Costs, and Ownership Structure." *The Journal of Financial Economics,* 3, no. 4 (October 1976): 305-360.

Maitland, Ian. "Virtuous Markets: The Market as School of the Virtues." *Business Ethics Quarterly*, January 1997: 17-31.

Milgrom, Paul, Douglass C. North, and Barry Weingast. "The Role of Institutions in the Revival of Trade: The Law Merchant, Private Judges, and the Campagne Fairs." *Economics and Politics*, 2, no. 1 (March 1990): 1-23.

Ronen, Joshua. "Post Enron Reform: Financial Statement Insurance and GAAP Revisited." *Stanford Journal of Law, Business, and Finance*, 8, no. 1 (2002): 39-68.

PERIODICALS, NEWSPAPERS, AND MAGAZINES

"A Bleak Future." *The Economist*, 28 February, 2004, 71.

"A Damning Verdict." *Economist Global Agenda*, 25 August 2004, 1.

"Ahold: The Fall-out." *Financial Times*, 25 February 2003, 16.

Anders, George. "As Scandals Mount, Fund Boards Feel the Heat." *Wall Street Journal*, 17 March 2004, A1.

Barta, Patrick. "Restatement by Freddie Puts Fannie Mae on Spot," *The Wall Street Journal*, 12 January 2004, C1.

Bassing, Tom. "Five ex-HealthSouth executives sentenced." *Birmingham Business Journal*, 12 December 2003, 15.

"Blodget Pays Out $4m and Gets Life Ban." *Financial Times*, 29 April 2003, 21.

Bowie, Norman E. "Companies are Discovering the Value of Ethics," *USA Today* magazine, January 1998.

Brancaccio, David. *Marketplace News*: Wednesday 29 May 2002.

Burns, Judith. "MFS Deal Cracks Down On Company, Two Top Executives," *Dow Jones Newswires*, 5 February 2004.

"Special Report: Corporate America's Woes, continued—Enron: one year on," *The Economist*, 30 November 2002, 69.

Covey, Stephen R. "Why Character Counts." *Reader's Digest*. January 1999, 132-135.

Cummings, Jeanne and Tom Hamburger. "Enron's Washington Clout Before Collapse Draws Scrutiny – Congressional Democrats Pore Over Contracts With Government for Clues." *Wall Street Journal*, 15 January 2002, A18.

Damato, Karen. "Strong's Fund Sale Faces a Hurdle." *The Wall Street Journal*, 28 January 2004, D11.

Damato, Karen and Judith Burns. "Quarterly Mutual Funds Review: Cleaning Up the Fund Industry; Regulators and Congress Propose 'Unprecendented' Changes, but Critics Say Some Moves Would Hurt Investors." *Wall Street Journal*, 5 April 2004, R1

Davis, Ann. "Fidelity Wants Trading Costs Broken Down." *Wall Street Journal*, 15 March 2004, C1.

Davis, Ann. "'Soft' Punch: Dreyfus Says A Mutual-Fund Reform Would Give Investors Less." *Wall Street Journal,* 26 January 2004, C1.

Day, Kathleen and Ben White. "NYSE Fundraisers Draw Scrutiny." *Washington Post,* 26 September 2003, A01.

Eisner, Jane. "What's behind our high tolerance for the sin of greed?" *Tallahassee Democrat,* 31 July 2002, 9A.

Elkind, Peter. "The Untold Tale of the Great Mutual Fund Rip-off." *Fortune,* 19 April 2004, 106.

Emshwiller, John R. And Kathryn Kranhold. "Publicized Letter to Lay Involved Struggle Over Enron's Direction." *Wall Street Journal,* 16 January 2002, A4.

"Enron Justice." Review & Outlook *Wall Street Journal,* 15 January 2004, A14.

Etzioni, Amitai. "When It Comes to Ethics, B-Schools Get an F," *Washington Post,* 4 August 2002, B04.

"Federal Reserve Flow of Funds." *Federal Reserve Bulletin* 1989–2003.

"Former Enron Chief Financial Officer Andrew S. Fastow Charged With Fraud, Money Laundering, Conspiracy." *United States Department of Justice Press Release,* 2 October 2002.

Francis, Theo. "Fund Track—Open Secrets: How Variable Annuities Can Gnash Investors; Sellers, Brokers Do Well on Fees But Some Buyers Turn Sour When They Read the Fine Print." *Wall Street Journal,* 6 February 2004, C1.

"Freddie Mac Scandal Deepens." *The Banker,* 3 November 2003, 12.

Gallagher, Kathleen. "Word on Strong May Come Next Month." *Milwaukee Journal Sentinel,* 21 January 2004, D2.

"Garry Winick Should Go To Jail." *The New York Observer,* 1 April 2002, 4.

Goldberg, Laura. "Enron seeks bankruptcy alternatives Company may sue Dynergy over termination of merger." *Houston Chronicle* (Business Section), 17 January 2002.

Goodman, Peter S. "7 More Executives Arrested in Parmalat Probe." *Washington Post Foreign Service,* 1 January 2004, E01.

Gordon, Marcy. "SEC Pushing for Dramatic Reforms for Mutual Funds." *Tallahassee Democrat,* 12 February 2004, E1.

Grone, Jack. "Financial Scandals Test Regulators European Authorities Are Under Pressure to Show They Are Up to the Task." *DOW Jones Newswires,* 20 January 2004.

"Grubman The Poster Child for Conflict of Interest." *Financial Times,* 29 April 2003. 21.

Hayashi, Yuka. "Tainted Funds Hurt by Withdrawals." *Wall Street Journal,* 1 April 2004, D7.

Hechinger, John. "Deciphering Funds' Hidden Costs: Mutual-Fund Study Reveals How Much Investors Actually Pay in Undisclosed Charges." *Wall Street Journal,* 17 March 2004, D1.

Hechinger, John. "Fidelity's Johnson Seeks to Keep Both His Jobs." *Wall Street Journal,* 17 March 2004, C1.

Hechinger, John. "MFS Ends Soft Dollar Payments on Concerns Over Ethics." *Wall Street Journal,* 16 March 2004, C1.

Hechinger, John. "Putnam to Pay $110 Million in Settlement." *Wall Street Journal,* 9 April 2004, C1.

Hechinger, John and Laura Johannes. "Regulation: MFS to Pay $50 Million In SEC Case; Regulators Also Consider Action Against Edward D. Jones & Co. As Mutual-Fund Probe Widens." *Wall Street Journal,* 31 March 2004, C1.

Hodgson, Paul. "Golden Parachutes and Cushion Landings: Termination Payments and Policy in the S&P 500." *The Corporate Library,* Portland, ME February 2003, 3.

Horovitz, Bruce. "Scandals grow out of CEOs' warped mind-set," *USA TODAY,* 11 October 2002, 2B.

Jensen, Michael. "Agency Cost of Free Cash Flow, Corporate Finance, and Takeovers." *AEA Papers and Proceedings,* 76:323-9, 323.

Kochan, T.A. "Addressing the Crisis in Confidence in Corporations: Root Causes, Victims, and Strategies for Reform." Papers presented at the special presidential panel, *Academy of Management Annual Meeting,* August 2002.

Laing, Jonathan R. "Mercurial Man." *Barron's,* 26 January 2004, 27-29.

Lauricella, Tom and John Hechinger. "SEC's Agreement with MFS Puts Mutual Funds on Notice." *Wall Street Journal,* 1 April 2004, C1.

Lauricella, Tom and John Hechinger. "Alliance Settles Charges, MFS in Talks." *Wall Street Journal,* 19 December 2003, C1.

Leitch, Matt. "Take A Perp Walk With Me: A Scandalous Score Card." *Registered Rep.,* 1 January 2004.

Lublin, Joann S. "Companies Seek To Recover Pay." *Wall Street Journal,* 7 January 2004, B1.

MacDonald, Ian. "Mutual Fund Regulation Primer: The SEC's Flurry of New Rules." *Wall Street Journal,* 14 April 2004, C1.

McCarty, Phil. "MFS Settlement Funds To Be Returned To Shareholders: CNBC." *Dow Jones Newswire,* 5 February 2004.

McDonald, Ivan. "Janus Executive Quits Amid Probe: Investigators Say Garland Approved Rapid Trading of Mutual-Fund Shares." *Wall Street Journal,* 18 November 2003, D9.

McDonald, Ian. "Putnam board chief targets the gaps that lead to timing." *Wall Street Journal,* 13 January 2004, C1.

"MFS Settles Market-timing Issues." *Office of New York Attorney General, Press release,* 5 February 2004.

Nowell, Paul. "Bank of America confirms three executives fired." *The Atlanta Journal-Constitution,* 12 September 2003.

Oster, Christopher. "Janus to Repay Fund Shareholders." *Wall Street Journal*, 22 December, 2003, C13.

Oster, Christopher and Carrick Mollenkamp. "Mutual-Fund Indictment Against Broker Reveals Startling Phone Dialogue." *Wall Street Journal*, 6 April 2004, C1.

"Pitt the Gamekeeper." *The Economist*, 14 February, 2002, 82.

Pitts, Leonard. "Your kid's going to pay for cheating—eventually." *Tallahassee Democrat*, 24 June 2002, 7A.

Plender, John. "What Price Virtue?" *Financial Times*, 2 December 2002, 21.

Schmitt, Richard B. "Bankruptcy Judge for Enron Case is a Stickler for Detail." *Wall Street Journal*, 7 December 2001, A8.

"SEC Details Quattrone's Influence." *Financial Times*, 29 April 2003. 21.

"SEC, NYSE, NASD and Elliot Spitzer settle with U.S. Investment Banks." *SRI Media*, 28 April 2003.

Shipman, John. "Federated to Compensate Investors." *Wall Street Journal*, 4 February 2004, D9.

Shipman, John. "Schwab's Role in Mutual-Fund Probe Adds New Dimension." *Wall Street Journal*, 14 November 2003, C1.

Sidel, Robin and Tom Lauricella, "Funds Allure Survives." *Wall Street Journal*, 9 January 2004, C3.

Simon, Ruth. "Why Your Broker Is Pushing That Fund." *Wall Street Journal*, 14 January 2004, D1.

Skapinker, Michael. "CEO: Greedy Liar with Personality Disorder." *Financial Times*, 2 July 2003, 8.

Sloan, Allan. "Grasso's Gone, but Plenty of Corporate and Political Excesses Remain." *Washington Post*, 23 September 2003, E03.

"Spitzer, S. E. C. Reach Largest Mutual Fund Settlement Ever." Press Releases, Office of New York State Attorney General Eliot Spitzer, 15 March 2004.

SRI Media News Corporate Governance, Joint Press Release, SEC, NYSE, NASD and New York Attorney General, 28 April 2003

Statement by Attorney General Eliot Spitzer Regarding Mutual Fund Fee Reduction," Office of New York Attorney General Eliot Spitzer, Press Release, 18 December 2003.

"The Bull Market Hero at Bay." *Financial Times*, 30 August 2003, 7.

"The Grasso Resignation." *Financial Times*, 19 September 2003, 20.

Time magazine cover, 28 October 1929.

"Tyco to cut costs by $3 billion in next 3 years." *Reuters*, 29 December 2003.

"Unsure of Shell." *Financial Times*, 23 January 2004, 15.

White, Ben and Brooke Masters. "Exchange Looks for New Leader." *Washington Post*, 19 September 2003, E01.

White, Ben and Kathleen Day. "NYSE to Fine Five Floor-Trading Firms." *Washington Post,* 16 October 2003, E01.

White, Ben. "Grasso Backer to Quit NYSE's Board." *Washington Post,* 26 September 2003, E01.

_____. "New NYSE Head Plans Changes." *Washington Post,* 27 September 2003, E03.

_____. "NYSE's Interim Chief A Master of Analysis." *Washington Post,* 14 October 2003, E01.

_____. "Pension Fund Officials Seek NYSE Split: Group Wants Business Regulation Separated." *Washington Post,* 25 September 2003, E01.

Willoughby, Jack. "Smoldering." *Barron's,* 80, no. 40 (2 October 2000), 38-42.

Zucherman, Gregory and Randall Smith. "Bear Shakes Up Its Clearing House." *Wall Street Journal,* 1 April 2004, C1.

INTERNET

"140M Payday For Big Board Chief." *CBSNews.com* [Article on-line]; available from http://news.codewind.com/go,10997; Internet; accessed 28 August 2003.

"Adelphia execs arrested for fraud." *BBC News Co.* United Kingdom [Article on-line]; available from http://news.bbc.co.uk/1/hi/business/2149956.stm; Internet; accessed 24 July 2003.

"Andersen Wreckage Means Higher Fees." *BBC News Co.* United Kingdom [Article on-line]; available from http://news.bbc.co.uk/1/hi/business/2049021.stm; Internet; accessed 17 June 2002.

Andrejczak, Matt. "Franklin In Talks to Settle SEC Charges." CBS Marketwatch.com [Article on-line]; available from http://www.1800lawinfo.com/practice/news.htm?story_id=7578&topic=mutual1%20funds%20fraud; Internet; accessed 9 February 2004.

Butler, Eamon. "Preface." The Theory of the Moral Sentiments. Available from http://www.adamsmith.org/smith/tms-intro.htm; Internet; accessed 25 January 2004.

"Cable flop sues former auditor." *BBC News Co.* United Kingdom [Article on-line]; available from http://news.bbc.co.uk/1/hi/business/2415145.stm; Internet; accessed 7 November 2003.

Caux Round Table. "Principles for Business." [Homepage on-line]; available from http://www.cauxroundtable.org/principles.html; Internet; accessed 3 April 2004.

Derivative Instrument. [Glossary on-line]; available from http://www.riskglossary.com/articles/derivative_instrument.htm; Internet; accessed 10 April 2004.

Dugas, Christine. "Spotlight hits whistle-blower," *USAToday.com,* [Article on-line]; available from http://www.usatoday.com/money/perfi/funds/2003-12-09-whistleblow_x.htm; Internet; accessed 10 December 2003.

"Global Crossing accounts probed." *BBC News Co.* United Kingdom [Article on-line]; available from http://news.bbc.co.uk/1/hi/business/1801871.stm; Internet; accessed 22 February 2004.

Goff, John. "So Who Was Arthur Andersen Anyway?" *CFO.com,* [Article on-line]; available from http://www.CFO.com/article/1,5309,7639,00.html; Internet; accessed 13 March 2004.

Goldstein, Matthew. "A.G. Edwards Fired Brokers Over Fund Practices." Thestreet. com [Article on-line]; available from http://www.thestreet.com/_tscana/markets/marketfeatures/10132167.html; Internet; accessed 15 December 2003.

Goldstein, Matthew. "Back-Office Figure Emerges in Bear Stearns Investigation." Thestreet.com [Article on-line]; available from http://www.thestreet.com/_yahoo/markets/matthewgoldstein/10158333.html; Internet; accessed 5 May 2004.

Goldstein, Matthew. "Three Merrill Brokers Fired in Hedge Fund Scandal." Thestreet.com [Article on-line]; available from http://www.thestreet.com/_yahoo/markets/matthewgoldstein/10117370.html; Internet; accessed 3 October 2003.

"HealthSouth Timeline." *NBC13.com.* [Article on-line]; available from http://www.nbc13.com/news/2101600/detail.html; Internet; accessed 17 April 2004.

"How Did Tyco Defraud Shareholders?" *SecuritiesFraudFYI.com* [Article on-line]; available from http://www.securitiesfraudfyi.com/tyco.html; Internet; accessed

"ImClone founder jailed." *BBC News Co.* United Kingdom [Article on-line]; available from http://news.bbc.co.uk/1/hi/business/2979672.stm; Internet; accessed 10 June 2003.

Krajicek, Dave. "The Crime Beat: Perp Walks." [Article on-line]; available from http://www.justicejournalism.org/crimeguide/chapter01/sidebars/chap01_xside5.html; Internet; accessed 8 January 2004.

MacDonald, Elizabeth. "Tyco's Goodwill Games." Forbes.com [Article on-line]; available from http://www.forbes.com/2002/06/13/0613tycaccount.html; Internet; accessed 13 June 2002.

"Martha Stewart sued by investor." *BBC News Co.* United Kingdom [Article on-line]; available from http://news.bbc.co.uk/1/hi/business/2210598.stm; Internet; accessed 22 August 2003.

O'Donnell, Jayne. "The guy who blew the whistle on Putnam." *USAToday.com/* [Article on-line]; available from http://www.yourlawyer.com/practice/news.htm?story_id=7077&topic=Putnam%20Mutual%20Funds; Internet; accessed 20 November 2003.

"Parmalat Timeline." Available from http://news.bbc.co.uk/go/pr/fr/-/1/hi/business/3369079.stm; Internet; accessed 21 February 2004.

Public Company Accounting Oversight Board. [Homepage on-line]; http://www.pcaobus.org/; Internet; accessed 10 April 2004.

"Putnam settles with SEC." *CNN Money,* [Article on-line]; available from http://money.cnn.com/2003/11/13/funds/fundsfire_putnam/index.htm; Internet;

accessed 13 November 2003.

"Sarbanes-Oxley Act of 2002." Perkins Coie Law Firm [Library on-line]; available from http://www.thecorporatelibrary.com/special/practices/; Internet; accessed 21 January 2004.

Schepp, David. "Bush delivers too little too late." *BBC News Co.* United Kingdom [Article on-line]; available from http://news.bbc.co.uk/1/hi/business/2118700.stm; Internet; accessed 9 July 2002.

Schneider, Mica. "Learning to Put Ethics Last." *Business Week,* 11 March 2002 [Article on-line]; available from http://www.businessweek.com/bschools/content/mar2002/bs2002038_0311.htm; accessed 4 June 2002.

"SEC Sues Former Tyco Director and Chairman of Compensation Committee Frank E. Walsh Jr. for Hiding $20 Million Payment From Shareholders." *SEC Government News 2002-177* [Article on-line]; available from http://www.sec.gov/news/press/2002-177.htm; Internet; accessed 17 December 2003.

Second Exodus. "Catholic Definitions: Capital Virtue." [Definitions on-line]; available from http://www.secondexodus.com/html/catholicdefinitions/capitalvirtue.htm; Internet; accessed 22 December 2002.

Smith, Adam. Preface to *The Theory of the Moral Sentiments* by Dr. Eamonn Butler, Director of the Adam Smith Institute, London [Book on-line]; available from http://www.adamsmith.org/smith/tms-intro.htm; Internet; accessed 25 January 2004.

"Spitzer Slams Putnam Settlement." Money.cnn.com [Article on-line]; available from http://money.cnn.com/2003/11/17/funds/spitzer_oped/; Internet; accessed 17 November 2003.

"Stewart resigns as company head." *BBC News Co.* United Kingdom [Article on-line]; available from http://news.bbc.co.uk/1/hi/business/2964478.stm; Internet; accessed 5 June 2003.

The Internet Encyclopedia of Philosophy. "Virtue Theory." [encyclopedia on-line]; available from *http://www.utm.edu/research/iep/v/virtue.htm;* Internet; accessed 5 October 2003.

"There's No Magic in Mergers." *Businessweek Online* [Article on-line]; available from http://www.businessweek.com/magazine/content/02_41/b3803160.htm; Internet; accessed 14 October 2002.

"Timeline: Enron—Key dates surrounding the Enron collapse." Guardian Unlimited. [Special Report on-line]; available from http://www.guardian.co.uk/enron/story/0,11337,638640,00.html; Internet; accessed 24 October 2004.

"Tyco Fraud." Securities Fraud FYI (Online). "Tyco Timeline." Available from http://www.securitiesfraudfyi.com/tyco.html; Internet; accessed 14 January 2004.

"UK strives to avoid Enron-style scandals." *BBC News Co.* United Kingdom, [Article on-line]; available from http://news.bbc.co.uk/1/hi/business/2096445.stm; Internet; accessed 5 July 2002.

"US financial regulator resigns." *BBC News Co.* United Kingdom [Article on-line]; available from http://news.bbc.co.uk/1/hi/business/2408157.stm; Internet; accessed 6 November 2003.

"Watchdog probes Qwest accounts." *BBC News Co.* United Kingdom [Article on-line]; available from http://news.bbc.co.uk/1/hi/business/1867238.stm; Internet; accessed 11 March 2003.

"WorldCom Fraud." Securities Fraud FYI (Online). Available from http://www.securitiesfraudfyi.com/worldcom_fraud.html; Internet; accessed 14 January 2004.

INDEX

A

Accountability, definition, 257
Accounting firms, plight, 95–96
Adelphia Communications, 241
    collapse, 67–68
    executives, arrest, 266, 288
    indictments, 91
A.G. Edwards, 150, 153
Agency costs/problem, 166
Agency theory, 164–166, 178
    problem, 166–167
Alliance Capital Management, 146,
    150–152
Allied Irish Banks, scandal, 95
Altruism, definition, 257
American Assembly of Collegiate
    Schools of Business (AACSB), 231
American Continental, 40
American Stock Exchange, 97
Anders, George, 271, 284
Andrejczak, Matt, 270, 288
Angelides, Phil, 124
Aristotle, 194, 213, 225–226
Armstrong, Michael, 118
Arthur Andersen
    accounting, role, 65, 66, 80
    conviction, 53
    demise, 4–5, 92–94, 288
    political contributions, 197
    SEC investigation, criticism, 104

AT&T, analyses (problems), 117–118
Audit committee standards, improve-
    ment, 87–88
Avineri, Shlomo, 273, 279
Avolio, Bruce, 275, 281
Axelrod, Robert, 183, 273, 279
Ayers, Angela C., 89

B

Bacanovic, Peter, 69
Bailey, Brian, 264, 279
Baker, George B., 274, 283
Ballen, John, 145
Banc One, 136
Bank Act of 1845, repeal, 22
Bank Act of 1933, 33–36
Bank funds, borrowing, 13
Bank of America (BofA), Nations Funds
    family, 136–139
Bank of the United States (bankruptcy),
    28
Bank One, 140, 150
Banque Générale, 15–16
Barta, Patrick, 284
Barzel, Yoram, 273, 279
Baskin, John, 264, 265, 279
Bassing, Tom, 267, 284
Bazerman, Max, 5, 263, 283
Bear Stearns & Co., Inc., 109, 147
Beatty, Randolph, 94

Bebel, Christopher, 106

Behavior factor, 209

Bell, Daniel, 279

Belnick, Mark, 58–59

Benevolence, definition, 257

Berle, Adolf A., 165, 272, 279

Blodget, Henry, 246
    payments, 268
    resignation, 114–115

Blue Sky law, 27, 106, 131

Blunt, John, 18–19

Board Audit Committees, 179

Boardman, Calvin M., 221, 275, 276, 283

Bobbitt, Max, 62

Boesky, Ivan, 39–40, 226

BofA. *See* Bank of America

Boom era (1920s), swindles, 27–28

Bowie, Norma E., 3, 263, 284

Bradley, Harold S., 130

Brancaccio, David, 267, 284

Bravery, definition, 257

Breckler, S.J., 274, 283

Brendsel, Leland, 97

Brown, James, 68

Bruenn, Christine, 109

Bryceland, Charles, 138

Bubbles, guarding (failure), 236–238

Buchanan, Allen, 279

Buchholz, Rogene A., 279

Buffett, Warren, 123, 155, 179

Burger, Warren, 4

Burns, Judith, 270, 284

Burrough, Bryan, 272, 279

Business
    behavior, 252

economic/social impact, 251–252
    principles, 249
    responsibilities, 251
    transactions (support), virtues (impact), 218

Business ethics
    education, impact, 229–231
    endnotes, 274–277
    virtue, impact, 207

Business scandals, 40–45
    endnotes, 263–265
    history, 13
    questions, 45

Butler, Eamon, 274

C

California Public Employees' Retirement System (CalPERS)
    investor influence, 45
    limited partnership interest, 52

Cameron, Kim S., 279

Canadian Imperial Bank of Commerce, 147

Canary Capital Partners, 87, 134, 136–138, 141–143

Candor, definition, 257

Capital sins/virtues, 228

Capitalism, dynamism, 195

Caring, definition, 257

Carswell, John, 263, 279

Caux Round Table, 222, 249, 275
    principles, 251–253

Cendant Corporation, fraud, 95

Chancellor, Edward, 263–265, 279

Character development, virtuous behavior (impact), 224–226

Charity, definition, 257

Charles Schwab, 149

Chase National Bank, 30–31

Chastity, definition, 257

Chen, Li-Fu, 275, 279

Chew, Jr., Donald H., 279

Chewco, 52–53

Chief Executive Officer (CEO)
  charisma, 5–6
  compensation
  excess, 200–201
  reduction, 85
  honesty, measurement, 210
  payment, appropriateness, 242–244
  profit reduction, 85
  report certification, 84–85

Chief Financial Officer (CFO)
  compensation/profits (reduction), 85
  honesty, measurement, 210
  report certification, 84–85

Chung, Tsai Chih, 276, 280

CIT Group, 57–59

Citigroup Global Markets Inc., 109–110

Civil War, investment banking, 24

Clark, Jr., George W., xix

Clauses Consolidation Act, violation, 22

Cleary, Thomas, 219, 275, 279–280

Coase, R., 283

Collins, Jim, 243, 280

Colonial Realty, fraud/prosecution, 92, 93

Commission bundling, 156–157

Commission on Public Trust and Private Enterprise, 6

Committee of European Securities

Regulators (CESR), 78

Communities, treatment, 256

Compagnie d'Occident, 15

Compassion, definition, 257

Compensation. See Executive officers
  excess. See Chief Executive Officer
  systems, improvement methods. See
    Management compensation
    systems

Competitors, treatment, 255

Conflict of interest, 199, 268

Confucius (K'ung Fu-Tse), 208, 219–224

Consideration, definition, 257

Cooke, Jay, 23–26

Cooper, Cynthia, 87

Corporate equities/foreign depository
  receipts, market value, 177

Corporate legal/ethical violations, 70

Corporate malfeasance, 47, 99, xix
  effects, 98–99
  endnotes, 265–266
  questions, 82

Corporate misdeeds, U.S. response, 33–37

Corporate scandals, 1
  assessment, 99–101
  attention, 83
  endnotes, 263, 267, 277
  examination, 235
  key questions, 236–245
  questions, 12, 101, 248

Corporate self-regulation, 84–85

Corporations, collapse, 49–70

Corruption. See Wall Street

Costa, John Dalla, 276, 280

Coster, F. Donald, 37–38

Courage, definition, 257
Courtesy, definition, 257
Covey, Stephen R., 225, 276, 284
Credit Suisse First Boston (CSFB),
   104–105, 109–110, 118
Csikszentmihalyi, Mihaly, 280
Cultural influences, impact. *See* Greed
Cultural institutions, social institution
   (role), 192–193
Cummings, Jeanne, 284
Curiosity, definition, 257
Curry, Timothy, 265, 283
Customers, treatment, 253

D

Damato, Karen, 269, 284
Davis, Ann, 271, 284
Day, Kathleen, 268, 284, 287
Dean Witter Reynolds, 104
Decency, definition, 258
Dependability, definition, 258
Derivative instruments, 267, 288
Diligence, definition, 258
DiPiazza, Jr., Samuel A., 280
Directed brokerage, 152
Directors, personal loans (bans), 86
Dividends
   buybacks, substitute, 171–172
   conventions, violations, 169–170
Donaldson, William H., 92, 99, 109,
   122, 125–130
Dow Jones Industrial Average (DJIA),
   237
   increase, 47
   monthly closings, 48

Drexel Burnham Lambert, 167
   receivership, 39, 40
Drucker, Peter, 272, 283
Dugas, Christine, 269, 288
Dutton, Jane E., 279
Duty, definition, 258
Dwyer, Paula, 281
Dynegy, prosecution, 92

E

Eamon, Butler, 288
Earnings per share (EPS), 171, 175–
   176, 179
East India and China Company, 15
East India Company, 24
Ebbers, Bernard, 62–63, 81, 246
Eccles, Robert G., 280
Economic boon (1990s), 168–169
Edison, Thomas, 29
Eisenhardt, M., 272, 283
Eisner, Jane, 276, 277, 284–285
Elan, scandal, 75–76
Elder, Linda, 277, 282
Elkind, Peter, 269, 285
Empathy, definition, 258
Employees, treatment, 254
Emshwiller, Peter, 56, 285
Enforcement actions, 112–113
Enron, 48, 87, 265
   Bush administration contacts, 51
   collapse, 45, 49–57
   timeline, 54–56, 290
Environment, respect, 252–253
Equity, definition, 258
Ernst & Young, 94, 144

financial documents, request, 90
IRS charges, 95
Ethics training, 230
Etienne de Callatay, 75
Etzioni, Amitai, 280, 285
Europe
corporate ethical violations, 76
scandals, 71–76
Excellence, definition, 258
Executive officers
compensation, 198–201
payment/salary
objective performance, 176–178
transparency, 201–203
performance, payment (relationship), 198–200
personal loans, bans, 86

F

Fairness, definition, 258
Faith, definition, 258
Family, social institution (role), 190–191
Fastow, Andrew S., 56, 241
fraud, 49–53, 265, 285
Federal Deposit Insurance Corporation (FDIC), creation, 35
Federal Drug Administration (FDA), 68–69
Federal National Mortgage Association (FNMA)
profit suppression, 96–98
scandal, 267
Federal Open Market Committee (FOMC), 237, 277
Federal Reserve System, 238, 277

establishment, 25
Flow of Funds databAse, 176, 177
interest rates, reduction, 98–99
market control, 32
Federated Investors, 148
Ferguson, Niall, 264, 265, 280
Ferrell, Linda, 276, 277, 280
Ferrell, O.C., 276, 277, 280
Fidelity Investments, board reform (proposal), 154–156
Filial piety, definition, 258
Financial Accounting Standards Board (FASB), 6, 176, 238–239
Financial caretakers, failure (reasons), 236–238
Financial management, executive perversion, 163
endnotes, 272
Firewalls, enforcement, 112
FleetBoston Financial Corp, 138
Forbes, Walter A., 95
Ford, Henry (Dodge lawsuit), 200
Forgiveness, definition, 258
Fortitude, definition, 258
Fraedrich, John, 276, 277, 280
Francis, Theo, 271, 285
Frank, Jerome, 36
Franklin, Charles, 264, 280
Franklin Resources, 147–148
Franklin Templeton, 154
Fraud, 47
endnotes, 265–266
Fred Alger and Company, 148
Free enterprise system, disrepair (degree), 238–240
Frieder, Larry A., xix
Frugality, definition, 258

G

Gallagher, Kathleen, 269, 285
Garland, Richard, 143
Gendelman, Jim, 137
Generosity, definition, 258
Gerth, Erich, 143
Gillan, Stuart L., 279
Glass, Carter, 34
Glass-Steagall Act, 33–36
Glauber, Robert, 109
Global Crossing, 48, 64–65
  accounts, probe, 266, 288
  bankruptcy, 1
  collapse, 64–67
  prosecution, 92
Global settlement, summary, 114
Goff, John, 288–289
Goldberg, Laura, 56, 285
Golden Rule, 211, 212
Goldman, Sachs & Co., 109–110, 140
Goldstein, Matthew, 270, 271, 289
Good judgment, definition, 258–259
Good temper, definition, 259
Goodman, Peter S., 266, 285
Goodness, definition, 259
Goodwin, Andrew, 136
Gordon, Joel, 89
Gordon, Marcy, 271, 285
Government regulation, 33–37
Government sponsored enterprise
  (GSE), scandal (involvement),
  97–98
Grant, Ulysses S., 25
Grasso, Richard, 130, 201
  compensation, 122, 127, 243
  resignation, 120–126, 268, 287

role, 103
Gratitude, definition, 259
Gray, Kenneth, xix
Great Depression (1929), 27, 29, 42
Greed, 226–228. *See also* Wall Street
  cultural influences, impact, 241–242
  media, impact, 241–242
Greenspan, Alan, 99, 236–238, 277
Grone, Jack, 266, 285
Grubman, Jack, 107, 246
  conflict of interest, 268
  securities industry disbarment,
    117–118

H

Haliburton, prosecution, 92
Hamburger, Tom, 284
Hamilton, Early, 264, 283
Hammond, Bray, 263, 280
Harken Energy, 106
Harrington, Noreen, 87, 134–135
Harris, Emery, 89
Hayashi, Yuka, 272, 285
HealthSouth Corporation, 48, 210
  SOA test, 88–91
  timeline, 267, 289
Healthy, definition, 259
Hechinger, John, 269–271, 285, 286
Heckman, James, 277, 280
Hegel, Georg F.W., 190–194, 216–217,
  273, 275, 280
Helyar, John, 272, 279
Hevesi, Alan G., 124
Hewitt, Patricia, 76–77
Hobbes, Thomas, 272, 280

Hodgson, Paul, 274, 286
Honesty, definition, 259
Hope, definition, 259
Horovitz, Bruce, 276, 286
Hudson, George, 22–24
Huffington, Arianna, 280
Humility, definition, 259
Hunter, Ian, 76

I

Ickes, Harold, 36, 265, 280
Illicit operations, avoidance, 253
ImClone, 48, 225
    collapse, 68–70
    founder, jail sentence, 266, 289
Incentives, leadership (contrast),
    195–196
Independent research, penalties/reduc-
    tion/funds, 111–114
Industry, definition, 259
Inferior virtue, 214
Information Revolution, changes, 21
Insider trades, reporting (acceleration),
    86
Institutions. *See* Social institutions
    choices, meaning, 194–195
    creation, 188–190
    transaction costs, impact, 188–190
Insull, Samuel, 29
Insurance companies, malfeasance, 157
Integrity
    definition, 259
    restoration, 3–5
Internal Revenue Service (IRS) system, 7
International Postal Union coupons,

    purchase, 26–27
Internet Encyclopedia of Philosophy,
    274
Invesco, 149
Investment Act of 1940, 36–37
Investment analysts, investigations,
    114–120
Investment bankers/analysts, 120
Investment banks, global settlement,
    109–111
Investment Company Institute (ICI),
    151, 157, 239, 246
Investors
    education, penalties/reduction/
        funds, 111–114
    treatment, 254
Invisible Hand, 208, 214–219

J

Janus Capital Group, 142–144
Jensen, Michael C., 166, 198, 272, 274,
    283, 286
Jingpan, Chen, 276, 279
Johannes, Laura, 271, 286
Johnson, Edward (mutual fund board
    reform proposal), 155–156
Josephson, Matthew, 265, 280
Junk bonds, 39
Justice, definition, 259

K

Kato, Hideaki Kiyoshi, 221, 275, 276,
    283
Kautilya, Arthashastra, 275, 280
Keating, Charles, 40

Kelly, Marjorie, 280–281
Kennedy, Joseph P., 36
Keynes, John Maynard, 192, 226, 276, 281
Khurana, Rakesh, 263, 281
Kindleberger, Charles, 14, 263, 264, 281
Kindness, definition, 259
Klein, Maury, 264, 281
Kmart, bankruptcy, 238
Knight, Jack, 183, 273, 281
Kochan, Thomas A., 5, 263, 286
Kopper, Michael J., 51–53
Kozlowski, Dennis, 57–60, 81, 215, 242
Krajicek, Dave, 289
Kranhold, Kathryn, 56, 285
Kravis, Kohlberg and Roberts (KKR), 167–168
Kreuger & Toll, 28–29, 38
Krueger, Alan, 277, 280
Krueger, Ivar, 28
Krueger and Toll Company, bankruptcy, 28

L

Laing, Jonathan R., 269, 286
Lasser, Lawrence, 139
Lauricella, Tom, 269, 270, 286, 287
Law, John, 15–17
Law Merchants, 185
Lay, Kenneth, 50, 57, 241, 246
Leadership, usage, 196, 227
Lefkowitz, Louis, 107
Lehman Brothers, 109–110, 140
Leitch, Matt, 286

Leonard, Joseph, 276, 282
Lernout & Hauspie, scandal, 75
Leveraged buyouts (LBOs), 39, 164
    junk bonds, relationship, 267
    options, impact, 167–168
Levitt, Arthur, 281
Lewin, H.G., 264, 281
Leys, Simon, 275, 281
Liberality, definition, 259
Lietch, Matt, 270
Lincoln Savings & Loan, 40
Livesay, Ken, 89
Living Omnimedia, stock value (reduction), 69
LJM interests, 49, 51–52
Loewenstein, George, 263, 283
Love, 209
    definition, 259
Loyalty, definition, 260
Lublin, Joann S., 267, 286
Luthans, Fred, 275, 281

M

MacDonald, Elizabeth, 265, 289
MacDonald, Ian, 272, 286
Maitland, Ian, 275, 283
Management compensation systems, improvement methods, 242–244
Market
    economy, institution role, 185–186
    negative effects, 190–194
    spill-over effects, 196–198
Market system
    endnotes, 272–274
    questioning, 181

questions, 205

Martin, Alice H., 92

Martin, Warren, 96

Martin Act, 42, 131

impact. *See* Wall Street

prohibitions, 135

usage, 8, 27, 106

Massachusetts Financial Services (MFS) Company, 145–146, 156

Masters, Brooke, 268, 287

Mayer, Martin, 281

McCall, H. Carl (trading/regulation separation advocacy), 123, 126–127

McCarty, Phil, 270, 286

McDonald, Forrest, 264, 281

McDonald, Ian, 269, 286

McDonald, Ivan, 286

McDonough, William J., 100

McGill, Andrew R., 282

McKesson & Robbins Company, 37–38

Means, Gardiner C., 165, 272, 279

Meckling, William H., 166, 272

Meeker, Mary, 115–116

Meekness, definition, 260

Mercy, definition, 260

Mergers, magic, 265

Merrill Lynch, 109–110, 150, 154

settlement, 107

Micklethwait, John, 264, 265, 272, 281

Middle West Utilities Holding Company, 29–30

bankruptcy, 28

Milgrom, Paul, 273, 284

Milken, Michael, 40, 64, 167

Miller, William Curtis, 90

Minow, Neil, 281

Miranti, Paul J., 264, 265, 279

Mississippi Company bubble (France), 14–16, 19–20, 41

Mitchell, Charles E. (financial supermarket), 31–33

Mobley, Sybil C., xx

Moderation, definition, 260

Modesty, definition, 260

Mollenkamp, Carrick, 269, 286

Monks, Robert A.G., 281

Moore, Don, 263, 283

Morgan, Rebecca Kay, 89

Morgan Stanley, investments, 116

Morgenthau, Robert, 106

Mulcahey, Michael, 68

Muller, Jerry, 190, 273, 281

Multilateral trade, support, 252

Murphy, Antoine E., 264, 281

Murphy, Kevin J., 198, 274, 283

Mutual funds

directed brokerage businesses, 152–154

endnotes, 269–272

fees

questions, 150–152

reduction, Spitzer (comments), 271

late trading, scandals, 134–137

market timing, scandals, 134–137

questions, 162

sales practices, illegality, 152–154

scandals, 133

SEC reform, 158

size, cash withdrawals, 157–158

trustees, 155

N

Nader, Ralph, 88

Nappier, Denise L., 125

National Association of Investment Professionals, 123

National Association of Securities Dealers (NASD), 2, 104, 107, 124, 154

National City Bank (NCB), 31–34

National City Company (NCC), 31–32

National Westminster Bank, 52

Nations, institution (role), 192–193

Neal, Larry, 264, 281

New Deal legislation, 33

New York Stock Exchange (NYSE), 2, 238

design, 36

Grasso payment, 201

self-regulation failure, 120–129

Newkirk, Thomas C., 59

Niceness, definition, 260

Non-market institutions, 182, 190–194, 196

North, Douglass C., 273, 274, 281, 283, 284

Northern Pacific Railroad (NPR), 24–25

Nowell, Peter, 269, 286

O

O'Donnell, Jayne, 269, 289

Office of Federal Housing Enterprises Oversight (OFHEO), 97–98

O'Keefe, T. Sheridan, 123

Optimism, definition, 260

Organization theory, 195–196

Organizations, role, 184–185

Oster, Christopher, 269, 270, 286

Owners, treatment, 254

Oxley, Michael, 7

P

Pandit, Vijaya Lakshmi, 229

Park, Nansook, 274–276, 281

Parke, Kevin, 145

Parmalat Finanziaria SpA, scandal, 48, 73–75, 77

timeline, 74–75, 289

Parseghian, Gregory, 97

Partnoy, Frank, 282

Patriotism, 192–193

Paul, Richard, 277, 282

Pension fund blackout periods, insider trades (prohibition), 86–87

Perquisites (perks), 198

Peterson, Christopher M., 274–276, 281

Philosophies, 209–210

Piety, definition, 260. See also Filial piety

Pilgram, Baxter & Associates, 146–147

PIMCO, 154

Pimco Advisors, 148

Piper Jaffray, 109–110

Pitt, Harvey, 99, 131, 267

Bush reaction, 105–106

controversy, 103–105

reform, reluctance, 9

Pitts, Leonard, 276, 287

Plato, 211, 213

Playfulness, definition, 260

Plender, John, 263, 287

Ponzi, Charles (Carlo), 26

Ponzi pyramid scheme, 26–27

Price-book value (P/VB) ratio, 171, 173

Price-earnings (P/E) ratio, 171, 173

Price-Waterhouse-Coopers (PwC), scandal involvement, 95–96

Professional associations/organizations, responsibility, 193–194

Promises (keeping), definition, 259

Property rights, impact, 188–190

Propriety, 223

Prudence, definition, 260

Prudential Securities, 149

Public Company Accounting Oversight Board (PCAOB), 8, 84, 131, 239, 267, 289

   controversy, 105

   creation, 83, 100

Public education, necessity, 186–188

Public-spiritedness, definition, 260

Putnam Investments, 139–140

   SEC settlement, 271, 289

Q

Quanyu, Huang, 276, 282

Quattrone, Frank (impact), 246. *See also* Technology IPOs

Quinn, Robert E., 279

Qwest, 48, 66–67

   accounts, watchdog probe, 266

   prosecution/lawsuits, 92, 107

   SEC civil fraud charges, 67

R

Railroads, scandals, 21–23

Railways

   history, 20

   mania, 21

   stocks, 23–26

Reed, John S., 103, 118, 125, 127–129

Regulatory laxity, 47

   endnotes, 265–266

Reid, T.R., 275, 282

Remuneration practices, 202

Resilience, definition, 260

Resolution, definition, 260

Resolution Trust Corporation (RTC), creation, 38

Respect, definition, 260

Responsibility, definition, 260

Restraint, definition, 260

Rigas, John, 67–68, 81, 241

Righteousness, definition, 260

RJR Nabisco, purchase, 167

Roiter, Eric, 156

Ronen, Joshua, 263, 284

Roosevelt, Franklin D., 33, 36, 42

Rosenthal, Sandra B., 279

Royal Ahold, scandal, 48, 72–73, 77

Royal Dutch/Shell Group, reserves (overstatement), 71

Rules, respect, 252

Runes, Dagobert, 275, 282

Ryckmans, Pietter, 281

S

Salomon Smith Barney Inc. (SSB), 109, 117

Sarbanes, Paul, 7

Sarbanes-Oxley Act (SOA) (2002), 83, 131, 267, 289
  criticism, 7–8
  endnotes, 267
  impact, 83–84
  implementation/enactment, 181, 203
  questions, 101
  results, 91–92
  test. *See* HealthSouth

Savings and Loans (S&Ls), scandals, 38–40

Scandals. *See* Business scandals; Corporate scandals; Europe; Mutual funds; Railroads; Savings and Loans
  conclusion, 78–81
  crisis
    remedies, 7–8
    root causes, 5–6
  definition, 1
  increase. *See* Wall Street
  international reaction, 76–78
  overview, 9–12

Scannell, Peter, 139

Schepp, David, 267, 268

Schmitt, Richard B., 287

Schneider, Mica, 290

Schumpeter, Joseph, 273, 282

Schwartz, Benjamin I., 275, 276, 282

Scrushy, Richard M., 88–91, 215, 246

Second Exodus, 277, 290

Securities and Exchange Commission (SEC), 2, 238
  civil fraud charges. *See* Qwest
  controversy, 104–105
  Bush reaction, 105–106
  creation, 29
  funding, 84
  reform, 7. *See* Mutual funds
  initiatives, 159–161
  regulation, unwillingness, 103

Securities Exchange Act of 1934, 36–37

Security Trust, 148

Self-control, definition, 260

Self-regulated organization (SRO), 122, 246

Self-respect, definition, 261

Self-sacrifice, definition, 261

Sen, Amartya, 3, 263, 282

Share buybacks
  results, 175–176
  usage, 172–173
  value, 173–175

Share repurchase strategy (SRS), 170–173, 178

Share repurchases, dividends (comparison), 172

Sheehy, Gail, 276, 282

Shell, missing oil reserves, 71–72

Shibut, Lynn, 265, 283

Shipman, John, 270, 287

Shleifer, Andrei, 282

Sidel, Robin, 269, 287

Sihpol III, Theodore C., 138

Simon, Ruth, 271, 287

Sincerity, definition, 261

Skapinker, Michael, 274, 287

Skilling, Jeff, 50, 57, 246

Sloan, Allan, 268, 287

Smith, Adam, 43–44, 214–219, 265, 273, 274, 276, 282, 290
  moral sentiments, 223–224
  populace, development, 186–187
  praise, 191–192
  relationship idea, 64
  self-interest, 185

Smith, Randall, 270, 288

Smith, Richard C., 92

Smith Barney (Citigroup), 149, 153

SOA. See Sarbanes-Oxley Act

Sobel, Robert, 264, 282

Social institutions
  endnotes, 272–274
  questioning, 181
  questions, 205
  rules, establishment, 182–184

Soft dollar payments, 156–157

Sommers, Christina, 276, 282

Sommers, Fred, 276, 282

South Sea Company bubble (England), 14, 17–20, 41
  comparison, 25

Spacek, Leonard, 93

Special Purpose Entity (SPE), problems, 49–53, 80

Specialist firms, 129

Spinning, 113

Spitzer, Eliot, 106–108, 287
  comments. See Mutual funds
  impact, 150–152, 201, 244–246, 290
  leadership role, 134
  reforms, 9, 27, 103, 109–111
  legacy, 240–241
  settlements, 109, 111

SRI Media News Corporate Governance, 268, 287

Stakeholders, principles, 252–256

Standard & Poor's 500 (S&P500)
  dividend yield, 169
  share repurchases/equity issuance, 174

State, social institution (role), 191–192

Steagall, Henry, 34. See also Glass-Steagall Act

Steidlmeier, Paul, 282

Stern, Edward, 136–137

Stern Asset Management, 134

Stewart, Martha, 225, 289
  indictment, 69
  resignation, 266, 290

Stiglitz, Joseph E., 282

Stock market crash (1873), 23–26

Stock market crash (1929), 30
  U.S. response, 33–37

Strong, Richard, 140

Strong Funds, 140–142

Sullivan, Scott, 62

Sunbeam, prosecution, 92, 93

Suppliers, treatment, 255

Swartz, Mark, 58–59, 242

Syron, Richard, 97

T

Tanzi, Calisto, 73

Taylor, Frederick, 195

Technology IPOs, Quattrone (impact), 118–120

Temperance, definition, 261

Theft, 47

Thompson, Larry, 67, 92

Tichy, Noel M., 282

Tolerance, definition, 261

Tong, Chen, 276, 282

Tonna, Fausto, 73

Trade-through rules, violations, 129–130

Transaction costs, impact. *See* Institutions

Transcendence, definition, 261

Treaty of Utrecht, 17

Trump, Donald, 242

Trust
definition, 3
restoration, 3–5, 9

Trustworthiness, definition, 261

Truthfulness, definition, 261

Turley, James, 94

Tyco, 48, 96
collapse, 57–61
costs, reduction, 265
fraud, 45, 265, 289, 290
SEC investigation, 57, 59
timeline, 60–61

Tzu, Hui-nan, 276, 282

U

UBS AG, 150, 153

UBS Warburg LLC, 109–110

Universal symmetry, 212

Uprightness, definition, 261

Useem, Michael, 263, 282

V

Value-added services, 156

Virtues, 209. *See also* Inferior virtue
core virtues, 227
endnotes, 274
examination, 210–224
listing, 257
questions, 234

Virtuous life, reflections, 209–210

Volcker, Paul, 123

W

Wachovia Securities, 154

Waksal, Samuel, 68–69

Wall Street
corruption/greed, 8–9
scandal, increase, 103
endnotes, 267–268
questions, 132
wrongdoing, Martin Act (impact), 106–108

Wallis, John, 273, 283

Walsh, Frank, 58–60

War of Spanish Succession, 17

Waste Management, prosecution, 92, 93

Waters, Maxine, 106

Watkins, Sherron, 50, 87

Watts, Sir Phillip, 71

Wealth (shift), social problem (question), 244–245

Weber, Max, 274, 283

Webster, William, 105

Weill, Sanford, 117–118

Weingast, Barry, 284

Welch, Jack, 232–233

Wells Fargo, 140